THE LIGHT SHINETH IN DARKNESS

Udo Schaefer studied first music and then law at
Heidelberg University. He also became a member of
the Bahá'í Faith there, and chose to write his
doctoral thesis about it. He was Chairman of the
National Spiritual Assembly of the Bahá'ís of
Germany for several years and still serves as a
member of the German Bahá'í Publishing Trust.
His time is divided among several interests—his
career as a lawyer in Heidelberg, his writing,
lecture tours throughout Germany, and his family.

The Light Shineth In Darkness

Five studies in revelation after Christ

Udo Schaefer

Translated from the German by
Hélène Momtaz Neri and Oliver Coburn

 George Ronald · Oxford

George Ronald, Publisher
46 High Street, Kidlington, Oxford OX5 2DN

Original German-language editions
Was es heisst, Bahá'í zu sein © Copyright Bahá'í-Verlag GmbH Frankfurt 1973
Die missverstandene Religion © Copyright Bahá'í-Verlag GmbH Frankfurt 1968
'Muḥammad—ein Lügenprophet?' from *Bahá'í Briefe* © Copyright Bah-á'í
Verlag GmbH Frankfurt 1969
Bahá'í—Religion nach Mass? © Copyright Verum-Verlag GmbH Stuttgart 1970
This translation © George Ronald 1977

Reprinted 1979

EXTRACTS FROM THE FOLLOWING WORKS
PUBLISHED IN THE UNITED STATES OF AMERICA
REPRINTED BY PERMISSION:

By Bahá'u'lláh: *Epistle to the Son of the Wolf*, Copyright 1941, © 1969 by National
Spiritual Assembly of the Bahá'ís of the United States; *Gleanings from the Writings of
Bahá'u'lláh*, Copyright 1939, by National Spiritual Assembly of the Bahá'ís of the
United States; *The Kitáb-i-Íqán · The Book of Certitude*, Copyright 1931, by National
Spiritual Assembly of the Bahá'ís of the United States; *Prayers and Meditations*,
Copyright 1938 by National Spiritual Assembly of the Bahá'ís of the United States.
By 'Abdu'l-Bahá: *The Promulgation of Universal Peace: Discourses by Abdul Baha during
His Visit to the United States in 1912*, published 1921–22, 1925. By Bahá'u'lláh and
'Abdu'l-Bahá: *Bahá'í World Faith: Selected Writings of Bahá'u'lláh and 'Abdul'l-Bahá*,
Copyright 1943, © 1976 by the National Spiritual Assembly of the Bahá'ís of the
United States. By Shoghi Effendi: *The Advent of Divine Justice*, Copyright 1939, ©
1967 by National Spiritual Assembly of the Bahá'ís of the United States; *The World
Order of Bahá'u'lláh: Selected Letters*, Copyright 1938, © 1974 by National Spiritual
Assembly of the Bahá'ís of the United States. Miscellaneous: *Bahá'í Year Book*,
copyright 1926 by National Spiritual Assembly of the Bahá'ís of the United States;
Bahá'í Procedure, copyright 1937, 1942 by National Spiritual Assembly of the Bahá'ís of
the United States.

ISBN 0 85398 072 1

*Printed in Great Britain by
Fletcher & Son Ltd
Norwich*

To my late friend Hermann Grossmann, the mentor and guide in
my studies of religion

Contents

Acknowledgements

This book is a collection of studies originally published in German under four separate titles. The text has been revised in certain respects and a new introduction has been written.

I wish to express my thanks to those who have assisted in the preparation of this English edition: to Mrs. Hélène Momtaz Neri who translated *Die missverstandene Religion*, 'Muḥammad–ein Lügenprophet?' (published in April 1969 in *Bahá'í Briefe*), and *Was es Heisst, Bahá'í zu sein*, and to Mr. Oliver Coburn who translated *Bahá'í—Religion nach Mass?*; to Bahá'í-Verlag of Frankfurt and Verum-Verlag of Stuttgart, the publishers of the original German editions; to Mrs Janet Rawling who reviewed the translation; to Mr. Ian Semple for his many valuable editorial suggestions; to Dr. Iḥsán Halabi, to whom I owe a deeper understanding of Islám. Above all, I wish to thank my editor Miss May Hofman for her help in putting the book together and for her cooperation; to Mr. Rustom Sabit and Mrs. Wendy Manners for reading proofs; and to my wife Sigrun, without whose aid this book could never have been presented to the public.

I am much indebted to the several authors and publishers who have permitted me to quote from their copyright publications. Full acknowledgement is given in the bibliography to these publishers, their authors and titles. Extracts from the Authorised Version of the Bible, the Copyright of which belongs to the Crown, are used with permission. Quotations from *The Koran* (*Qur'án*) are in the translation by J. M. Rodwell published in the Everyman's Library series. The quotation on p. 136 from Dante's *Inferno* is in the translation by F. H. Cary and used by permission of the Oxford University Press. Unless otherwise noted, the quotations from German texts have been translated by Mrs. Neri and Mr. Coburn.

And the light shineth in darkness; and the darkness comprehended it not.
John 1:5

Nay, we will hurl the truth at falsehood, and it shall smite it, and lo! it
shall vanish.
Qur'án 21:18

Introduction

The attitude of the West to the non-Christian religions has always been a critical one. Christianity was its perfect standard and at the same time the yardstick which it applied to the rival great religions. Little was changed in that respect when scholars of religion emancipated themselves from Christian missionary theology whose only real concern was to find in the non-Christian religions points of contact for teaching the heathen. However, none of these religions has been so detested, vilified, misunderstood and misrepresented as the sister religion of Christianity: Islám. Here the Christians' annoyance was of a special character: not only was a claim to revelation made to which the Bible did not bear witness, but, worse still, the doctrine that the history of the Salvation of Man had ended once and for all with Jesus Christ was denied. The 'Son of God' was demoted to the rank of a mere prophet. Whoever made such a statement was clearly in error; this is why Islám was, from the beginning, looked upon as an infamous fraud and a wicked heresy. It could not be a revelation, therefore for the Western scholar it remains to this day an eclectic mixture of ideas and teachings which its founder borrowed from religious concepts which he found in Judaism, Christianity and among the pagan Arabs, and which he partly misunderstood.

The same accusation has been made against the Bahá'í Faith, which has sprung from Islám and has still hardly been investigated by religious scholars; to the viewer with a Christian bias, it too appears as a 'syncretism' (Rosenkranz, Visser't Hooft), as 'a strange mixture' (Kellerhals), as 'a dervish order' (Roemer), when it is not altogether dismissed as a 'miserable sect' (Gottfried Simon). The one-sided bias—mainly towards Protestant dogma—the use of secondary literature and the preference given to unreliable sources inevitably led to misunderstanding and false interpretations.

Whoever wants to be properly informed about a religion would first do well to get hold of literature which is both self-descriptive and self-interpretative, which shows what the religion in question is and what its claims are according to its own teachings and history. This is a matter of course. He who really wants to know whether a retailer's merchandise is good and worth the money will buy from him before he criticises; he will not be satisfied merely with information given him by competitors. He who would like to know what Catholicism is, and how it sees itself, should not seek information from its declared enemies before he is familiar with its followers. Otherwise his research is unscientific; he bars himself from the way to a personal evaluation and a proper understanding.

He who wants information about Islám should start by reading works written by believers before he concentrates his attention on the premises of Western scholars of Islám, and can look at the religion only from their point of view. Obviously this is easier said than done, for the choice of literature is not very wide although the best material available is written in English.[1] The works of non-religious European writers offer an abundance of interesting and useful facts and details. But as soon as these scholars start to evaluate their material—and evaluation as well as classification are prerequisites to understanding—the calamity begins: the results are determined by the scholar's attitude to his subject and the premises on which his research has been based. The image projected is not concordant with the reality; as in a concave mirror, it is strangely distorted. The believing Christian, on the other hand, exploring a religious world foreign to him, has more understanding of the original religious element than the atheist scholar for whom the world of religion is nothing more than a reflection of the human mind's imaginative power and of specific social and economic conditions.

The same is true of the Bahá'í Faith. Whoever wants to inform himself in an objective manner, and believes he can find this objectivity in the scientific works available to the general public—which, incidentally, are not very numerous—will find it difficult to reach an unbiased conclusion and a fair-minded evaluation.

---

1. Syed Ameer Ali, *The Spirit of Islam*, London, 1965; Seyyed Hossein Nasr, *Ideals and Realities of Islám*, London, 1972.

Most of the descriptions in the encyclopedias[2] are based on early European publications and are hopelessly obsolete. As a rule the Bahá'í Faith is dealt with under the heading 'Islamic sects'[3] in the reference books and collective works on Islám.

The orientalist[4] who deserves best for his research on the Bahá'í Faith and especially on the Bábí Faith—one of the few Europeans who entered the presence of Bahá'u'lláh[5] and one who handed down to posterity a priceless report about this meeting[6]— has to a considerable extent drawn from sources which were partly falsified or which came from authors frankly opposed to Bahá'u'lláh and 'Abdu'l-Bahá.[7] The image he conveys is therefore self-contradictory.

Most of the other writers on the Bahá'í Faith have been Christian theologians and missionaries—often embittered enemies of the religion of Bahá'u'lláh.[8] It is therefore obvious that an objective presentation cannot be expected of them.

2. A notable exception is the article 'Bahá'í Faith' in *Encyclopaedia Britannica*, 15th ed., Chicago, 1974.

3. Ignaz Goldziher, *Vorlesungen über den Islam*, p. 272 ff. See also E. E. Kellett, *A Short History of Religions*, London, 1954; A. C. Bouquet, *Sacred Books of the World*, London, 1962; G. Parrinder, *The Handbook of Living Religions*, London, 1967.

4. 'No Western scholar has ever equalled the effort of Edward Granville Browne in seeking and preserving for generations to come the story of the birth and the rise of a Faith which was destined, as he foresaw at the onset of his distinguished career, to have a significance comparable to that of the other great religions of the world' (H. M. Balyuzi, *Edward Granville Browne and the Bahá'í Faith*, p. 121).

5. 1890 at Bahjí, near 'Akká.

6. Browne (ed.), *A Traveller's Narrative*, vol. II, pp. xxxix–xl.

7. See Balyuzi, *Edward Granville Browne and the Bahá'í Faith*.

8. The first book to have been published on the Bahá'í Faith in Germany was by the Jesuit Hermann Roemer (*Die Babi-Beha'i*, Potsdam, 1912) who recognises in his foreword that 'My work sprang from the practical need to take steps against Bahá'í propaganda in Germany . . . At the same time this work should be of use to Christian missionaries *vis-à-vis* the Muhammadan world'. This is the main work of reference on which Gerhard Rosenkranz, professor of Evangelical (Protestant) theology in Heidelberg and Tübingen bases his book *Die Bahá'í* (Stuttgart, 1949). His merit is that he fully recognises the independence of the Bahá'í' Faith and does not look upon it as an Islamic sect. However, the book contains a series of misconceptions and misinterpretations. And the last two pages are one single hymn to the uniqueness of the Christian Faith.

The Protestant theologian Kurt Hutten, in his book *Seher, Grübler, Enthusiasten* (1966) has devoted a chapter to the Bahá'í Faith. He is concerned to render an objective image of the Faith but his evaluation, however, is wholly influenced by the Christian claim to exclusiveness.

William Miller (*Bahá'ísm, Its Origin, History and Teachings*, New York, 1931; *The Bahá'í Faith: Its History and Teachings*, South Pasadena, California, U.S.A., 1974) was for many years a missionary in the Presbyterian church in Mashhad, Irán, and is

The present work, written because of the need to proclaim the Bahá'í Faith in the West, presents this religion and its basic teachings in the first two studies. Limited space allows only a restricted presentation of its history. However, the author does not simply present a purely descriptive image of the Bahá'í Faith but tries to go further and lead the reader to an understanding both of the redemptive hour in which we are living and of the meaning and aim of this great revolution in human history. This is an opportunity for him to set forth the teachings of Bahá'u'lláh and contrast them with ideas prevalent in present-day society, and to show to what extent the decadence of our culture is to be attributed to the decline of religion.

In the third study, in answer to a rather biased criticism of the Bahá'í Faith by a Protestant theologian, the author discusses a number of theological questions which crop up in every dialogue held with representatives of the Christian Faith and which need to be answered. This study is designed to help the theologically inclined reader to form a deeper concept of the true meaning of the revelation of Bahá'u'lláh.

The fourth study sets forth the relationship of the Bahá'í Faith to Islám—a relationship similar to that of Christianity to Judaism. The reproach, so often heard, that the Bahá'í Faith is a sect of Islám, is also dealt with, as are the theological similarities and differences between the two religions.

The fifth study stems from the religious conviction that the history of the Salvation of Man did not end once and for all with Jesus Christ but continued with the post-Biblical religions—Islám and the Bahá'í Faith. Here, questions are discussed which have particularly excited Western critics of Islám. The study investigates some traditional misconceptions which can still be found today in works by Western scholars of Islám as well as in school history textbooks. At the same time, methods of research into Islám will be critically assessed. The reproach, made time and again, that Islám and the Bahá'í Faith are basically nothing more than earthly products of a powerful synthesis of previous religious convictions, i.e. syncretisms, is answered here in detail.

One thing, however, must be stressed. The attitude of the

known as an embittered enemy of the Bahá'í Faith. His work places great emphasis on a document (Nuqtatu'l-Kaf) of doubtful authenticity.

Bahá'í towards Christianity is clear: he acknowledges its divine origin and believes in the Word of God as testified by the Gospels, but he does not acknowledge as divinely guided the historical development of Christianity, which, even in its earliest period, diverged from its source and assimilated essentially alien elements. Bahá'u'lláh testifies: 'Know thou that when the Son of Man yielded up His breath to God, the whole creation wept with a great weeping. By sacrificing Himself, however, a fresh capacity was infused into all created things. Its evidences, as witnessed in all the peoples of the earth, are now manifest before thee. The deepest wisdom which the sages have uttered, the profoundest learning which any mind hath unfolded, the arts which the ablest hands have produced, the influence exerted by the most potent of rulers, are but manifestations of the quickening power released by His transcendent, His all-pervasive, and resplendent Spirit.

'We testify that when He came into the world, He shed the splendour of His glory upon all created things . . . He it is Who purified the world. Blessed is the man who, with a face beaming with light, hath turned towards Him.'[9]

May this contribution to modern religious history lead to a deeper understanding of both Islám and the Bahá'í Faith.

9. *Gleanings*, XXXVI.

The vitality of men's belief in God is dying out in every land: nothing short of His wholesome medicine can ever restore it.

Bahá'u'lláh

Belief and Unbelief Today

The great revolutionary events in the history of the world arrive—as Friedrich Nietzsche once said—'on doves' feet.'[10]

These words are especially relevant to the appearance of the great religions—those events in the history of mankind which have influenced and changed people's lives in a particularly lasting way. In their early periods, none of the universal religions known to us allowed an unbelieving world to see their creative spiritual impulse which was transforming and reviving everything anew. The quality of dynamic power inherent in the Word of God was perceived only by the small group of those who believed in this creative Word of God and were filled with it. At first the world at large scarcely took any notice of it. Thus Jesus Christ was virtually ignored by contemporary historians. The historians of Palestine, Greece and Rome took no notice of the event which was to change the world of that time and without which the spiritual life of the West would be inconceivable. They paid no attention to the life, works and death of the founder of Christianity. Only Tacitus mentions in his Annals—and the authenticity of this evidence is questioned—a 'Christ' who, in the reign of the Emperor Tiberius, was killed by order of the governor Pontius Pilate, and he continues: 'For the moment the destructive superstition had been repressed, but it broke out again not only in Judea, the starting-point of this evil, but also in the capital where all that is hideous and shameful congregates and gains adherents.'[11]

Even Philo of Alexandria, the Jewish scholar, knows nothing of Jesus—Philo, who left to posterity a voluminous bulk of works, who was a great expert on the Bible and the Jewish sects and who

10. 'It is the stillest words which bring the storm; thoughts that come on doves' feet guide the world' (*Thus spoke Zarathustra*, p. 168).
11. *Annals*, XV:44.

also mentions Pilate. The report about Christ in *The Antiquities of the Jews* by the Jewish historian Flavius Josephus, born shortly after Jesus's crucifixion, is very likely an interpolation from the third century. 'The New Testament is the only source of information about Jesus,' writes Romano Guardini. To the cultivated Roman of the second century, Christianity was an obscure Jewish sect, a 'corrupt superstitious belief', an 'evil', as Tacitus calls it; only a small part of the population, the Christians themselves, believed in the triumphant progress of this religion. It certainly seemed much more probable that the future belonged to any other of the many religious movements, for instance the mystery cults, some of which were quite eminent. We can see the same process taking place in the history of other great religions: every faith in its early period has had to experience first ignorance, then derision and persecution. At no time have contemporary non-believers visualised a great future for the new-born religion.

We, too, are witnesses of an event which has arrived on 'doves' feet' and is destined to change the world: the rise of a new religion, the Bahá'í Faith, which claims to fulfil the promises of the religions of the past and to be the religion of the future. Its history[12] began in 1844 when a twenty-five-year-old merchant, Siyyid 'Alí Muḥammad, declared himself in Shíráz to be the revealer of God's will for our time. He assumed the title of 'Báb' (Gate) and described himself as the herald of 'Him Whom God shall make manifest'—one who would be greater than he. The Báb gathered a handful of eighteen followers, the 'Letters of the Living' (i.e. of God), as he called them, and sent them into the provinces of Persia to announce his message. The Faith, which very quickly found many followers in all parts of the country, was soon attacked by the orthodox Shí'ah clergy; at their instigation, the Persian government, on which the duty of protecting Islám rested, persecuted the Faith with a great deal of bloodshed. The Báb, whose ministry lasted only six years, was publicly executed

12. The historical facts here are kept to the necessary minimum. For further information see Shoghi Effendi, *God Passes By*, Wilmette, Ill., 5th repr. 1965; Nabíl-i-A'ẓam, *The Dawn-Breakers*, Nabíl's Narrative of the Early Days of the Bahá'í Revelation, Wilmette, Ill., 1932. London, 1953. E. G. Browne (ed.), *A Traveller's Narrative written to illustrate the Episode of the Báb*, Cambridge, 1891, re-issued 1976; H. M. Balyuzi, *The Báb*, George Ronald, Oxford, 1973; *Bahá'u'lláh*, George Ronald, Oxford, 1963; *'Abdu'l-Bahá*, George Ronald, Oxford, 1971. *The Bahá'í World*, An International Record, vol. XV, Bahá'í World Centre, Haifa, 1976. *Encyclopaedia Britannica*, 15th ed., Chicago, 1974.

in 1850 in a barracks square in Tabríz after several years of imprisonment. In 1863 in Baghdád, Mírzá Ḥusayn 'Alí, who had assumed the title 'Bahá'u'lláh' (The Glory of God)—a title confirmed by the Báb—and who had gathered around himself the disheartened group of the Báb's followers, declared himself as the promised one of all religions and as 'Him Whom God shall make manifest'. On the request of the Persian government, Bahá'u'lláh was banished to Constantinople and from there to Adrianople as a prisoner of the Turkish Government. In the following years he wrote his first tablets to the crowned heads of East and West: Napoleon III, Emperor Wilhelm I, Emperor Franz Joseph, Queen Victoria, Tsar Alexander II, Náṣiri'd-Dín Sháh, Sulṭán 'Abdu'l-'Azíz, Pope Pius IX and others. He announced his message and called upon the sovereigns to follow the principles of his teachings in their politics, to reduce their armaments and to establish world peace. With the greatest clarity, he revealed his task of giving the world new life, of reforming its order under divine guidance and of leading the whole of mankind on the path of spiritual progress. He saw the purpose of his mission as the bringing together of humanity in an all-encompassing order in a spirit of harmony, peace and unity. The means of achieving this goal would be the unification of mankind in the all-embracing Faith which he revealed and in obedience to his counsels. He left no doubt as to the fact that the present inadequate and diseased human order would be laid aside by the hand of the Almighty and that a new one would be established in its place: 'Soon will the present-day order be rolled up, and a new one spread out in its stead.'[13] Bahá'u'lláh warned the peoples about the divine judgment which was at hand and of the misery which would come upon mankind: 'Bestir yourselves, O people, in anticipation of the days of Divine Justice, for the promised hour is now come.' 'Abandon that which ye possess, and seize that which God, Who layeth low the necks of men, hath brought . . . We have fixed a time for you, O people! If ye fail, at the appointed hour, to turn towards God, He, verily, will lay violent hold on you, and will cause grievous afflictions to assail you from every direction . . . Know verily that an unforeseen calamity is following you and that grievous retribution awaiteth you.'[14] According to Bahá'u'lláh, this divine punishment

13. *Gleanings*, IV.
14. Quoted by Shoghi Effendi, *The Promised Day is Come*, p. 3.

is at the same time a purification of the human race. Through it humanity will be welded together into an organic, indivisible and world-wide community to whom he promises a radiant future, the coming of the 'Most Great Peace'. He was finally banished to Palestine in 1868 and imprisoned in the Turkish penal colony, the Crusaders' fortress of 'Akká. He died in 1892 nearby at Bahjí where, after mitigation of his imprisonment, he had spent the latter years of his life.

In the West the Bahá'í Faith was made known through the interest which the 'episode of the Báb' aroused among European savants (such as Tolstoy, Renan, Gobineau and Browne) and pre-eminently through the journeys undertaken by the eldest son of Bahá'u'lláh, 'Abdu'l-Bahá, after he was freed from prison by the Young Turks' Revolution in 1908. These journeys took him to Egypt, Europe and North America. Bahá'u'lláh had appointed him the authoritative interpreter of his writings. Innumerable contemporary publications testify to the deep respect accorded him in public by churches, universities and renowned personalities. He died in Haifa in 1921, leaving in his Will and Testament a charter for the future development of the Bahá'í Faith under the guidance of Shoghi Effendi, whom He appointed Guardian of the Faith, and of the Universal House of Justice. Authority to interpret the revelation was vested in the Guardian, while authority in the legislative and administrative realms had been given to the Universal House of Justice by Bahá'u'lláh himself.

During the thirty-six years of Shoghi Effendi's ministry, Bahá'í teachings were disseminated in over two hundred and fifty countries and Bahá'í communities began to grow in the farthest corners of the earth. In 1963, one hundred years after Bahá'u'-lláh's declaration, the Universal House of Justice was elected for the first time by representatives of the whole Bahá'í world, and is now the supreme administrative body of the Bahá'í Faith, deriving its powers from the express command of Bahá'u'lláh and endowed by him with binding authority.

Bahá'u'lláh's call to the leaders of his time remained unheeded. None of the rulers addressed by Bahá'u'lláh was mindful of his warning and counsels. Today we are experiencing the significance of those monitory words. It becomes more and more obvious that we are living in a period of crisis, the most critical phase in the history of mankind, that the future of mankind is threatened as

never before by its own destructive forces, that man is on the way
to a catastrophe, to self-annihilation. Since the report of the Club
of Rome about the situation of mankind[15] has been published and
become a bestseller, wider circles of the population are now aware
of what eminent scientists and philosophers have been observing
for a long time: mankind is on the way to destruction, if it does
not come to a fundamental change in consciousness.

Our contemporary way of thinking is characterised by the loss
of belief in God and the loss of values which are universally
acknowledged. Atheism is a world-wide phenomenon. The
'absence' of God is the stigma of our time. Bahá'u'lláh clearly
predicted this situation over one hundred years ago: 'The face of
the world hath altered. The way of God and the religion of God
have ceased to be of any worth in the eyes of men.' 'The vitality
of men's belief in God is dying out in every land . . . The corrosion
of ungodliness is eating into the vitals of human society.'[16] For
about thirty or forty years theologians and philosophers have been
noting and describing the rapid increase of atheism and the total
secularisation of our society. Gustav Mensching[17] describes the
phenomenon of the secularisation of the masses and calls the
religious situation in the West a 'sham-churchism'. He draws
attention to the fact that the number of church-taxpayers—in
Germany about 95 per cent of the population—throws no light on
people's faith and on the real significance of religion in their lives.
In communist countries militant atheism is a component of the
prevailing philosophy of the state. Religion is regarded as a 'drug',
the 'opium of the people' (Karl Marx). But also in the West sceptical atheism is taking hold of more and more people. For many of
the younger generation God is no longer a reality.[18] In Rome in

15. Dennis L. Meadows, *The Limits to Growth*, New York, Universe Books, 1972.
The essay by the American futurologist Grover Foley, in *Frankfurter Hefte*, no. 10,
October 1971, p. 741 ff.: 'Sind wir am Ende?' (Have we come to the end?) is also
noteworthy.

16. Quoted by Shoghi Effendi, *The Promised Day is Come*, p. 117.

17. *Soziologie der Religion*, p. 213 ff. and 257.

18. In 1974 in the state of Hesse, 550 Protestant primary schoolchildren in Oden-
wald and in the city of Giessen were asked about religious concepts. The results
showed that for most pupils the terms 'God', 'church' and 'Christ' were 'foreign
words' that mean little or nothing to them. The fact that they had no concept of
religion was discovered to be connected with the experiences of the children in the
parental home: most parents avoid any discussion of religious topics or strongly
criticise everything connected with religion (*Frankfurter Allgemeine Zeitung*, 17 Sep-
tember 1974).

the autumn of 1974 an assembly of bishops consulted both about this situation which was causing great anxiety, and about the ever-increasing difficulties of proclaiming the Gospel. Religion, which used to be the centre of man's life and gave him a yardstick to act by, has lost its importance, as Bahá'u'lláh predicted. It plays scarcely any part in the running of society. The considerable power of the churches in public life cannot disguise this fact. The desolate situation of the religions is described by the religious philosopher and former state president of India, Sarvapalli Radha-krishnan: 'Millions of people wish to believe, but they cannot, even though these orphaned children make use of the outer frame-work of religions. We are christened, or baptised, married, buried or cremated according to our religious rites, but all the time we are victims of an involuntary hypocrisy.'[19] For most of those who still follow a religion, it is little more than a mechanical participa-tion in traditional forms and customs and a passive submission to dogma. For modern man is increasingly sceptical and attached to things of this world; he is so deeply involved in this life that the life to come has scarcely any meaning for him. The Church is, therefore, to a great extent reduced to the degrading level of an institution for baptism, marriage and burial. Religious ties are often maintained only for the sake of convention, out of consider-ation for the family or even on economic grounds. But the great multitude of adherents do not in any way direct their lives accord-ing to the laws to which they are morally bound. Radhakrishnan writes: 'We keep up the forms of religion, which seem to be of the nature of play-acting' and rightly concludes: 'If religion is not dynamic and pervasive, if it does not penetrate every form of human life and influence every type of human activity, it is only a veneer and not a reality.'[20] While the great masses of spiritually-indifferent people consider religion with apathy—most of them not by virtue of a conviction acquired after deep consideration but on the strength of a materialistic view-point, of a licentious and materialistic striving after gain which today has so much hold over everybody—most of the intellectuals of the younger genera-tion adopt towards religion an attitude which is aloof or even hos-tile. They imagine themselves to be in possession of a scientific approach to human nature and are convinced that mankind's reli-

19. *The Recovery of Faith*, p. 36.
20. ibid., p. 22.

gious life will some day be overcome just like the demonism of primitive tribes or the belief in witchcraft of the Middle Ages.

It is not the aim of this book to trace back the manifold causes which brought about the world-wide process of the decay and abandonment of religious faith, which is by no means confined to the Christian world alone but affects all great religions.[21] This change has caused the decadence in traditional systems of the world, the rise of nihilism and the depreciation of all values: 'Nihilism is the last word of metaphysics which refuses to go beyond the surface appearances. We see, on all sides, a violent loosening of the familiar bonds, a snapping of the strands that hold a civilisation together.'[22] Bahá'u'lláh has made no secret of the outcome of the decline in religion: 'This cannot but lead in the end to chaos and confusion.' For 'Religion is verily the chief instrument for the establishment of order in the world, and of tranquillity amongst its peoples.'[23] It is 'a radiant light and an impregnable stronghold for the protection and welfare of the peoples of the world, for the fear of God impelleth man to hold fast to that which is good, and shun all evil. Should the lamp of religion be obscured, chaos and confusion will ensue, and the lights of fairness, of justice, of tranquillity and peace cease to shine.'[24]

In this atmosphere of growing atheism, many claim that a new revealed religion no longer stands a chance because the conditions in which religions have arisen in history no longer prevail and because the enlightenment of the age in which we live not only causes the power of the great religions to vanish but excludes at the same time the birth of a new religion. What is remarkable, however, is that, at the same time as the old religions have lost their original impulse and used up their vital energy, the Bahá'í Faith has spread over the whole earth and found numerous followers, especially in Africa, South America, India and the islands of the Pacific Ocean.[25] Millions of people who have long

21. Compare the remarkable analysis of H. J. Schoeps (note 442) and Shoghi Effendi's diagnosis of the present world condition (note 473).

22. Radhakrishnan, p. 39.

23. Quoted by Shoghi Effendi, *The Promised Day is Come*, p. 117.

24. Quoted by Shoghi Effendi, 'The Unfoldment of World Civilization', *The World Order of Bahá'u'lláh*, p. 186.

25. There are in 1977 approximately 72,000 Bahá'í centres and communities; the number of National Spiritual Assemblies has grown to 124; Bahá'í literature has

since realised that the problems of our private and community lives cannot be solved by scientific knowledge and reason alone, and that the organisation of human communities and the establishment of freedom, justice and peace are not only intellectual acts but above all spiritual and moral processes, who refuse to recant their faith in the spiritual nature of man and refuse to see in him nothing but a highly-developed animal, who long for a spiritual awakening and the birth of a new religion, millions of whom Radhakrishnan writes that they would like to believe but cannot do so because they find no satisfaction in the old religions, whose tenets have long since become unacceptable yet are still obstinately proclaimed from the pulpit while religious scholars are puzzled and confused about these very teachings,[26] in the message of Bahá'u'lláh these millions find a new, more developed presentation of the eternal verities which form the foundation of all past religions. They see in this Faith a 'unifying force instilling into the adherents of these religions a new spiritual vigour, infusing them with a new hope and love for mankind.'[27] They know that this is 'not a new path to immortality' but 'the ancient path cleared of the debris of imaginations and superstitions of men, of the debris of strife and misunderstanding and is again made a clear path to the sincere seeker, that he may enter therein in assurance, and find that the word of God is one word, though the speakers were many'.[28]

---

been translated into 546 languages and the number of countries opened to the Faith has reached 330.

26. The unreliability of the Church is already demonstrated by the fact that the message it proclaims from the pulpit is different from the one it teaches from the academic chair; 'The Church lives from the fact that the results of scientific research it makes into the life of Jesus are not made public' (Conzelmann, *Zur Methodik der Leben-Jesu-Forschung*, p. 8).

27. Shoghi Effendi, 'The Faith of Bahá'u'lláh', a statement prepared for the United Nations Special Palestine Committee, 1947.

28. 'Abdu'l-Bahá, quoted in *Principles of the Bahá'í Faith*.

To live the life is to be no cause of grief to anyone. To be kind to all people and to love them with a pure spirit. Should opposition or injury happen to us, to bear it, to be as kind as ever we can be, and through all, to love the people. Should calamity exist in the greatest degree, to rejoice, for these things are the gifts and favours of God. To be silent concerning the faults of others, to pray for them, and help them, through kindness to correct their faults. To look always at the good and not at the bad. If a man has ten good qualities and one bad one, to look at the ten and forget the one. And if a man has ten bad qualities and one good one, to look at the one and forget the ten. Never to allow ourselves to speak one unkind word about another, even though that other be our enemy. To do all of our deeds in kindness. To cut our hearts from ourselves and from the world. To be humble. To be servants of each other, and to know that we are less than anyone else. To be as one soul in many bodies, for the more we love each other, the nearer we shall be to God; but to know that our love, our unity, our obedience must not be by confession, but reality. To act with cautiousness and wisdom. To be truthful, to be hospitable. To be reverent. To be a cause of healing for every sick one, a comforter for every sorrowful one, a pleasant water for every thirsty one, a heavenly table for every hungry one, a star to every horizon, a light for every lamp, a herald to everyone who yearns for the kingdom of God.

'Abdu'l-Bahá

What it means to be a Bahá'í

Being a Bahá'í is first a matter of consciousness and belief, for in the essential questions of life, Bahá'í beliefs and principles are often different from—and even diametrically opposed to—generally prevalent views. But it is also a question of conduct and behaviour, for it is essentially in one's actions that one must show what it means to be a Bahá'í.

God is not dead

The Bahá'ís are immediately distinguished by their belief that this world is more than the outcome of coincidence or the resultant of blind forces, that man is more than nature's 'lucky strike', that our life has a meaning and an aim—a belief looked upon by many of their contemporaries as old-fashioned.

Bahá'ís believe in an almighty creator who has fashioned the universe and has made man in his own image; they believe in a non-created cause of all existence, in a single God. The word 'God' is a symbol for that transcendent reality by which all existence is ruled and maintained. What we call God is not, as the critics of the concept of God[29] believe, a product of human imagination, a creation of the mind, a fanciful invention which has no reality, or the reflection of particular social and economic circumstances. And although it is true that the ideas of God, religion and religious teaching have often been used for very ungodly, selfish motives and repeatedly misused to justify the existing social and economic differences which, apparently nature-born and willed by God, were therefore sacred, it is equally true—and especially in

29. Ludwig Feuerbach (German philosopher, 1804-72): 'God did not create man in his image but man created God in his image.'

Christian thought—that conditions on earth were considered un-
real, transitory and unessential and responsibility for this world
was neglected, for only one thing seemed important: the salvation
of the soul in need of redemption from its sinfulness. And it is also
true that the theories of Ludwig Feuerbach and Karl Marx, which
are written on banners above the Soviet prisoners' camps, and
according to which man is the God of man, and man is the highest
reality for man, appear a mockery when one regards the situation
of the world today.

To evaluate a phenomenon in its degeneration and decadence is
prejudice and can only lead to erroneous conclusions. Religious
history very clearly shows that the religions—including Christianity—not only legitimised the prevailing order of things and upheld ownership by the feudal government, the nobility and the
bourgeoisie, but also, that in the beginning they were the revolutionary *élan* for renewal and change. The misuse of a thing does
not disprove the thing itself; the misuse of the idea of God and
religion does not make absurd that which we call God, 'the One
Power which animates and dominates all things'.[30]

God is transcendental—beyond our comprehension and our
imaginative power. Therefore all speculation about the reality of
God, such as the ideas of the Incarnation and the Trinity in
Christian theology, is vain and condemned to failure. Bahá'u'lláh,
the founder of the Bahá'í Faith, proclaims the absolute transcendence of God: 'God, singly and alone, abideth in His Own Place
which is Holy above space and time, mention and utterance, sign,
description and definition, height and depth'.[31]

God cannot be conceived, perceived or objectively known. He
is beyond our rational understanding. According to Bahá'u'lláh's
teachings, His essence will always be hidden from man. He is the
Hidden One [32] for there is no direct way leading to the knowledge
of Him: 'The way is barred and all seeking rejected.'[33] But He is
also the 'Manifest One', for He reveals Himself to men through
His manifestations, as religious history testifies.

30. Bahá'u'lláh, *The Hidden Words, Words of Wisdom and Communes*, p. 61.
31. ibid.
32. 'He is the first and the last; the Seen and the Hidden; and He knoweth all
things!'(*Qur'án* 57:4).
33. Bahá'u'lláh, *Kitáb-i-Íqán*, p. 91 (Brit.), p. 141 (U.S.).

The Lord of history

God is more than the creator of man, He is also the Lord of history. Through His revelations He has made a covenant with men. From time immemorial, through His divine messengers, He has been leading His people to 'safeguard the interests and promote the unity of the human race, and to foster the spirit of love and fellowship amongst men'[34] and 'to carry forward an ever-advancing civilization'.[35] These are the purposes of religion: the spiritual education of the human race and the establishment of an ever-advancing civilisation.

The divine messengers, the central figures of the religions, are the necessary mediators between God and man. They are the perfect mirrors of God's bounties and attributes. God is manifest in them. It is in this sense that Jesus said: 'I am the way, the truth, and the life: no man cometh unto the Father but by me';[36] 'he that hath seen me hath seen the Father';[37] 'I and my Father are one'.[38]

Two more essential beliefs characterise the consciousness of the Bahá'í. First, that no essential difference exists between these divine messengers:[39] 'There is no distinction whatsoever among the Bearers of My Message'.[40] Abraham, Moses, Krishna, Buddha, Christ and Muḥammad, all came with the same mission: the education of the human race. Secondly, the claim that today, when all the old religions have consumed their life force and are being questioned, and when, following the philosophers, even the theologians now proclaim the death of God and see in Him nothing more than a symbol for 'a particular form of love for others',[41] God, through Bahá'u'lláh, has once again spoken to mankind.

To modern man the very claim seems a shocking, unreasonable assertion, a pure presumption. Like the Gospel in former times, it is considered scandalous. As with the appearance of all the divine messengers in the past, at the appearance of Bahá'u'lláh today the souls of men measure themselves against him. A study of religious history shows that the advent of every prophet was

---

34. Bahá'u'lláh, *Gleanings*, CX.   35. ibid., CIX.

36. John 14:6.   37. John 14:9.   38. John 10:30.

39. The term 'prophet' is ambiguous; the *Qur'án* uses the concept of *rasúl*, i.e. messenger and Bahá'u'lláh that of *ẓuhúr*, i.e. manifestation.

40. Bahá'u'lláh, *Gleanings*, XXXIV.

41. Herbert Braun, *Gesammelte Studien zum Neuen Testament und seiner Umwelt*, p. 325 ff.

accompanied by rejection, derision, conflict, turmoil, violence and rebellion. 'And whensoever the portals of grace did open, and the clouds of divine bounty did rain upon mankind, and the light of the Unseen did shine above the horizon of celestial might; they all denied Him, and turned away from His face—the face of God Himself.'[42] On this point the *Qur'án* says: 'Oh! the misery that rests upon my servants! No apostle cometh to them but they laugh him to scorn.'[43] The objection is self-evident: anyone could make such a claim! How is it possible to discover, in the clamour of rival claims, where truth is and where falsehood?

A minimum of intellectual humility is a prerequisite to the recognition of truth. The divine kingdom is no *Schlaraffenland*,[44] it must be earned. In order to recognise the truth, one must first make a personal effort and hold a certain attitude towards life. Whoever encounters the light of truth with a prejudiced mind set on the religious traditions of the past and their conventional interpretation, whoever is guided by his self-made concept of the world, whoever is crammed with ideas of his own which he has come so to cherish that he is unwilling to correct them, for him truth will remain hidden behind the veil of his 'idle fancies and vain imaginations'.[45] Only he who seeks the truth will find it. And a true seeker is only he who purifies 'his heart . . . from the obscuring dust of all acquired knowledge':[46] 'He must so cleanse his heart that no remnant of either love or hate may linger therein, lest that love blindly incline him to error or that hate repel him away from the truth'.[47] This is the purity of heart referred to by Jesus when He said: 'Blessed are the pure in heart: for they shall see God'[48] and 'Every one that is of the truth heareth my voice'.[49] Bahá'u'lláh gives us the assurance that 'He hath endowed every soul with the capacity to recognize the signs of God'[50] and that

---

42. Bahá'u'lláh, *Kitáb-i-Íqán*, p. 4 (Brit.), p. 4 (U.S.).
43. 36:30.
44. *Schlaraffenland:* A fairy-tale land of milk and honey where roast chickens fly into the mouths of the indolent and hot dogs grow on fences. Idleness is the highest virtue and diligence the worst vice. The laziest in the land is king. The stories about *Schlaraffenland* go back to myths of a lost paradise.
45. *Gleanings*, C.
46. *Kitáb-i-Íqán*, p. 123 (Brit.), pp. 192–3 (U.S.).
47. ibid.
48. Matthew 5:8.
49. John 18:37.
50. *Gleanings*, LII.

to the sincere seeker who tears away the veils of preconceived ideas, the light of divine truth will appear as manifest as 'the sun in its noontide glory'.[51]

This discernment excels by far a purely intellectual understanding. It is bestowed upon the seeker in his encounter with light and truth. But for him both rational thinking and the experience itself are necessary. The words of Jesus are noteworthy on this point: 'My doctrine is not mine, but his that sent me. If any man will do his will, he shall know of the doctrine, whether it be of God, or whether I speak of myself.'[52] And whoever reflects on the warning according to which false prophets, like true ones, must be recognised by their fruits,[53] and considers with an unbiased mind what is beginning to take shape on a small scale in the Bahá'í community—the unity of mankind in which all men of all races, nations and religions are integrated—he will be able to recognise how Bahá'u'lláh quickens the hearts and unites men: 'The proof of the sun is the light thereof, which shineth and envelopeth all things. The evidence of the shower is the bounty thereof, which reneweth and investeth the world with the mantle of life. Yea, the blind can perceive naught from the sun except its heat, and the arid soil hath no share of the showers of mercy.'[54] It is the profound experience of the Bahá'í that the God who is said to be dead is alive and that He has fulfilled the promise He made to the prophets by leading mankind to peace and unity through Bahá'u'lláh.

But Bahá'u'lláh does not represent the final stage in the history of the Salvation of Man. He proclaims that God will continue in the future to send His messengers to mankind 'to summon all mankind to truthfulness and sincerity, to piety and trustworthiness, to resignation and submissiveness to the Will of God, to forbearance and kindliness, to uprightness and wisdom' and 'to array every man with the mantle of a saintly character, and to adorn him with the ornament of holy and goodly deeds'.[55]

The unity of religion
This is the fundamental belief of Bahá'u'lláh's followers: that religion is not static but dynamic, that God did not manifest Him-

---

51. ibid. 52. John 7: 16–17. 53. Matthew 7: 16.
54. *Kitáb-i-Íqán*, p. 133 (Brit.), p. 209 (U.S.).
55. *Gleanings*, CXXXVII.

self once and for all in the past but has done so at irregular cyclic
intervals and will continue to do so in the future. They believe
that the birth of each revealed religion was as the 'tide of For-
tune'[56] and that the progressive development of the human race is
dependent on the appearance of the divine manifestations.

Bahá'u'lláh teaches that with the coming of each prophet of God
a new force was released into the world which had the power to
transform man as well as the order of things, an impulse which,
however, was consumed in the course of history. Man's mental
capacity and his cultural situation were relative to his environment and to the time in which he lived. Earthly conditions are
constantly changing. All living things, including religions, are
exposed to time's process of deterioration. This is why God
speaks to mankind anew whenever He pleases: 'for every age
requireth a fresh measure of the light of God. Every Divine
Revelation hath been sent down in a manner that befitted the
circumstances of the age in which it hath appeared.'[57]

All that lives, and this includes the religions, have a springtime,
a time of maturity, of harvest and a winter-time. Then religion
becomes barren, a lifeless adherence to the letter uninformed by
the spirit, and man's spiritual life declines. When we look at
religious history, we see that God has spoken to men precisely at
times when they have reached the nadir of their degradation and
cultural decadence. Moses came to Israel when it was languishing
under the Pharaoh's yoke, Christ appeared at a time when the
Jewish Faith had lost its power and the culture of antiquity was
in its death throes. Muḥammad came to a people who lived in
barbaric ignorance at the lowest level of culture and into a world
in which the former religions had strayed far away from their
origins and nearly lost their identity. The Báb addressed Himself
to a people who had irretrievably lost their former grandeur and
who found themselves in a state of hopeless decadence. Bahá'u'-
lláh came to a humanity which was approaching the most critical
phase of its history.

'Abdu'l-Bahá writes: 'God leaves not His children comfortless,
but, when the darkness of winter overshadows them, then again
He sends His Messengers, the Prophets, with a renewal of the

---

56. 'Sternstunden der Menschheit.' This notion is from Stefan Zweig (1881–1942)
who gave this title to a volume of essays published in 1927.
57. *Gleanings*, XXXIV.

blessed spring. The Sun of Truth appears again on the horizon of the world shining into the eyes of those who sleep, awaking them to behold the glory of a new dawn. Then again will the tree of humanity blossom and bring forth the fruit of righteousness for the healing of the nations.'[58]

Some conclusions can be drawn from this fundamental belief. First, all religions are divine in essence and consequently there are no religions which contradict or exclude each other, but only one indivisible divine religion which is renewed periodically and according to the requirements of the age, in cycles of about a thousand years: 'Our command was but one word.'[59] It is therefore hardly surprising if many of Bahá'u'lláh's teachings are to be found in former religions either expressly or in an embryonic form. As 'Abdu'l-Bahá says, the Bahá'í Faith is 'not a new path to immortality'.[60] On account of this transcendent oneness of all religions, Bahá'u'lláh exhorted His people to associate with followers of all religions in a spirit of loving-kindness and to make of religion a cause of harmony and peace, not of discord and strife, of hate and division.

The second conclusion is that we cannot perceive what the essence of religion is and what it has the power to achieve if we examine the traditional great religions in their present form. They have achieved much but have reached the end of their road; they were the foundation of great cultures and for thousands of years they were the guiding-star of millions of people in their everyday life and activities. But during the course of history they have also accumulated large amounts of historical ballast. They have moved a long way from their origin and are burdened with their followers' misdeeds and cravings for power. They are no pleasant sight today, least of all to young people, who no longer see in these religions the 'salt of the earth' as Jesus called his disciples,[61] but rather the 'opium of the people' (Karl Marx). And one is easily inclined to pass judgment on religion as a whole, and to see in it an anachronism of past times, long since overcome, like the belief in demons in former times. But a withered plant does not give us the faintest idea of its blossoming time. In reality, religions are the

58. *Paris Talks*, p. 32.
59. *Qur'án* 54:51.
60. Quoted from *Principles of the Bahá'í Faith*.
61. Matthew 5:13.

'light of the world' and, according to Bahá'u'lláh's teachings, the foundation of human culture. It is important to understand that they are as necessary for mankind as sunlight for the plant. Without divine revelation, there would be neither progress nor culture: 'Were this revelation to be withdrawn, all would perish.'[62]

The new society

The main cause behind the fast accelerating decline of our culture is the loss of religious feeling and the subsequent collapse of the sets of values originally given by religions. Unanimous answers to the question of what is good and what is evil, what is allowed and what is not are no longer to be found anywhere. But a culture, in which a minimum of agreement on value concepts does not exist, in which there is only a pluralism of opinions that are not binding about the essential questions of life, is bound to fall.

Bahá'ís differ in their belief on an all-important point from Christian and especially Protestant thought. They visualise religion as an encompassing power which embraces all aspects of our existence and brings order to it. Religion is not confined to the individual and his relationship to God. It is also the power which stabilises society and gives it order: 'Religion is verily the chief instrument for the establishment of order in the world, and of tranquillity amongst its peoples.'[63] It is 'a radiant light and an impregnable stronghold for the protection and welfare of the peoples of the world, for the fear of God impelleth man to hold fast to that which is good, and shun all evil. Should the lamp of religion be obscured, chaos and confusion will ensue, and the lights of fairness, of justice, of tranquillity and peace cease to shine.'[64]

This point of view, according to which a religion is the glue which holds society together, is in no way new, but it has been forgotten. Francis Bacon already knew that 'Religion being the chief Band of human Society, it is a happy thing, when it self, is well contained within the true Band of Unity',[65] and Jakob Burckhardt writes 'that religion is the chief bond in human society for it is the only satisfactory guardian of that moral condition which

62. Bahá'u'lláh, *Gleanings*, XCIII.
63. Bahá'u'lláh, quoted by Shoghi Effendi, *The Promised Day is Come*, p. 117.
64. Bahá'u'lláh, quoted by Shoghi Effendi, 'The Unfoldment of World Civilization', *The World Order of Bahá'u'lláh*, p. 186.
65. *Essays:* 'Of Unity in Religion'.

holds society together'.[66] It is therefore no wonder if the moral decadence of our society and the consequent brutalisation of our lives[67] and barbarisation of our manners[68] are rapidly advancing and nations are being visited by waves of violence, terrorism and lawlessness, with today's spreading unbelief.

Bahá'u'lláh's influence over society is not restricted to the behaviour of the individual believer. He has also laid down the foundations of a new order in which all peoples, united by their common belief in God and His revelation, will live together in peace and justice. Bahá'u'lláh has come to establish the promised kingdom of God on earth. This kingdom is neither a supernatural, supraterrestrial place nor a metaphor for the abode of the deceased, but it is a kingdom on this planet. It is none other than the realisation of the unity of mankind and of world peace, the creation of an all-embracing and just order, in which every human being can live in security and fulfil himself in conformity with God's law, a kingdom in which God Himself rules His people.

To be a Bahá'í does not mean therefore that one only works selfishly, with an eye on the next world, for one's own salvation, but rather that one participates fully in this earthly life and co-operates in the building of this kingdom of peace as envisioned by the prophets. This will be realised neither in the way Christian zealots have imagined nor as so many socialists envision the creation of a new order, neither by God's cosmic interference in our order of existence with the consequent transformation of human nature which would then no longer be capable of evil, nor simply by the resolute adherence to the commandment to love one's neighbour, nor by the wholehearted observation of the exhortations in the Sermon on the Mount, as Leo Tolstoy vaguely dreamt. It will not come about simply by destroying the old social structures in revolutionary civil wars or by trying to build a new society free from contradictions in which man, no longer sup-

---

66. *Weltgeschichtliche Betrachtungen*, chapter 3, part 3, p. 104.

67. G. Hacker, *Conflict*, Thomas Nelson and Sons, New Jersey, 1969.

68. One small symptom of our cultural decadence is the gutter vocabulary used to-day even in university discussions—n.b. between educated people. The persuasive power which faeces apparently seem to have in discussion is noteworthy! Another symptom is the vocabulary relating to the anal and genital parts of the body and which playwrights seem incapable of doing without. If their intention is to shock, they can no longer achieve their aim for meanwhile the public has become used to this vocabulary. Besides, the so-called four-letter word has become acceptable even in polite society.

pressed or exploited, can fulfil himself and will spontaneously become 'good'. The kingdom of peace will come to men neither as
a cosmic event, as some Christians, on the basis of a literal interpretation of the Scriptures, expect,[69] nor 'from the barrel of a gun'
(Mao Tse Tung). Peace and justice cannot be bombed on to the
planet. They will be the fruit of a complete transformation of
human consciousness and of a laborious building process by a
new race of men.

Man's effort to tread the path of virtue and lead a life pleasing
to God and inspired by the norms of Christian ethics will not by
itself save mankind from its torments and troubles. For this
striving, even in the few places it still exists, is becoming intoler-
ably limited by men's superstitions and prejudices and by the con-
straints of a sick society. How can the commandment to love one's
neighbour overcome the basic illness of mankind, its division and
disunity, when to this day that commandment—and the events in
Northern Ireland and Lebanon are sad examples of it—is still
restricted literally to the 'neighbour', that is to the member of the
same race, the same nation, the same class, the same confession,
and mankind is not seen as one? Has this command ever prevented unjust social structures from being formed? Is it not precisely in 'God's own land', in puritanical America, a country
where the Pilgrim Fathers wanted to build a Christian state inspired by the precepts of the Sermon on the Mount, that the
division between rich and poor and black and white is most un-
bearable and gives rise to confrontations reminiscent of civil war?
A man born in the slums of Harlem or Calcutta does not see the
light of this world but its gloom. What chance does he stand of
leading a virtuous life when poverty, hunger, dirt and crime sur-
round him from early childhood and when he lacks the barest
necessities for his material and spiritual development? Unless all
prejudices are overcome, as Bahá'u'lláh so urgently commands,
and the great social contradictions solved, mankind will not find
peace nor will the individual be able to fulfil his high destiny.

On the other hand, unless man has an elevated goal and is
answerable to a power superior to the institution of society, even
the best imaginable social order will not cause him to control his
ego and master his own aggressiveness, to overcome his baser
instincts, improve his character and be more than a mere wolf

69. e.g. Jehovah's witnesses.

among wolves.[70] It is undeniable that there is a cause-and-effect connection between crime and society. But it is equally true that criminal behaviour can be caused to some extent or even entirely by a bad disposition, an evil way of life, or bad character: social conditions do not force the individual to act in a certain way; they only encourage certain inclinations.[71]

Bahá'ís believe that two forces—the elements of a historical dialectic already taking place—will bring about mankind's golden age: first, the transformation of man, his spiritual rebirth through God's creative word; secondly, the transformation of society both through the change in its structures according to the divine will proclaimed by Bahá'u'lláh, and through the establishment by means of Bahá'u'lláh's world order, of universal justice in which all men can live in peace.

The old and the new order

We are experiencing this process of the fall of the old order and the building up of the new one. The collapse of the old order, however painful and dangerous, is necessary and cannot be stopped; it is as necessary as the sweeping away of the leaves from the trees by the cold wind in winter, which makes room for the tender buds, already perceptible.

But there is one point we must not lose sight of: it is not our duty to tear down the old order which we find unacceptable. Over a hundred years ago, at a time when people thought 'We've really come a long way', and when no one could imagine the extent of the present cultural decadence, Bahá'u'lláh foretold the breaking down of the old social order and the rise of a new one: 'Soon will the present-day order be rolled up, and a new one spread out in its stead.'[72] Today we are realising the meaning of these words. Our forms of government are being questioned. Young people are rebelling against the existing social order. The entire world is crying out for reforms and—one cannot help feeling—the more it is reformed, the more disastrous is the confusion and the more insoluble become our problems and conflicts.

70. The English philosopher Thomas Hobbes (1588–1679) put forward the well-known theory that man in his natural state behaves like a wolf towards his fellow-men: 'Homo homini lupus', *Elementa philosophiae*, Paris, 1642.

71. 'The fault, dear Brutus, is not in our stars, But in ourselves, that we are underlings' (Shakespeare, *Julius Caesar*, I. ii).

72. *Gleanings*, IV.

Why? Because the foundations of our cultures, the great religions, have lost their power and are breaking up, because the values given to us by the religions and which form the basis of our culture are no longer considered binding; people no longer 'believe' in them. Thus, our epoch is no longer an epoch of reforms, nor of reformations.[73] The sick body of mankind can no longer be healed with palliatives but only with a radical cure. Radical means 'from the root' and healing from the root implies laying a new foundation for a stable society. This foundation is a new faith inspiring man with a new consciousness, a world consciousness, giving him a new set of values, a goal and a meaning to his life and showing him a way out of his hopelessness. Thus Bahá'ís are actually the real 'radicals' and the Bahá'í Faith is the most radical movement today. But Bahá'ís are not radical in their methods; they are neither subversive nor violent. They are no fermenting-agents in the process of decomposition and no revolutionaries climbing the barricades and throwing bombs. They know that this old, mouldy system will burst apart by itself like rotten fruit without their intervention, and they know what their task is: the building up of the new order.

This explains why Bahá'ís do not engage in political activities and may not belong to any political party. For today every political activity must be carried out within a system and must use the methods of that system which is destined to fall. Moreover, the Bahá'í Faith would lose its power to unite if its believers were to become involved in political disputes as a 'party'—that is, restricted in a separatist way—or as members of the different existing parties. Shoghi Effendi has convincingly demonstrated that the Faith of God suffers when believers enter 'the arena of party politics'. 'We Bahá'ís', his secretary wrote on his behalf, 'are one the world over; we are seeking to build up a new World Order, divine in origin. How can we do this if every Bahá'í is a member of a different political party . . . Where is our unity then? . . . The

73. The real core of our lives, the 'dimension of depth' (Paul Tillich) has been lost and cannot be made good by human means. All attempts to breathe new life into old religions will fail. For true reformation comes from God: 'The vitality of men's belief in God is dying out in every land; nothing short of His wholesome medicine can ever restore it. The corrosion of ungodliness is eating into the vitals of human society; what else but the Elixir of His potent Revelation can cleanse and revive it?' (Bahá'u'lláh, *Gleanings*, XCIX). Thus the revelation of Bahá'u'lláh is also the judgment upon the old religions, since it purifies the genuine and true from the artificial and false, from human trimmings and misunderstandings. See also p. 86.

best way for a Bahá'í to serve his country and the world is to work for the establishment of Bahá'u'lláh's World Order which will gradually unite all men and do away with divisive political systems and religious creeds.'[74]

The law of strict abstinence from party politics seems surprising in a religion which is directed so much towards altering and transforming this world. To many this attitude seems inconsistent and self-contradictory, and quite often the Bahá'ís are reproached with holding themselves back from the 'real problems' of society and of their fellow human beings, and with passively watching the world hastening to its destruction.

Is this reproach justified? The question is: what is 'reality', what is the 'real world'? For someone who only accepts as reality what can be perceived, what can be actually experienced or empirically verified, or who sees the reality of society only in its socio-economic conditions, the political abstinence of the Bahá'ís may appear as a refusal to cooperate in the building of a humane and just world, and a refusal to eliminate the evils of this world.

The Bahá'ís know, however, that the visible world is only a part of reality and 'that the working of the material world is merely a reflection of spiritual conditions and until the spiritual conditions can be changed there can be no lasting change for the better in material affairs'.[75]

In this context it should be realised that most of those who expect the world to be saved by political action alone themselves 'have no clear concept of the sort of world they wish to build, nor how to go about building it. Even those who are concerned to improve conditions are therefore reduced to combatting every apparent evil that takes their attention. Willingness to fight against evils, whether in the form of conditions or embodied in evil men, has thus become for most people the touchstone by which they judge a person's moral worth. Bahá'ís, on the other hand, know the goal they are working towards and know what they must do, step by step, to attain it. Their whole energy is directed towards the building of the good, a good which has such a positive strength that in the face of it the multitude of evils—which are in essence negative—will fade away and be no more. To

---

74. *Principles of Bahá'í Administration*, p. 31.
75. Quoted from a letter dated 7 July 1976 from the Universal House of Justice to a believer.

enter into the quixotic tournament of demolishing one by one the
evils in the world is, to a Bahá'í, a vain waste of time and effort.
His whole life is directed towards proclaiming the Message of
Bahá'u'lláh, reviving the spiritual life of his fellow-men, uniting
them in a divinely-created World Order, and then, as that Order
grows in strength and influence, he will see the power of that
Message transforming the whole of human society and progressively solving the problems and removing the injustices which
have so long bedevilled the world.'[76]

Bahá'u'lláh clearly states that mankind's political leaders are at
a standstill and will not find a way out of the distress which is
growing worse day by day; He says that in its present troubles
what the world needs is an 'All-Knowing Physician' who 'hath
His finger on the pulse of mankind' and who 'in His unerring
wisdom' perceives the disease and prescribes the remedy: 'We can
well perceive how the whole human race is encompassed with
great, with incalculable afflictions. We see it languishing on its bed
of sickness, sore-tried and disillusioned. They that are intoxicated
by self-conceit have interposed themselves between it and the
Divine and infallible Physician. Witness how they have entangled
all men, themselves included, in the mesh of their devices. They
can neither discover the cause of the disease, nor have they any
knowledge of the remedy. They have conceived the straight to be
crooked and have imagined their friend an enemy'.[77]

Thus the salvation of the world cannot be expected from political action alone. Without spiritual rebirth mankind will not be
cured. The task of the Bahá'ís is therefore a constructive one,
theirs is the duty to proclaim the glad-tidings, to bring the divine
remedy to a sorely-stricken humanity, to quicken the hearts of
men, to educate them and unite the peoples of the world. And it
is in this sense that Bahá'u'lláh's command of obedience to one's
government must be understood: rebellion and strife have a
destructive effect and make the evil worse. Bahá'u'lláh, therefore,
warns His people not to take part in the uproar and conflict that
have seized the rest of mankind: 'Address yourselves to the pro-
motion of the well-being and tranquillity of the children of men.
Bend your minds and wills to the education of the peoples and
kindreds of the earth, that haply the dissensions that divide it may,
through the power of the Most Great Name, be blotted out from

76. ibid.   77. *Gleanings*, CVI.

its face, and all mankind become the upholders of one Order, and the inhabitants of one City. Illumine and hallow your hearts; let them not be profaned by the thorns of hate or the thistles of malice. Ye dwell in one world, and have been created through the operation of one Will. Blessed is he who mingleth with all men in a spirit of utmost kindliness and love.'[78]

Respect for the law and obedience to government are unconditional prerequisites, for without the loyalty of men no order can last. In the just world order of the future, this law of Bahá'u'lláh will be equally important.

Authority and obedience

If we consider what determines the attitude and the actions of a Bahá'í we must start with a concept that people do not like to hear of nowadays: obedience. After the way this word has been misused it is no wonder that it is no longer much valued. Obedience implies authority, and what kind of authority is acknowledged today when everything is being questioned? And yet, religion is unthinkable without obligations and obedience. Religion is the 'encounter with the sacred', the purely absolute: 'The essence of religion is to testify unto that which the Lord hath revealed, and follow that which He hath ordained in His mighty Book.'[79] The word which the manifestation proclaims is the Word of God. Thus the divine messenger speaks with the highest degree of authority. This authority must be carefully examined. If it is accepted, then all that the manifestation says and does is 'absolute wisdom, and is in accordance with the reality. If some people do not understand the hidden secret of one of His commands and actions, they ought not to oppose it, for the universal Manifestation does what He wishes.'[80] Bahá'u'lláh says quite clearly, 'Whenever My laws appear like the sun in the heaven of Mine utterance, they must be faithfully obeyed by all, though My decree be such as to cause the heaven of every religion to be cleft asunder. He doth what He pleaseth. He chooseth; and none may question His choice. Whatsoever He, the Well-Beloved, ordaineth, the same is, verily, beloved . . . Well is it with him that hath turned thereunto, and apprehended the meaning of His decisive decree.'[81]

78. *Gleanings*, CLVI.
79. Bahá'u'lláh, Words of Wisdom, *Bahá'í World Faith*, p. 140.
80. 'Abdu'l-Bahá, *Some Answered Questions*, VL.
81. *Gleanings*, CLV.

A partial acceptance of the revelation of Bahá'u'lláh is not possible because from the moment parts of His message are rejected, Bahá'u'lláh is put on the level of a fallible human being. There are people who whole-heartedly agree with the pacific, inter-racial and humanitarian strivings of the Bahá'ís and with their goal, the unity of mankind. But they have their own ideas as to the way to achieve this goal and refuse to follow Bahá'u'lláh when His word does not suit them for some reason. 'These people with one hand cling to the verses . . . which they have found to accord with their inclinations and interests, and with the other reject those which are contrary to their selfish desires. "Believe ye then part of the Book, and deny part?"'[82, 83] Such a selective attitude is impossible for a true believer. Shoghi Effendi's secretary wrote on his behalf:

> Allegiance to the Faith cannot be partial and half-hearted. Either we should accept the Cause without any qualification whatever, or cease calling ourselves Bahá'ís. The new believers should be made to realise that it is not sufficient for them to accept some aspects of the teachings and reject those which cannot suit their mentality in order to become fully recognised and active followers of the Faith. In this way all sorts of misunderstandings will vanish and the organic unity of the Cause will be preserved.[84]

This is where religion differs from philosophy. However inspiring the teaching of a philosopher and however convincing his arguments, it is a fallible man who speaks, one with no greater authority than the convincing power of his words. Error is always possible. One can adopt part of his statement and reject another part.

The Word of God belongs to a different category. It demands unconditional obedience even when one does not grasp the profound wisdom it contains. Each person comes in contact with the Cause of God from a different angle and with different personal convictions and it often happens that precisely what attracts one is looked upon with reserve by another. Faith is a process of inner growth and it is absolutely legitimate to put aside articles of faith

82. *Qur'án* 2:79.
83. *Kitáb-i-Íqán*, p. 108 (Brit.), p. 168 (U.S.).
84. *Bahá'í Procedure*, p. 18.

which one cannot understand at first until one's knowledge has grown—always mindful of Bahá'u'lláh's exhortation: to 'cleanse and purify his heart ... from the obscuring dust of all acquired knowledge'[85] and to consider the book itself as the 'unerring balance established amongst men'.[86]

What is freedom ?

For the believer the required submission he is expected to show to the will of God,[87] which is the essence of religion, means that he has to come to terms with his ego and with God, with his selfish, worldly desires and the divine command. Bahá'ís are not enjoined to flee this life as ascetics, but to turn to God, to strive for an inner detachment from everything transitory, and to subordinate their whole lives to their faith. 'O Son of Spirit! There is no peace for thee save by renouncing thyself and turning unto Me.'[88] 'Say: Deliver your souls, O people, from the bondage of self, and purify them from all attachment to anything besides Me.'[89] But the self-knowledge and self-conquest required from the believers is rewarded at the end by everlasting happiness: 'O My servants! Sorrow not if, in these days and on this earthly plane, things contrary to your wishes have been ordained and manifested by God, for days of blissful joy, of heavenly delight, are assuredly in store for you.'[90]

The fulfilment of God's commands demands effort and striving on the part of the believer.[91] Observance of the divine prohibitions means the restriction of his own freedom of action. This is obvious; all forms of ethics set limits to one's freedom of action and every religion has done this. Absolute freedom of action, the unlimited exercise of one's own will, as is demanded by some today, does not lead to man's liberation but to chaos. Unrestricted freedom in which the autonomous person does not observe any limits other than those which he sets himself—and these are not binding in the end—must 'lead to sedition, whose flames none can

85. *Kitáb-i-Íqán*, p. 123 (Brit.), p. 192 (U.S.).
86. *Gleanings*, XCVIII.
87. This is the true meaning of the word 'Islám': submission to the will of God.
88. Bahá'u'lláh, *The Hidden Words*, Arabic 8.
89. *Gleanings*, CXXXVI.
90. *Gleanings*, CLIII.
91. '... strait is the gate, and narrow is the way, which leadeth unto life, and few there be that find it' (Matthew 7:14).

quench ... That which beseemeth man is submission unto such restraints as will protect him from his own ignorance, and guard him against the harm of the mischief-maker. Liberty causeth man to overstep the bounds of propriety, and to infringe on the dignity of his station.'[92]

This striving for unlimited freedom condemned by Bahá'u'lláh is widespread today and the concept is clearly expressed by Arno Plack[93] when he says that man's aggressiveness is not original but has been learnt only through frustration of his impulses; and only when his sexuality is no longer suppressed and he is allowed to live out his spontaneous instincts to the full can he achieve true fulfilment. This idea can only be understood if one accepts a popularised libido-theory which lies at the basis of this purely materialistic, pansexual vision of man. If we took seriously the demand to abolish all institutionalised forms of behaviour and to leave all sexual relationship to the personal will of the individual, we would soon have a culture reminiscent of a rabbit hutch: 'to act like the beasts of the field is unworthy of man'.[94] And if we were to abolish penal law, as Plack also demands,[95] we would have complete chaos.

The laws of Bahá'u'lláh are not an expression of divine caprice, nor do they suppress or violate human nature. They are 'not imposition of will, or of power, or pleasure, but the resolutions of truth, reason and justice'.[96] They are 'the lamps of My loving providence among My servants, and the keys of My mercy for My creatures', 'the highest means for the maintenance of order in the world and the security of its peoples'.[97] This is why true freedom consists in 'man's submission unto My commandments, little as ye know it ... The liberty that profiteth you is to be found nowhere except in complete servitude unto God, the Eternal Truth.'[98]

Life as preparation
With the same conviction as that with which they have proclaimed the unity of mankind and the changing of our conditions on earth,

92. *Gleanings*, CLIX.
93. *Die Gesellschaft und das Böse.*
94. *Gleanings*, CIX.
95. *Plädoyer für die Abschaffung des Strafrechts.*
96. 'Abdu'l-Bahá, *Paris Talks*, p. 154.
97. Bahá'u'lláh, *Gleanings*, CLV.
98. *Gleanings*, CLIX.

so do Bahá'ís know that this world is only transitory, a preparation for the next world. 'Abdu'l-Bahá draws the analogy with one's life before birth: 'In the beginning of his human life man was embryonic in the world of the matrix. There he received capacity and endowment for the reality of human existence. The forces and powers necessary for the world were bestowed upon him in that limited condition. In this world he needed eyes: he received them potentially in the other. He needed ears; he obtained them there in readiness and preparation for his new existence. The powers requisite in this world were conferred upon him in the world of the matrix, so that when he entered this realm of real existence he not only possessed all necessary functions and powers but found provision for his material sustenance awaiting him.

'Therefore in this world he must prepare himself for the life beyond. That which he needs in the world of the kingdom must be obtained here. Just as he prepared himself in the world of the matrix by acquiring forces necessary in this sphere of existence, so likewise the indispensable forces of the divine existence must be potentially attained in this world.

'What is he in need of in the kingdom which transcends the life and limitation of this mortal sphere? That world beyond is a world of sanctity and radiance; therefore it is necessary that in this world he should acquire these divine attributes. In that world there is need of spirituality, faith, assurance, the knowledge and love of God. These he must attain in this world so that after his ascension from the earthly to the heavenly kingdom he shall find all that is needful in that life eternal ready for him . . .'[99]

It is therefore evident that the way one lives is not at all a matter of indifference. As all sacred writings testify, one is answerable for one's acts: 'Bring thyself to account each day ere thou art summoned to a reckoning; for death, unheralded, shall come upon thee and thou shalt be called to give account for thy deeds.'[100]

Death, that decisive change which is part of man's life, the complete change into another sphere of existence, has no place or value in the thinking of modern man. Killing and being killed is an integral part of our society, to a large extent because of its continual demonstration on the cinema and television screens; natural death, on the other hand, is made taboo, the thought of

99. *The Promulgation of Universal Peace*, p. 220 ff.
100. Bahá'u'lláh, *The Hidden Words*, Arabic 31. See also Matthew 7:19-23.

death is repressed and the last act which is in store for everyone is banished into the loneliness of sick-rooms, and death (and thus life as well) has no meaning.

In the past, people's attitude to death was different: life was considered from the perspective of death; the hour-glass was the reminder, the *memento mori*, the constant and vivid representation of our transitoriness and the proof of how relative is earthly longing for happiness. We must remember that for Bahá'ís, too, this is the right attitude for death, which terminates this earthly life, is at the same time, the gateway to true life into which we are born. Here man is suddenly faced with what he has done on earth, with the divine perfections he has achieved, in a word with what he is. Now it is that he has to account for his life on earth.

It is very fashionable today to question this responsibility by saying that man, being driven by his impulses and social pressures, has no freedom of action. This attitude has grave consequences for the individual who believes in it as well as for the society which treats him according to this belief. That man is, to a great extent, exposed to pressures and determined by them, is undeniable. But that man has the freedom of choice between good and evil is a fact which each one of us can experience every day and a truth proclaimed by all religions. And just as everyone is able to recognise God and His manifestations,[101] everyone also has the capacity to accomplish the will of God as it manifests itself in the divine law; 'God will not burden any soul beyond its capacity.'[102] 'Man has the power both to do good and to do evil.'[103] The idea that God, the law-giver, provides men with an absolute rule of conduct and imposes upon them the duty 'to testify unto that which the Lord hath revealed, and follow that which He hath ordained in His mighty Book',[104] and that at the same time as creator, he has not endowed them with the capacity to fulfil this law,[105] contradicts the concept of God's justice and is absolutely unacceptable to religious thought. In this context, the statement: 'Thou canst for thou shouldst'[106] is important. Therefore no one *has* to steal, no one *has* to commit adultery, no one *has* to get drunk, no one *has* to

101. See Bahá'u'lláh, *Gleanings*, LXXV.
102. *Qur'án* 2:287.
103. 'Abdu'l-Bahá, *Paris Talks*, p. 60.
104. Bahá'u'lláh, Words of Wisdom, *Bahá'í World Faith*, p. 140.
105. Compare p. 90 ff.
106. Immanuel Kant (1724–1804).

smoke hashish. The theory which denies all human responsibility, on the assumption that man, bound by society's restrictions and his own impulses has no freedom of action, is the logical consequence of atheism: 'If God does not exist', Dostoyevsky makes Ivan Karamazov say, 'then everything is permitted; if there is no God, then everything is indifferent.' Dostoyevsky means here that when man is his own law-giver and acknowledges no higher responsibility than the state courts, he can justify any crime.

The new man

A new idea and a new society requires a new kind of people. Like all former prophets, Bahá'u'lláh urges man to change and be born again spiritually, and he proclaims that God's kingdom on earth must first be established in the hearts of men: 'The purpose of the one true God in manifesting Himself is to summon all mankind to truthfulness and sincerity, to piety and trustworthiness, to resignation and submissiveness to the Will of God, to forbearance and kindliness, to uprightness and wisdom. His object is to array every man with the mantle of a saintly character, and to adorn him with the ornament of holy and goodly deeds.'[107]

Being a Bahá'í is not a matter of name, nor merely of belonging to a community. Once when 'Abdu'l-Bahá was asked what a Bahá'í was, he answered: 'To be a Bahá'í simply means to love all the world; to love humanity and try to serve it; to work for universal peace and universal brotherhood.' In one of his talks in London, he said that someone could be a Bahá'í even if he had never heard the name of Bahá'u'lláh: 'The man who lives the life according to the teachings of Bahá'u'lláh is already a Bahá'í. On the other hand, a man may call himself a Bahá'í for fifty years, and if he does not live the life he is not a Bahá'í. An ugly man may call himself handsome, but he deceives no one.'[108] These words show briefly but clearly what the decisive factors are: our life and our actions. In the sacred writings of the Bahá'í Faith no idea recurs as often as this one: man must bring forth fruits; he must not waste these days which will never return. Here are a few quotations on this subject: 'The essence of faith', Bahá'u'lláh writes, 'is fewness of words and abundance of deeds; he whose words exceed

---

107. *Gleanings*, CXXXVII.
108. J. E. Esslemont, *Bahá'u'lláh and the New Era*, p. 69.

his deeds, know verily his death is better than his life.'[109] 'The companions of God are, in this day, the lump that must leaven the peoples of the world. They must show forth such trustworthiness, such truthfulness and perseverance, such deeds and character that all mankind may profit by their example.'[110] 'O army of God!' writes 'Abdu'l-Bahá, '. . . should any one of you enter a city, he should become a centre of attraction by reason of his sincerity, his faithfulness and love, his honesty and fidelity, his truthfulness and loving-kindness towards all the peoples of the world, so that the people of that city may cry out and say: "This man is unquestionably a Bahá'í, for his manners, his behaviour, his conduct, his morals, his nature, and disposition reflect the attributes of the Bahá'ís."'[111]

An oft-recurring exhortation of Bahá'u'lláh is: 'Beware, O people of Bahá, lest ye walk in the ways of them whose words differ from their deeds . . . Let your acts be a guide unto all mankind, for the profession of most men, be they high or low, differ from their conduct. It is through your deeds that ye can distinguish yourselves from others.'[112] And 'Abdu'l-Bahá shows us why the world is in such a sad plight: 'What profit is there in agreeing that universal friendship is good, and talking of the solidarity of the human race as a grand ideal? Unless these thoughts are translated into the world of action, they are useless. The wrong in the world continues to exist just because people talk only of their ideals, and do not strive to put them into practice. If actions took the place of words, the world's misery would very soon be changed into comfort.'[113]

Modern man basically respects only two things: credible theories and observable facts. The credible theory is at hand in the world order of Bahá'u'lláh. The observable facts must be brought forth by the Bahá'ís. Modern society, which is so deeply influenced by the technical and mathematical sciences, will lend no ear to an intellectualised proclamation of teachings. 'As a matter of fact no one cares very much what we say,' writes Ruḥíyyih Rabbání. 'Everyone is saying something these days: from every loudspeaker in the world, in Chinese, Czech, Spanish and so on, people

---

109. Words of Wisdom, *Bahá'í World Faith*, p. 140.
110. Quoted by Shoghi Effendi, *The Advent of Divine Justice*, p. 19.
111. ibid., p. 21.
112. *The Divine Art of Living*, p. 77.
113. *Paris Talks*, p. 16.

are shouting good plans, good precepts, good ideas—many of them are in fact similar or identical with our Bahá'í plans, precepts and ideas—but they are, as we can see from the state of the world, largely ineffectual. Why? Because nothing goes on behind them, there is no right action, no upright conduct backing them up and everyone knows it.'[114] And Mark Twain's remark is very much to the point: 'The great pity with world-reformers is that they do not start with themselves.' As long as the Bahá'í is swallowed up in the general current, he cannot hope to serve as the guide or the lighthouse in this dark period of history. What characterises a true believer is the unreserved earnestness with which he conforms his practical actions to the teachings of Bahá'u'lláh. This requires detachment from the world, this pleasure-seeking, consumer society with its superficial pastimes, and it also requires sacrifice. Whoever is not ready to take these consequences upon himself and allows himself to be assimilated by a decadent society—and we are living in one—whoever has not the courage to swim against the current, perishes with this society.

To be a Bahá'í today means—since society is deteriorating so rapidly—to swim against the current. This calls for courage. For instance he who, in accordance with Bahá'u'lláh's teachings, avoids all alcoholic drinks in a society where social life is charac- terised by the offering of alcohol, and where drinking customs actually amount to an obligation to drink, such a man will be looked upon, at least in Europe, as an odd sectarian and an eccen- tric outsider. But the Bahá'í must come to terms with this state of affairs. 'The indifference and scorn of the world matters not at all.'[115] In our epoch of transition, the Bahá'í may well feel at times that he is in the same position as the character described by Schopenhauer 'whose watch gives the right time in a town where all the clocks are wrong. He alone knows the right time: but of what use is that to him? Everybody is guided by the town-clocks which give the wrong time.'[116]

It is a well-known fact that whoever goes in for something new exposes himself to a certain degree of ridicule, for man's herd- instinct is great. As Ruḥíyyih Rabbání rightly remarks, people are in this respect very similar to sheep: 'they all "baa" together, they

114. *Success in teaching.*
115. 'Abdu'l-Bahá, *Paris Talks*, p. 118.
116. *Aphorismen zur Lebensweisheit*, V, 27.

all graze together, and they all stampede together. For a Bahá'í not to be able to realise that through identifying himself with the most progressive, constructive movement in the whole world, he has risen above the herd and covered himself with distinction, is pitiful.'[117]

It is certain that this detachment, as well as the constant effort towards self-knowledge and self-education enjoined upon us, is a lofty goal which requires constant vigilance and the readiness to correct one's self. But it would be a great error to calm our consciences by thinking that this goal is unattainable, in the same way that it has become usual to describe the exhortations of the Sermon on the Mount as unrealisable 'ethics of idealistic zealots'.[118] This goal can be attained, these ethics can be realised. A man—'Abdu'l-Bahá—has set the example for us and we can attempt to emulate him.

The people of the new covenant
Accordingly, to be a Bahá'í means to strive after human perfection but also to work for a new social order. The Bahá'í should not, therefore, lead a life of contemplation and self-engrossment in seclusion, far from the trivialities and the real problems of society. Instead, he should be engaged in the changing and forming of himself in conformity with the demands of these new ethics, as well as in the building up of a new order and the creation of a better world. He cannot pursue and reach this goal alone, in isolation, but only as a member of a community. To be a Bahá'í means, therefore, to belong to the Bahá'í community, to the people of Bahá.

There is only one condition attached to this membership, the recognition of Bahá'u'lláh as manifestation of God and the unreserved acceptance of his teachings and commands. No one who espouses his Faith is expected to show a specific measure of perfection. The only important things are the sincere wish to live according to the teachings of Bahá'u'lláh and the effort to advance on the path of perfection. And only God knows the degree to which each one of us is ready to progress spiritually.

Whoever becomes a Bahá'í must, therefore, be aware that the community he is joining is not a heavenly group of angelic beings

117. *Success in Teaching.*
118. Gerhard Szczesny, *Die Zukunft des Unglaubens*, p. 51.

but a community of imperfect people. And the more society breaks up, the more will those come to Bahá'u'lláh 'that labour and are heavy laden',[119] the rejected, the under-privileged, the oppressed, the hopeless, the sick in body and soul, the addicts. Bahá'u'lláh has come for them too. And just as Bahá'u'lláh never rejects a man on account of his imperfections, a believer is not allowed to reject another on account of the latter's failings. 'Among the sons of men some souls are suffering through ignorance, let us hasten to teach them; others are like children needing care and education until they are grown, and some are sick—to these we must carry Divine healing.'[120]

On no point is the Bahá'í Faith more categorical than in asking the believer to refrain from fault-finding and backbiting: 'O Son of Man! Breathe not the sins of others so long as thou art thyself a sinner. Shouldst thou transgress this command, accursed wouldst thou be, and to this I bear witness.'[121] The self-righteous —according to Confucius, the 'worst robbers of virtue'—are exhorted by Bahá'u'lláh: 'O Son of Being! How couldst thou forget thine own faults and busy thyself with the faults of others? Whoso doeth this is accursed of Me'[122] . . . 'If the fire of self overcome you, remember your own faults and not the faults of My creatures, inasmuch as every one of you knoweth his own self better than he knoweth others.'[123] The true believer 'should forgive the sinful, and never despise his low estate, for none knoweth what his own end shall be'.[124]

Backbiting is 'grievous error'; it 'quencheth the light of the heart, and extinguisheth the life of the soul'.[125] 'Abdu'l-Bahá asks us 'to be silent concerning the faults of others, to pray for them and to help them through kindness, to correct their faults', and 'to look always at the good and not at the bad'.[126] This attitude of tolerance and loving-kindness, which Jesus Christ so emphatically enjoined upon His followers (compare Matthew 7:1–5), is the only guarantee that in a community of people with such different

119. Matthew 11:28.
120. 'Abdu'l-Bahá, *Paris Talks*, p. 121.
121. Bahá'u'lláh, *The Hidden Words*, Arabic 27.
122. ibid., Arabic 26.
123. ibid., Persian 66.
124. *Kitáb-i-Íqán*, p. 124 (Brit.), p. 194)U.S.).
125. ibid., p. 124 (Brit.), p. 193 (U.S.).
126. Quoted by Esslemont, *Bahá'u'lláh and the New Era*, p. 80.

backgrounds and education, love and harmony prevail instead of strife and dissension.

These exhortations and maxims concern the individual believer in his relationship with his fellow-men. The institutions of the community, on the other hand, should help believers to correct their faults and protect the community from law-breakers. Nor should the institutions look passively on if some believers were openly to undermine the common cause or intended to destroy God's Cause from within. Bahá'u'lláh and 'Abdu'l-Bahá have made provisions for the protection of the divine Covenant and for the foundation of society and its order is justice and not mercy.[127]

Why withdraw from the Church?

It is evident that he who joins this community must break away from the religious institution to which he has formerly belonged. This request is not a sign of narrow-minded confessionalism, it is a logical consequence. No one can serve two masters at the same time. Unless he be a schizophrenic no one can believe in the future return of Christ (as a Christian) and at the same time believe (as a Bahá'í) that Christ has returned in the person of Bahá'u'lláh. And just as no one can be of the Jewish Faith and at the same time Christian or Muslim, nor belong to two different denominations of one and the same religion, like the Catholic and Protestant churches, the Bahá'í cannot be a member of another religious community. To leave the Church is therefore a logical act. But it is also an act of honesty even towards the community to which one has until now belonged. 'We as Bahá'ís can never be known as hypocrites or as people insincere in their protestations and because of this we cannot subscribe to both the Faith of Bahá'u'lláh and ordinary church dogma. The churches are waiting for the coming of Jesus Christ; we believe He has come again in the glory of the Father. The Churches teach doctrines—various ones in various creeds—which we as Bahá'ís do not accept, such as the bodily resurrection, confession, or in some creeds, the denial of the immaculate conception. In other words, there is no Christian church today whose dogmas we Bahá'ís can truthfully say we accept in their entirety. Therefore to remain a member of the

127. 'The structure of world stability and order hath been reared upon, and will continue to be sustained by, the twin pillars of reward and punishment' (*Gleanings*, CXII). Compare with 'Abdu'l-Bahá, *Some Answered Questions*, ch. 77.

church is not proper for us, for we do so under false pretence. We should therefore withdraw from our churches but continue to associate, if we wish to, with the church members and Ministers. Our belief in Christ, as Bahá'ís, is so firm, so unshakeable and so exalted in nature that very few Christians are to be found nowadays who love Him and reverence Him and have the faith in Him that we have. It is only from the dogmas and creeds of the churches that we dissociate ourselves; not from the Spirit of Christianity.'[128]

Thus one is not disloyal to Christ. And as formerly the true Jew showed his fidelity to his prophet Moses by accepting Jesus,[129] the sincere follower of Christ shows his faithfulness to Christ by following Bahá'u'lláh unreservedly and with all his heart. But he who finds this venture too hazardous, who (out of consideration for his reputation, business and family) joins this religion without real commitment and without cutting the old ties, has not understood the true significance of religion. These words are meant for him: 'He that loveth father or mother more than me is not worthy of me; and he that loveth son or daughter more than me is not worthy of me',[130] and 'No man, having put his hand to the plough, and looking back, is fit for the kingdom of God'.[131]

The order of the community

The Bahá'í community is essentially more than a call to religious unity, a platform for the old world religions to meet on or a kind of vanguard for a world parliament of religions. It is not an association of like-minded world-reformers, but God's new people, the people of the latest covenant. Therefore it is not a loose, amorphous, spiritualistic movement, no 'spiritual anarchy' as Rudolf Sohm saw Christianity,[132] but a community based on law. The believers are not only united by the bond of faith and

128. Shoghi Effendi through his secretary, *Principles of Bahá'í Administration*, pp. 42–3.
129. John 5:45–7: 'Do not think that I will accuse you to the Father: there is one that accuseth you, even Moses, in whom ye trust. For had ye believed Moses, ye would have believed me: for he wrote of me. But if ye believe not his writings, how shall ye believe my words?'
130. Matthew 10:37. Compare also *Qur'án* 80:33–7.
131. Luke 9:62.
132. He based his argument on the Gospel of St. Matthew 18:20: 'For where two or three are gathered together in my name, there am I in the midst of them.'

love but also by the bond of law.[133] It is important for whoever
lives and works in this community to know its structure. A de-
tailed description is beyond the purpose of this book, but the
necessity and origin of this structure, and its significance to the
believer, are dealt with.[134]

Its legal structure has not come to the community as a result of
external necessity, but was given by its founder Bahá'u'lláh as an
integral part of his teaching. It is the first time in religious history
that the legal structure of the community has not been put in the
hands of men but has been given in documented form as part of
the divine Revelation. Bahá'u'lláh is 'the Judge, the Lawgiver and
Redeemer of all mankind' and also 'the Organizer of the entire
planet'.[135] He has given his community its unchangeable and unconditional legal form and has thus made sure that a dispute over
the right kind of structure cannot split the community of God as
has so often happened in religious history.

The necessity for some formal organisation is obvious. To be
able to assert itself and be active in this world, which is a world of
order, the community of God must have a legal structure. For this
is the only guarantee of the unity of the believers, the only protection against the community breaking up and becoming divided.
And were it not for this unity, the spiritual impulse bestowed
upon mankind through the Revelation of Bahá'u'lláh would
be dispersed and the spiritual forces latent within the Word
of God would be dissipated before they could even take effect.
This protection against schism and sect-forming is guaranteed
through the authenticity of the constitution of the Bahá'í community.

Besides, the legal institutions laid down by Bahá'u'lláh secure
the continuity of divine authority and guidance. With the passing

133. Dr. Kurt Hutten should consider this statement as well as the ones following
and bear them in mind when bringing out the new edition of his book (*Seher, Grübler,
Enthusiasten*, 10th edition, 1966, p. 317).

134. The administrative order of the Bahá'ís has the quality of law. It is a system
of spiritual law governing the institutions of the community and preserving the
rights and duties of the individual—in some ways comparable to canon law or the
Sharí'at of Islám. See my thesis, 'Die Grundlagen der Verwaltungsordnung der
Bahá'í (The Legal Basis of the Administrative Order of the Bahá'ís), Heidelberg,
1957 Diss. University Library. The existence of Bahá'í law does not lessen the
responsibility of the Bahá'í to obey the law of the country in which he lives. See
pp. 32–3 above.

135. Shoghi Effendi, *God Passes By*, p. 93.

away of the prophet the divine guidance of the people of God would have ceased. In the Book he left behind, divine guidance can be found, but the Book has been revealed to last over a long period of time and therefore offers only a framework as far as social norms are concerned. As the times and conditions change, it becomes necessary to have complementary laws. This cannot be dependent upon the more or less imperfect and above all uncontrollable guidance of individual believers. It must be possible for legal guidance of the community to be recognised on an objective basis. In the Bahá'í Faith divine guidance continues in an objective way, with an institution to which Bahá'u'lláh has promised his guidance and upon which he has conferred supreme authority. The Universal House of Justice has its residence in Haifa and leads the destinies of the Faith on the whole planet. The community order of Bahá'u'lláh is thus of a theocratic nature: God himself rules His people.

Moreover, this order has a democratic constitution. Through it, the demand for democracy is really taken seriously. Bahá'u'lláh emphasises the importance of the coming of age as well as the responsibility of modern man. Therefore no distinction is made in the Bahá'í Faith between clergy and laymen. There is no priesthood, no impersonal higher court which comes in between the believer and God and claims to confer grace, just as there are no sacraments. All legal power has been excluded from the realm of personal conscience. Bahá'u'lláh has expressly forbidden confession. For these reasons alone it is wrong to say that the Bahá'í Faith is taking on the structure of a church (*Verkirchlichung*).[136] In its nature the Bahá'í community is not a 'church'. Besides, individuals have no power of jurisdiction or executive authority at all, but what is accepted is the principle of collective guidance. The guidance and administration of the community on the local, national and international levels have been given to the 'Houses of Justice' instituted by Bahá'u'lláh, their duties and prerogatives elucidated by 'Abdu'l-Bahá and their election vested in the body of the believers. As these Houses of Justice are still at the embryonic stage of their development, they are called 'Spiritual Assemblies' on the local and national levels. They must be 'the trusted ones of the Merciful among men' and 'regard themselves

136. See, for example, Gerhard Rosenkranz, *Die Bahá'í*, p. 56, and Kurt Hutten, op. cit., p. 319.

as the guardians appointed of God for all that dwell on earth'.[137]
But the 'principle of council' does not exist in the Marxist sense
where a member of the institution is only a mouthpiece and can be
recalled by the electors whenever they choose. In the Bahá'í Faith,
neither the elected bodies nor their individual members are
responsible to their electors. There is no imperative mandate.

The democratic principle is realised with much greater consis-
tency than in parliamentary democracy, for each believer who is
of age can not only vote but is also actually—not only in theory—
eligible for election. The votes and deliberations of these institutions are religious acts. They must take place in a spirit of prayer.
All election campaigning, propaganda, electoral lists, election
proposals, arrangements and candidatures, all party-forming, and
therefore all compulsion coming from a party, in short, every
attempt to influence the election and manipulate the consultative
and voting processes are strictly condemned. This is not only
because these conventions which poison all political life are contrary to the spirit of prayer, to the atmosphere of spiritual purity,
humility and selflessness in which both election and consultation
must take place, but above all because through them the believer's
right to do only what prayer has inspired him to do would be
impaired and the theocratic principle which is the basis of
Bahá'u'lláh's order would be neglected.

To be a Bahá'í also means to work loyally with others in these
divinely-ordained institutions and to respect their authority, for
the order of Bahá'u'lláh is not just an end in itself. It is not a
substitute for the absence of spirit[138] but the instrument which
serves to spread the Cause of God, the 'pattern for future society'
and 'a supreme instrument for the establishment of the Most
Great Peace'.[139]

The duty to teach

Finally, to be a Bahá'í means to proclaim the teachings of Bahá'u'-
lláh. Today, as mankind stands on the precipice of its menacing
self-destruction, each believer is called upon to distribute widely
the remedy for the many sorrows and afflictions of a tormented
humanity—the message of Bahá'u'lláh. For only when the Word

137. Bahá'u'lláh, Kitáb-i-Aqdas, *Synopsis and Codification*, p. 13.
138. As Dr. Hutten seems to think.
139. Shoghi Effendi, *The World Order of Bahá'u'lláh*, p. 19.

of God reaches men will they wake from their sleep and experience their spiritual rebirth.

In the Bahá'í Faith there is no special class appointed to proclaim the teachings. Every believer is urged, according to his ability and possibilities, to proclaim the Word of God. 'Teach ye the Cause of God, O people of Bahá, for God hath prescribed unto every one the duty of proclaiming His Message, and regardeth it as the most meritorious of all deeds.'[140] 'Arise, and lift up your voices, that haply they that are fast asleep may be awakened. Say: O ye who are dead! The Hand of Divine bounty proffereth unto you the Water of Life. Hasten and drink your fill.'[141] 'O ye beloved of God! Repose not yourselves on your couches, nay bestir yourselves as soon as ye recognize your Lord, the Creator . . . Unloose your tongues, and proclaim unceasingly His Cause.'[142]

The duty of the Bahá'í is clear: 'God hath prescribed unto every one the duty of teaching His Cause' and Bahá'u'lláh continues by immediately explaining the conditions for successful teaching: 'Whoever ariseth to discharge this duty, must needs, ere he proclaimeth His Message, adorn himself with the ornament of an upright and praiseworthy character, so that his words may attract the hearts of such as are receptive to his call. Without it, he can never hope to influence his hearers.'[143] And in another passage He says: 'Such a deed is acceptable only when he that teacheth the Cause is already a firm believer in God.'[144] 'Whoso ariseth among you to teach the Cause of his Lord, let him, before all else, teach his own self, that his speech may attract the hearts of them that hear him. Unless he teacheth his own self, the words of his mouth will not influence the heart of the seeker. Take heed, O people, lest ye be of them that give good counsel to others but forget to follow it themselves. The words of such as these, and beyond the words the realities of all things, and beyond these realities the angels that are nigh unto God, bring against them the accusation of falsehood.'[145]

'Wholly for the sake of God' and 'unrestrained as the wind' must the believer carry forward the message and thus show such 'steadfastness in the Cause of God, that no earthly thing whatsoever will have the power' to deter him from his duty, from guiding his 'neighbour to the law of God, the Most Merciful'.[146]

140. *Gleanings*, CXXVIII. 141. ibid., CVI. 142. ibid., CLIV.
143. ibid., CLVIII. 144. ibid., CXXVIII.
145. ibid., CXXVIII. 146. ibid., CLXI.

The importance ascribed by Bahá'u'lláh to the teaching task in general should not lead one to think that the Bahá'í teaching method is importunate proselytism. Bahá'ulláh exhorts the believers to be 'guided by wisdom'[147] above all in their teaching work and to treat people with patience, friendliness and good-will: 'If ye be aware of a certain truth, if ye possess a jewel, of which others are deprived, share it with them in a language of utmost kindliness and good-will. If it be accepted, if it fulfil its purpose, your object is attained. If anyone should refuse it, leave him unto himself, and beseech God to guide him. Beware lest ye deal unkindly with him. A kindly tongue is the lodestone of the hearts of men. It is the bread of the spirit, it clotheth the words with meaning, it is the fountain of the light of wisdom and understanding.'[148]

To force people to the path of God is foolish and runs counter to the command of wisdom. Patience and understanding are indispensable and proselytising is to be avoided as well as every undignified or ostentatious way of teaching the Cause. 'O Son of Dust! The wise are they that speak not unless they obtain a hearing, even as the cup-bearer, who proffereth not his cup till he findeth a seeker.'[149] And just as He does not approve of the conduct of the 'fearful' who seeks 'to dissemble his faith', Bahá'u'lláh cannot 'sanction the behaviour of the avowed believer that clamorously asserteth his allegiance to this Cause. Both should observe the dictates of wisdom, and strive diligently to serve the best interests of the Faith.'[150]

Time and again Bahá'u'lláh urges the believers to respect those who wish to go their own way: 'Whosoever desireth, let him turn aside from this counsel, and whosoever desireth, let him choose the path to his Lord' we read in the Tablet of Aḥmad, and in another passage He says: 'Should any man respond to thy call, lay bare before him the pearls of the wisdom of the Lord, thy God, which His Spirit hath sent down unto thee, and be thou of them that truly believe. And should any one reject thy offer, turn thou away from him, and put thy trust and confidence in the Lord, thy God, the Lord of all worlds.'[151] Thus conversion with the

147. *Gleanings*, XCVI; see also CXXXVI.
148. Bahá'u'lláh, *Epistle to the Son of the Wolf*, p. 15.
149. Bahá'u'lláh, *The Hidden Words*, Persian no. 36.
150. *Gleanings*, CLXIII.
151. ibid., CXXIX.

Nürnberger-Trichter[152] is just as much out of the question as an 'awakening' in the style of the present 'Jesus-movement'. 'Blind zeal can only do harm', a German proverb says. Sectarian proselytism is wrong, for it is based on the erroneous assumption that it lies within one's power to convince others of the truth provided one starts correctly and is pressing enough. But in reality religious truth cannot be demonstrated like a mathematical rule. Therefore, if they are to become Bahá'ís, people should not be 'converted', i.e. talked and pushed into the religion, nor should they be 'awakened', i.e. manipulated in such a way that their critical judgment is befogged. Rather should they become acquainted with the message of Bahá'u'lláh and be taught the Bahá'í teachings as long as they so desire. From then on it is their concern whether they decide to become Bahá'ís or not. Only when a person has made this decision of his own free-will is there a good chance that he will hold to it.

Bahá'u'lláh warns his followers emphatically against engaging in vain disputes: 'Rid thyself of all attachment to the vain allusions of men, and cast behind thy back the idle and subtle disputations of them that are veiled from God. Proclaim, then, that which the Most Great Spirit will inspire thee to utter in the service of the Cause of thy Lord, that thou mayest stir up the souls of all men . . .'[153] And in another passage He says: 'Beware lest ye contend with any one, nay, strive to make him aware of the truth with kindly manner and most convincing exhortation. If your hearer respond, he will have responded to his own behoof, and if not, turn ye away from him, and set your faces towards God's sacred Court, the seat of resplendent holiness.'[154]

The attitude of a true Bahá'í, far from being that of arrogance and pride, is rather humility at the divine threshold: 'Show forbearance and benevolence and love to one another. Should any one among you be incapable of grasping a certain truth, or be striving to comprehend it, show forth, when conversing with him, a spirit of extreme kindliness and good-will. Help him to see and recognize the truth, without esteeming yourself to be, in the least, superior to him, or to be possessed of greater endowments.'[155] And success does not justify a proud attitude either: 'Should such

---

152. *Nürnberger-Trichter:* a funnel by means of which information is successfully crammed into the head of even the dullest dunce.
153. *Gleanings*, CXXXIX.   154. ibid., CXXVIII.   155. ibid., V.

a man ever succeed in influencing any one, this success should be attributed not to him, but rather to the influence of the words of God, as decreed by Him Who is the Almighty, the All-Wise. In the sight of God he is regarded as a lamp that imparteth its light, and yet is all the while being consumed within itself.'[156]

Each teacher of the Faith is assured of divine assistance: 'Whoso openeth his lips in this Day and maketh mention of the name of his Lord, the hosts of Divine inspiration shall descend upon him from the heaven of My name, the All-Knowing, the All-Wise.'[157]

But the believer has the right to express his own belief and thoughts regarding the revealed text: 'We should not restrict the liberty of the individual to express his own views so long as he makes it clear that these views are his own ... This does not, however, mean that the absolute authority does not remain in the revealed Words. We should try and keep as near to the authority as we can and show that we are faithful to it by quoting from the Words of Bahá'u'lláh in establishing our points. To discard the authority of the revealed Words is heretic and to suppress completely individual interpretation of those Words is also bad.'[158] The believers must strike a happy medium between 'extreme orthodoxy on the one hand, and irresponsible freedom on the other'.[159] Through frequent reading they must deepen themselves in their understanding and knowledge of the utterance of Bahá'u'lláh to be able 'to give it to others in its pure form'.[160] However, the believer who is teaching the Faith does not have any authority for only the revealed Word is authoritative.

It is not difficult to understand why Bahá'u'lláh has described teaching as 'the most meritorious of all deeds'[161] for the weal and ill of mankind depend on God's message reaching them. 'Can any one of us feel', writes Rúḥíyyih Rabbani, 'he can receive such a bounty and yet withhold it from others, rest quiescent in his own inner sense of security and leave others untaught and unhelped in these disastrous days the world is passing through? Today, if ever, must ring in our ears the battle cry of Mullá Ḥusayn, 'Mount your steeds, O heroes of God!'[162]

156. *Gleanings*, CXXVIII.   157. ibid., CXXIX.
158. Shoghi Effendi, *Principles of Bahá'í Administration*, p. 35.
159. *Bahá'í Administration*, p. 42.
160. *Principles of Bahá'í Administration*, p. 11.
161. *Gleanings*, CXXVIII.   162. *Success in Teaching*.

Say: this is a weighty message, from which ye turn aside.

Qur'án 38:68

How strange the way of this people! They clamour for guidance, although the standards of Him Who guideth all things are already hoisted. They cleave to the obscure intricacies of knowledge, when He, Who is the Object of all knowledge, shineth as the sun. They see the sun with their own eyes, and yet question that brilliant Orb as to the proof of its light. They behold the vernal showers descending upon them, and yet seek an evidence of that bounty.

Bahá'u'lláh

Answer to a Theologian

How does the public react to the phenomenon of a new religion? Here in Europe the overwhelming majority behave as did the citizens of Rome and Athens at the appearance of Christianity; even if the new religion is not persecuted, the predominant response is scepticism and rejection, and often scorn and mockery also. The new Gospel is a 'stumbling-block' to the Christians and 'foolishness' to those who do not believe in God.[163]

The Bahá'í Faith gives a particular challenge to orthodox Christians who cannot see its existence as other than a threat to their long-held and cherished beliefs. Many, unable to examine the claim of Bahá'u'lláh objectively because they are not sufficiently unbiased and detached from their old-fashioned traditional doctrines, nevertheless pass judgment on the Cause of God.

In 1968 in Germany, opposition was aroused by the publication of a book, *Der gespaltene Himmel*, by Huschmand Sabet.[164] This book, an introduction to the Bahá'í Faith for the general public, attracted reviews in the German press and radio, some sympathetic, others critical. A review by Dr. Kurt Hutten[165] in the *Deutsches Allgemeines Sonntagsblatt* moved the present writer to a reply published under the title 'Religion Made to Measure?'[166]

Although the virulent tone of Dr. Hutten's article weakened his argument, the questions he raised were of more than passing interest. It was clearly not the last time that a theologian would

163. Compare I Corinthians 1:23.

164. Verum Verlag, Stuttgart, 1967. (English edition: *The Heavens are Cleft Asunder*, George Ronald, Oxford, 1975.)

165. He was for many years the leader of an institution of the Protestant Church in Germany, the 'Evangelische Zentralstelle für Weltanschauungsfragen' in Stuttgart. He is also the author of the book *Seher, Grübler, Enthusiasten* (Seers, Meditators, Enthusiasts), 1966, in which one chapter is concerned with the Bahá'í Faith.

166. *Religion nach Mass?*, Verum Verlag, Stuttgart, 1970.

examine the Bahá'í Faith, and so it was felt worthwhile and necessary to offer an answer to the criticism in the review. Polemics was
far from being my main concern; but it was almost inevitable,
considering the style of the review, that my answer should in part
have turned out polemical. Dr. Hutten did not mince words: inability to carry on a serious dialogue, defective knowledge of the
Christian Faith, lack of theological 'further education'—these
were some of his charges, not to mention his comment on 'helplessness faced by the message of the Cross', and his attempts to
represent the Bahá'ís as a group of fanatical illusionists.

Can sympathy and deep understanding be expected from a
church dignitary for a phenomenon which claims to be a revelation of God to mankind and therefore seems to rival the Christianity represented by the Church? Merely to ask the question is to
answer in the negative. Someone who is accustomed to think only
in the hidebound categories of a dogmatic system that demands
exclusiveness, someone who throughout his life has inveighed
even against other Christian denominations, directly they deviate
from his credal dogmas, can certainly be expected to give a rigid
'no' when challenged from outside. Churchmen just cannot see
the rival great religions as other than 'lies' (Karl Barth) or at best
as attempts at self-redemption which are human and therefore
doomed to failure, as tissues of truth, half-truth, error, superstition, illusion and charlatanry, as—in the view of Dr. Hutten—a
mass of 'general religious concepts and general human hopes and
expectations'—in short as an amalgam of disparate elements. This
blindness is a fact which has to be accepted. But while expecting
the adamant rejection, I could not help being surprised at the
arguments used by Dr. Hutten and by his outlook. If he is indeed
familiar, as he claims to be, with all the writings of Bahá'u'lláh
which have been published in German, it is difficult to see how he
could have devised such a pathetic, dismal and distorted picture
of this religion that the reader can only wonder how such a pitiful
movement finds any followers at all!

A synthetic religion?

Dr. Hutten puts Bahá'u'lláh on a level with the founder of the
Aḥmadíyyah sect, <u>Gh</u>ulám Aḥmad. The Bahá'í Faith, as described
by Huschmand Sabet, and the views of the future derived from it,
are declared to be 'resplendent façades'; and the reader is eagerly

offered 'a look behind the scenes', at the convulsions to which the Bahá'í Faith was exposed through the rivalries and disputes about the succession to Bahá'u'lláh and 'Abdu'l-Bahá and through the breakers of the Covenant. And how was this religion formed? By a synthesis: Bahá'u'lláh 'unshackled, modernised and enriched Islam by elements of his own teaching, so that a new religion was formed'. It is as simple as that. Like the recipe, 'Anyone who wants to bake a cake must have seven ingredients', Bahá'u'lláh founded the Bahá'í Faith. Islám was the basic material, which he modernised and 'unshackled', and elements of his own teaching are the extras with which he enriched it. And because it is the product of an immense synthesis, it is also a 'Religion made to measure' (as the mocking title of Dr. Hutten's article had it), a deliberately modern religion, adapted to the thinking and general philosophy of modern man, sensible, rational, without difficulties of thought, paradoxes, mysteries or dogmas. Basically, in fact, nothing more than a flat, trivial rationalism and morality within the framework of a theosophical system, without 'spiritual profile', without originality.

Bahá'u'lláh—a false prophet?

In all ages there have been a great many religious usurpers who have caused confusion by the assumption of a prophetic office, have collected a crowd of followers round themselves and have eventually foundered and sunk into oblivion. Dr. Hutten, by his reference to Mírzá Ghulám Aḥmad, tried to put Bahá'u'lláh among their ranks.[167] Such phenomena can especially be observed in periods when the coming of the Messiah is tensely expected, as at the birth of Christ and also, significantly, around the middle of the nineteenth century. Judgment of truth and error becomes more difficult for those living at the time. The conservatives and the orthodox, who persist in their old traditions, have always been suspicious of true and false prophets alike, and if ever they commit themselves, it is quite often to the false ones. Was not the founder of Christianity also a trouble-maker, an innovator who disturbed the keepers of the old traditions in their rest? Was not he too rejected and persecuted by churchmen of his time as a usurper, while a Bar-Kochba, whose political activities matched

---

167. See also Parrinder, *Comparative Religion*, p. 108.

the ambition of the people who had rejected Christ, was later greeted jubilantly as the Messiah?

History gives judgment on whether the 'sun' rose or whether only a lamplighter was at work. The standard is 'By their fruits ye shall know them'.[168] Jesus and Muḥammad—to name only these two—transformed men and changed the world and so survived the 'crackpots' of their age. Who today remembers Mani, who knows of Musaylimah the 'Liar', the false prophet of Arabia, who proposed to Muḥammad to share the world between them? The future will show whether Bahá'u'lláh is to be seen as the Lord of a new era and a manifestation of the living God or only a usurper of the prophetic office. For 'If this Cause be of God, no man can prevail against it; and if it be not of God, the divines amongst you, and they that follow their corrupt desires, and such as have re-belled against Him, will surely suffice to overpower it.'[169]

The tribulations of betrayal

As for the look behind the scenes, the Bahá'ís have never made any secret of the fact that their Faith, which has developed in the bright light of history, has gone through a series of the severest internal crises, 'such as to exceed in gravity those from which the religions of the past have suffered'.[170] The plots to which Bahá'u'-lláh was exposed by his step-brother, Mírzá Yaḥyá, the succession disputes which shook the Faith after the deaths of both Bahá'u'-lláh and 'Abdu'l-Bahá, are all to be read in the standard work of the history of the Bahá'í Faith, Shoghi Effendi's *God Passes By*. These melancholy happenings are like illnesses, which shook and prostrated the young Faith and temporarily obscured its bright-ness; yet after they had been overcome, on each occasion it arose with new strength.

No religion has been spared similar experiences. The greatest and most dangerous adversaries to religions have grown up from within them and not outside them. Marcion, not Domitian, Dio-cletian or Julian, was the most dangerous threat to the unity of the young Christian community. Usually it was the nearest relatives, disciples or confidants who betrayed their Lord and master.

168. Matthew 7:20.
169. Bahá'u'lláh, quoted by Shoghi Effendi, *The Promised Day is Come*, p. 90. cf. Acts 5:38 et seq.
170. Shoghi Effendi, *God Passes By*, p. 410.

Joseph was 'sold into Egypt' by his blood-brothers, Jesus was betrayed to his enemies by one of his twelve chosen Apostles; Abú-Bakr, Muḥammad's father-in-law, and 'Umar, his closest confidant, acted against the Prophet's express directions, opposed his chosen successor, 'Alí, and usurped the Caliph's office. Here the words apply: 'For it must needs be that offences come; but woe to that man by whom the offence cometh.'[171] No human community, least of all a religious one,[172] is immune from such 'offences', from elements with a destructive urge, which aspire to leadership and rebel against authority, whether out of self-seeking ambition or from error. The question is only whether and how the community deals with them. Huschmand Sabet's book was both an attempt to offer an analysis of our present world situation and an introduction to the Bahá'í Faith. He had not the slightest reason to mention such events, which anyhow have only peripheral importance. However, that a Protestant theologian should consider these things so essential[173] need cause no surprise, in view of the history of Christianity.[174]

A religion's originality

There are only two possibilities. Either through Bahá'u'lláh an incursion of transcendence has taken place, a revelation of God to mankind, in which case his word is God's word, and the teaching he proclaims is not from him but from 'Him Who sent him'; or

171. Matthew 18:7.

172. It holds a special danger of conflicting views, because language is at its most inadequate in matters of eschatology.

173. In his book *Seher, Grübler, Enthusiasten* Dr. Hutten gave a good deal of space to a protest against the 'institutionalisation' of the Bahá'í Faith and showed where his sympathies lay: on the side of those who instead of the legally structured community have raised the banners of an inspired charismatic 'movement'. It is easy enough to see why: because in an 'inspired anarchy', such as Rudolf Sohm envisaged, or a 'movement without legal structure', as called for by Aḥmad Sohrab, the unity of those professing the religion would at once be lost and the enthusiasm flowing from it would soon ebb away. The advocates of a community without legal structure, who have shrunk meanwhile to complete insignificance, fail to recognise that the Bahá'í community's legal structure did not come about through external necessity but was already provided by its founder as an essential arrangement. Bahá'u'lláh called the institutions he set up 'Houses of Justice', thereby expressing the fact that the community he had founded was to be united by the bond of law as well as the bonds of faith and love. I have dealt in detail with this complex of problems in my thesis, 'Die Grundlagen der Verwaltungsordnung der Bahá'í'.

174. Church history itself is full of disputes about doctrine, authority, order, heresy and schism: a 'farrago of error and violence', as Goethe called it.

else his claim to be the promised one of all religions is false, in which case his work is of human construction, and the Bahá'í Faith an eclectic compound, the result of a synthesis, a 'new composite religion which replaces the old religions'.[175] Although on dogmatic grounds only the second alternative is conceivable to Christian theologians, this 'Either–Or' has come up with every religion, including Christianity. Judaism could not accept the truth that the expected redemption had already appeared with Jesus, and saw Jesus as a mischief-maker. The Jews of all ages have regarded Christianity as Dr. Hutten regards the Bahá'í Faith: as a human anticipation of the divine promise, a human creation which wrongly assumes divine origin, a compound of revelation and pagan philosophy, a ragbag of elements of truth collected up from various religions. There have been plenty of attempts from the earliest days of Christianity till the present age, whether from the Jews or from old or new paganism, to disprove the originality of Jesus or even declare him a synthesist, not the originator of a religious community. I can take these attempts as well enough known, and mention here only Celsus, who saw Christianity as a mixture of Stoic, Platonic, Jewish, Persian and Egyptian elements,[176] and Porphyry, who declared the Gospels a collection of myths and the Evangelists liars and falsifiers. Many theologians today call belief in the uniqueness of Jesus's teaching a naïve idea.[177] According to Rudolf Bultmann, Jesus's message is 'not new in its thinking'.[178]

With the method inherent in Dr. Hutten's attitude—to call it 'borrowing' if there are observable common features in thought and doctrine—the originality of any religion can be disputed. If common features in teaching, philosophy and terminology are proofs of a religion's lack of originality and synthetic character, why was Dr. Hutten not disturbed by the many references made by Jesus to Moses and the prophets and by the immense number of features common to Christianity and its 'mother religion'—which are so many and various that Christianity without Judaism is completely inconceivable?

It is often difficult to have a discussion with Christians: not only

175. Visser't Hooft, *No Other Name*, p. 45.
176. C. Andresen, *Logos und Nomos, Die Polemik des Celsus wider das Christentum*, p. 223.
177. e.g. H. Windisch, *Der Sinn der Bergpredigt*, p. 105.
178. *Glauben und Verstehen*, vol. I, p. 265.

because they are split up into many schools of thought and belief, and because everything to do with Christianity is a matter for multiple dispute within the Churches;[179] but above all because their eye for the parallels in religious history is blurred by their sense of uniqueness and exclusiveness and their belief that the Christians are a 'chosen people'. This prevents any real insight into the facts.

The originality of a religion, as I have pointed out elsewhere,[180] lies less in the proclamation of new ideas never thought of before than in the impulses transforming men and women, in the creative, formative power of the word of God and in the judgment on the superseded religions—of which I shall be speaking later on. Early Christianity and Islám in particular are testimonies to these impulses, which are behind religious concepts and imperatives both new and old. The ideas alone could not have produced the victorious campaign through which these religions conquered the world.

Religion made to measure?

As to the slogans Dr. Hutten bestowed on the Bahá'í Faith: religion 'made to measure', religion 'without any logical difficulties, without mysteries or paradoxes, religion deliberately modern, sensible and rational'. This judgment shows once more how much he judges a religious system alien to his own according to the concept of religion obtained from neo-Protestant theology. Anyone who sees the 'Skandalon', the message of paradox and mystery, as the central statement and real depth of the New Testament, is bound, of course, to be especially suspicious of the rationality of the Bahá'í Faith with its challenge to the phrase *credo quia absurdum*.[181] Anyone who has raised irrationality and contradictoriness to a principle is bound to find realism, application to present times, intelligibility and rational clarity, criteria of error. He is put off by just the qualities in the Bahá'í Faith which make it especially attractive to sceptical people in an enlightened and disenchanted

179. The Jew Isaac Orobio was already complaining about this in the seventeenth century in his disputation with the Christian Philipp van Limborch. Orobio pointed out that what was orthodox to one Christian was anathema to another (Hans-Joachim Schoeps, *Jüdisch-christliches Religionsgespräch in neunzehn Jahrhunderten*, p. 86).

180. See below, p. 115.

181. The phrase has just made a triumphant return with, naturally, the neo-orthodox Karl Barth,

world—its respect for reason and scientific judgment, its readiness
to attend to this world and its affirmation of it. Easy enough to see
why they upset him: because Christianity as encrusted in the
orthodoxy of the Church cannot cope with them. The phrases Dr.
Hutten used in his article and in his book ('all too harmonious, all
too conflict-free, all too lucid') are meaningless and unintelligible
for anyone who does not share his premises.[182] Quite a clever
trick perhaps: to turn a good epithet into its opposite by a dia-
lectical manoeuvre, using the words 'all too' without good cause
(and indeed without possible good cause). As if one can add 'all
too' to *any* epithet? Something can be too easy, too dangerous, too
frivolous, but not too true, too correct, nor 'all too lucid' and 'all
too harmonious'. To say 'all too lucid' is a form of pseudo-
argument which the uncritical reader accepts at its face value, but
logically the phrase is nonsense and it also exposes its user: anyone who has resort to such 'reasons' shows that he lacks real ones.

But this criticism shows something else: that Dr. Hutten does
not know the Bahá'í Faith well enough and has not grasped its
essential features. Human reason is certainly given a different
value than it is in the Protestant Church (Martin Luther spoke of
'that whore, Reason'). This, however, is not because the Bahá'í
Faith is 'a deliberately modern religion' in the sense that in order
to enhance its attractiveness, everything is geared to plausibility
and effect; but quite simply because the divine truths do not run
counter to human reason. Paradox is by no manner of means an
indispensable element in original religion. Judaism and Islám—to
mention only these two religions—get along without it, and, after
all, even Protestant theologians will agree that the God who
spoke in Judaism was the same God who revealed himself to man
in Jesus.

But the Bahá'í Faith with all its rationality is more than a dry
rationalism, more than a late product of Western 'enlightenment'.
The irrational, what Rudolf Otto called 'the numinous', is also its

182. What do these muddled sentences in his book mean, 'It [the Bahá'í Faith] has
many yeses and no noes', and 'It does not threaten, expose or judge'? Bahá'u'lláh
gives a decisive 'no' to man's rebellion against God, to moral depravity, to the
human order as it prevails today, to war, economic exploitation, materialism, hatred,
religious hatred, nationalism. He exposes and judges the religions in their petrified
dogmatic form, and their clergymen, the 'Doctors of Doubt' who speak 'in the name,
and yet are so far away from the spirit, of the Faith they profess' (Shoghi Effendi,
The Promised Day is Come, p. 107).

innermost being. The Bahá'í Faith is a religion of law, and its revealed laws are 'irrational' in that they acquire validity primarily through the Founder's statement, not through their special wisdom and rationality. The recognition that ethics has its ultimate source in revelation and can only be discovered *from* it, the refusal to admit the possibility of objective value judgments and therefore the rejection of 'natural law'—these are further evidence against Dr. Hutten's theme. Nor is it true that the Bahá'í Faith is without mystery. The status of 'Abdu'l-Bahá[183] and the short duration of the Báb's mission[184] are regarded by the Bahá'ís as hidden mysteries.

Another point: Dr. Hutten himself is familiar with the Bahá'í Faith at least well enough to know the importance it attaches to prayer and fasting.[185] I cannot understand how this point alone did not stop him from representing it in such a stunted form. He also completely missed a further aspect of the religion, which is an essential element in every living religion and does not fit at all into his scheme of things: mysticism. If the Bahá'í Faith were only, as he described it, an intellectual and moral system in traditional religious terms, there would be no room in it for the mystical element. But his aloofness from this subject is not to be wondered at: in great contrast to Catholic Christianity, the Protestant version has always maintained a very distant attitude to mysticism. The main theme of modern Protestant theology is the statement that there is no way from man to God but only from God to man, and Karl Barth, Friedrich Gogarten and Emil Brunner have castigated all mystical experience as 'the most monstrous human presumption', being an attempt 'on the part of a creature to surmount an absolute difference, that between creator and creature' (Gogarten). So the Protestant oriented to this theology has as little liking for mysticism as the Devil for holy water. It is not surprising, therefore, that Dr. Hutten made no effort to understand Bahá'u'lláh's *The Seven Valleys* or *Kitáb-i-Íqán*.

183. Bahá'u'lláh called him 'Sirru'lláh' (Mystery of God).
184. 'That so brief a span should have separated this most mighty and wondrous Revelation from Mine own previous Manifestation, is a secret that no man can unravel and a mystery such as no mind can fathom' (Bahá'u'lláh, quoted by Shoghi Effendi, 'The Dispensation of Bahá'u'lláh', in *The World Order of Bahá'u'lláh*, p. 124).
185. None of the historic religions possesses such an abundance of authentic prayers—prayers revealed directly by the Founder—as does the Bahá'í Faith.

World peace—a Utopia ?

Dr. Hutten said that he was without illusions about the goal of establishing the 'Most Great Peace', as Bahá'u'lláh envisaged and promised it; since in his view reliance on a transformation of the world is unrealistic and also goes against the testimony of the Bible. According to Biblical expectation of the Last Days, as Dr. Hutten interprets it, world history will end in a catastrophe, and this catastrophe is the destiny of the human race, which is moving not towards its self-perfection but to rebellion against God and the Law. From these premises Dr. Hutten simply declared the 'Twelve Principles'[186] a collection of 'pious hopes, commonplaces and mere illusions'.

On one point Bahá'ís are in complete agreement with Dr. Hutten; the human race will never by itself, through its own strength, be able to bring about this highest good of our temporal existence, world peace.[187] All human efforts, all the good will, all the appeals and resolutions, all the exertions of the politicians, will ultimately come to nothing. The total transformation of the world will finally come not from man but from God. Theologians have not recognised that the Lord of history has manifested Himself in Bahá'u'lláh and has spoken again to mankind, to bring about man's perfection; they cannot bring themselves to believe that behind the phenomenon they criticise so harshly, the transforming and re-creating power of the Word of God is at work, which can succeed where man relying only on himself and presuming his own independence, is bound to fail: this is why they find the Bahá'í hope of peace a Utopian illusion, a millennialist dream. But then the Bahá'ís do confidently believe that through Bahá'u'lláh the Lord has spoken and that He will redeem His promise of the

186. Among the many principles upheld by the Bahá'ís, the following are often quoted: the oneness of God; the oneness of religion which is progressively revealed to mankind according to its needs and capacities at the time of revelation; the oneness of mankind; the unfettered investigation of truth; the relinquishing of all prejudices whether religious, racial, class or national; the harmony of religion and science; world peace safeguarded by the necessary agencies, such as a world legislature and a world tribunal; the equality of men and women; the adoption of an international auxiliary language; universal compulsory education; certain general economic principles such as the abolition of extremes of poverty and wealth, and the principle that all must work—a work which, when performed in the spirit of service to mankind, is exalted to the rank of worship. These principles do not represent Bahá'í teaching in its entirety.

187. The 'Most Great Peace'. Humanity will, however, succeed in establishing the 'Lesser Peace'. See below, p. 70.

'Most Great Peace', that their religion is more than a sum of teachings, counsels and admonitions, that it is a living force, the same force which already in history has transformed men, established new orders and founded brotherly communities. Their expectations of the future are based on this confident belief.

The expected kingdom of peace will not come upon men like a cosmic event, as the millennialists envisaged, but will be the fruit of a universal process of change taking place within history, whose driving impulse is the new revelation: 'God's purpose is none other than to usher in, in ways He alone can bring about, and the full significance of which He alone can fathom, the great, the Golden Age of a long-divided, a long-afflicted humanity. Its present state, indeed its immediate future, is dark, distressingly dark. Its distant future, however, is radiant, gloriously radiant— so radiant that no eye can visualize it.'[188]

That man is in rebellion against God cannot be denied. Bahá'u'-lláh repeatedly gave warning of the impending judgment of God,[189] which is 'at once a visitation from God and a cleansing process for all mankind',[190] and for which 'the world's supreme leaders, both secular and religious, are to be regarded as primarily answerable'.[191] The catastrophe,[192] however, will not be the end of our temporal world, but the total break-up and overthrow of the existing order and the beginning of a new age, in which 'the folly and tumult of strife that has, since the dawn of history, blackened the annals of mankind, will have been finally transmuted into the wisdom and the tranquillity of an undisturbed, a universal, and lasting peace, in which the discord and separation of the children of men will have given way to the world-wide reconciliation, and the complete unification of the divers elements that constitute human society'.[193]

The promises of the prophets

I wonder how this vision of the future is supposed to be unbiblical. The Old Testament is full of promises of a time of peace when 'swords will be turned into ploughshares' and men will learn to

188. Shoghi Effendi, *The Promised Day is Come*, p. 120.
189. See pp. 11 and 117.
190. *The Promised Day is Come*, p. 2.
191. ibid., p. 116.
192. Compare *Qur'án*, Súrah 101.
193. Shoghi Effendi, op. cit., p. 122.

wage war no more; and *The Book of Revelation* foretells not only the
passing of the old but the beginning of a 'new Heaven' and a 'new
Earth'. The 'Last Days', which started in 1844,[194] do not end in
the destruction of the universe and the extermination of mankind.
The 'End', when the stars fall from Heaven and the sun is darkened, is the end of the aeon, the age of Adam, and also the turning-
point in time, the beginning of a new time, in which mankind will
achieve its perfection under the law of Bahá'u'lláh. I am well
aware that Christian theology gives a different interpretation of
the biblical expectations of the End. But there is one point to be
noted: whereas Christians have always ventured to claim all the
prophecies of the Old Testament, in allegorical interpretation, for
the people of the new Covenant and for the Church, they take the
same attitude towards their own Scripture with which they re-

194. Dr. Hutten rightly referred to the fact that in all centuries of Christian history
apocalyptic 'prophets' have recognised in their own age the signs that 'the end is
nigh' and have always been proved wrong. But when he said that God just cannot be
'read in the cards', he misrepresented the position of the Bahá'ís. It is not because
they dare to 'read God in the cards' that they believe in the start of the 'Last Days',
but because God Himself has broken the seal and made Himself known to mankind
in Bahá'u'lláh; also, the fact that past generations were wrong in imagining that the
Last Days had started is no proof that they have not started in our times—quite apart
from the many Christian sects which have recognised this and the gathering of the
People of Israel in the Holy Land. Almost all scientists, philosophers and even
theologians have seen that we live in a time of drastic upheaval and at a crisis of
world civilisation. They recognise the collapse of all orders and values. By contrast
with previous ages, this involves the whole of mankind; technology and the population explosion dominate life, and sharpen the crisis. Paul Tillich was writing as long
ago as 1941: 'We are in the midst of a world revolution, which embraces every
sphere of human existence and compels us to make a new interpretation of life and
the world. The only hope we can have for ourselves is to be a bridge between the
'ages' (quoted by Zahrnt, *Die Sache mit Gott*, p. 383). Romano Guardini too thinks
we are faced by a fundamental new orientation (*Das Ende der Neuzeit*). Jean Gebser,
who speaks of the end of an era and the beginning of a completely new one, stresses
that we are living in an extremely critical period, 'with very few parallels in intensity
in the history of mankind' (*In der Bewährung*, p. 9). The world changes at a very rapid
pace, and total secularisation is progressing even faster. Religion, having lost its
credibility, is pushed to the periphery of our life. As a result of the decline of religion,
chaos and anarchy are raising their head everywhere (as foreseen by Bahá'u'lláh).
The bewilderment of man, the perversion of his sense of right and wrong, the spread
of lawlessness, drunkenness and crime, the corruption of morals—grow daily more
obvious. With all acknowledgement of the positive sides of the revolt of youth today,
surely their materialistic, sex-obsessed, rebellious, anti-authority spirit bears the
mark of the Last Days? (II Timothy 3:1-9). How much worse must conditions on
earth get before the Dr. Huttens of this world can accept the beginning of the Last
Days so often prophesied? 'Ye can discern the face of the sky; but can ye not discern
the signs of the times?' (Matthew 16:2-3).

proach the Jews, namely that of 'sticking to the letter', and at least
in their eschatology banish any sort of allegorical interpretation.
What stands in contradiction to the Bahá'í vision of the future is
not the Bible but the theological interpretation of it.[195]

Law and order in Christian thought

Dr. Hutten's attitude to the possibility of world peace was marked,
it seems to me, by two errors of approach. The first, which the
Christians alone hold, is indeed typically Christian: the under-
estimation (despite the peace proclamation in Luke 2:14) of peace
in this world, combined with a complacent retreat to the peace of
the soul in pious expectation of 'eternal peace' in the hereafter.
'When a Christian speaks of redemption, he is thinking first of his
own soul . . . But human society and the structures which support
it do not come into these conceptions; for him they remain un-
redeemed. At most on the far distant horizon of the future there
rises a dimly reflected hope of an ultimate happening on Christ's
return, the great transfiguration of the whole world.'[196] To
Christians, the Kingdom of God is a transcendent, not an immanent kingdom, not a redeemed terrestrial order. Christian theologians, having failed to accept peace as a subject for theology, are
to blame for this false premise. In their eschatology they put
everything on to the hereafter, instead of acknowledging the task
of formulating peace for the whole of humanity as the final goal
for fulfilment and challenging Christians to be 'fellow workers for
peace'.[197] So they find peace, and the order which establishes it, a
'secondary task', to be left to secular political reform movements.

195. What a vast amount has been based and justified on an appeal to the Scriptures, which later has proved to be error—from forced baptism to the condemnation
of Bruno and Galileo, from the persecution of witches to discrimination against the
black race and even against the Jews in the so-called Third Reich, from the Crusades
to the atomic bomb! And were there not enough theologians too, both Protestants
and Catholic, to give consecration to Adolf Hitler's 'Thousand-Year Reich' by
appeal to Scripture?

196. Peter Mühlschlegel, 'Sozialisierte Erlösung', (Socialised Redemption),
Bahá'í-Briefe, no. 36, p. 927 ff. In fact, there is a big change taking place. A new
theology, the "Theology of Revolution," is being proclaimed and many of the
young theologians see in Jesus a (mere) social revolutionary. A protestant theologian,
who writes in a well-known German newspaper, explained to the author some
years ago: "Today one cannot be a good Christian without being an adherent of
Mao Tse Tung. For Mao has completed what Jesus proclaimed. The history of the
Church is nothing but error."

197. Eugen Biser at the Catholic Academy, Bavaria 1969.

The second mistake was to misunderstand peace on earth as a primitive paradise, as if it were dependent only on general good-will and could come about only when every single human being becomes an angel; and since that cannot be expected—even if we reject the pessimistic view of Man—it would follow that universal peace could never be reached and every hope of it would be a Utopian dream. This mistaken idea rests ultimately on the Protestant Church's inadequate relationship to law, justice and order. It is well known, indeed, that Luther saw law only as a 'work of necessity', an institution to protect the good from the wicked, and believed that mankind could dispense with law if all men were Christians.[198] But even if all men were Christians, and Christians not only in name, if every human being walked the paths of righteousness, peace would not come into being. For peace among the nations is not the fruit of love of one's neighbour but of justice: 'And the work of righteousness shall be peace; and the effect of righteousness quietness and assurance for ever.'[199] Peace is a question of order, not of individual compassion.

Of course man's individual relationship to God and to his neighbour is central to the New Testament, and here the law of love applies. But the order determined by the principle of justice, regarding which Jesus was basically for maintaining the *status quo*,[200] was surrendered to the secular realm when Paul declared not only ceremonial but also judicial law cancelled.[201] And when the Christians had to establish themselves in the world after Constantine, they took their law from pagan Roman law and later from pagan natural law with Christian elaborations and interpretations. 'You cannot govern' with the Gospel (Luther), you cannot solve the problems of our society with individual kindness and love. Concepts of a binding order are not valid for Christians, as

198. Martin Luther, *Von der weltlichen Obrigkeit, wie weit man ihr Gehorsam schuldig sei.* (On the authorities of the world, how far one owes them obedience), 1523.

199. Isaiah 32:17. Bahá'u'lláh also stresses this: 'Take heed, O concourse of the rulers of the world! There is no force on earth that can equal in its conquering power the force of justice and wisdom . . . Blessed is the king who marcheth with the ensign of wisdom unfurled before him, and the battalions of justice massed in his rear. He verily is the ornament that adorneth the brow of peace and the countenance of security' (*Gleanings*, CXII).

200. Matthew 5:17. As the Bahá'ís believe, until the law of the *Qur'án*, which brought a new model of ordered and united community life where people of all races and religions could live peacefully together.

201. Romans 10:4.

a Protestant theologian has clearly acknowledged: 'The problem of kindness could once be presented in the parallel of the Samaritan who helps the man fallen among thieves. But today the kindness of the individual is simply annulled by the lack of kindness of the group. Millions have fallen among thieves, and the kindness of individuals, even of many individuals, can make no difference to that. Love of one's neighbour has become a world-wide political problem. Moral appeals to individuals, however well meant, are not enough and individual kindness can all too easily become an alibi for group cruelty. Can a man remain human in an inhuman system? The moral questions of our time can no longer be answered by individual counsels or commandments. The New Testament has, as it were, a blind spot here. For the most part, it leaves us on our own.'[202] This is the reason why all the well-intentioned Christian peace movements and efforts achieve so little.[203] But where the New Testament is silent, Bahá'u'lláh offers the solution; a new, unified world order, and therewith the redemption not only of individual man but of the whole of mankind. The transformation of the individual, his sanctification (not justification), his turning to God, is just as much a central theme of the Bahá'í Faith as it is of all other religions. But redemption here is not confined to the personal God–man relationship, nor solely to the question of individual eternal salvation. As in Judaism and Islám, man is addressed in his totality, as an individual and also as a 'political animal'. Divine Providence is concerned, too, with human society and its order, of which Bahá'u'lláh demands the total transformation, according to the divine law he proclaimed.[204] The Bahá'í Faith has a theocratic goal: the realisation of God's will on this planet.[205]

'Saved' man and world peace

'Saved' man is not an indispensable condition for a political order of peace among the nations. For the world peace to be reached is not the Utopia of a peace in Paradise with the elimination of all

202. Wolfgang Kratz, 'Bibel—Hemmschuh oder Richtschnur', (Bible—brake or guideline) a radio talk broadcast by *Hessischer Rundfunk*, 16 March 1969.

203. The Bahá'ís by no means hold a monopoly on the realisation of peace. But in Bahá'u'lláh's mission they hold the key to the solution of this problem.

204. 'Soon will the present-day order be rolled up, and a new one spread out in its stead' (*Gleanings*, IV).

205. See below, p. 94.

conflicts, but relative peace with the elimination of violence in settling what conflicts there are, the exclusion of war as a method of policy. Just as the law of the jungle has been overcome as a method of solving individual conflicts, so the overcoming of war as a method of policy is possible without the need for all men to grow wings first.

Mankind has developed by stages and gone through various orders: from the family to the tribe, from the tribe to the city state, from the city state to the nation state. In the process it has abandoned the settlement by war of conflicts between the superseded orders, without all men having come to lead a saintlike life. Thefts and murders have still been committed, and yet the nation state has been created. The political task we are faced with, the outlawing and abolition of war and the creation of a universal order of peace, is far harder and more complex. But it can be achieved before men abandon, in Dr. Hutten's words, 'the roots of self-seeking, envy, greed and lust for power'. The 'Most Great Peace', a further stage in the development of world peace, is, of course, not possible without the realisation of the unity of mankind proclaimed by Bahá'u'lláh.[206]

Pious hopes, commonplaces, illusions?

Now a word on the 'Twelve Principles'. What Dr. Hutten wrote in this context in his review was, unfortunately, considerably below the level to which he aspired in his book on sects.

Take Bahá'u'lláh's commandments of independent and free search after the truth and of overcoming shibboleths, superstition and prejudices of all kinds: how is that a 'pious hope'? I don't know what to make of this wholesale criticism. If Dr. Hutten does not think such a proposition can be the content of a religious ethic at all, then it only exposes once more the inflexibility of his thinking: any other ethic than the Protestant one is obviously not conceivable for him. What can he have against this demand? Does it in any way contradict the Bible? Can he be in doubt of its usefulness? Would humanity not be a good bit further advanced if at

206. 'That which the Lord hath ordained as the sovereign remedy and mightiest instrument for the healing of all the world is the union of all its peoples in one universal cause, one common Faith' (*Gleanings*, CXX). 'The well-being of mankind, its peace and security, are unattainable unless and until its unity is firmly established. This unity can never be achieved so long as the counsels which the Pen of the Most High hath revealed are suffered to pass unheeded' (*Gleanings*, CXXXI).

least national and racial prejudices were overcome? Surely prejudices and superstition above all things have proved barriers to
kindness and compassion. Surely the Churches particularly have
taken on a burden of guilt through superstition and prejudices, in
their attitude to the advance of science, in the persecution of millions of innocent people as witches, in their attitude to the Jews.[207]
If the Christian message is so unutterably superior to all others as
the Christians always assert, why is it that in states like Germany
and the United States, where 95 per cent of the citizens are adherents of Christianity, the race question could gain such importance;
that six million people were wiped out like insects; that in the
United States civil strife between the races often occurs? Surely
it is only because love of one's neighbour is *limited* to neighbours,
and mankind is not conceived as a unity. Nothing will stop the
repetition of such occurrences and the worsening of such conditions except the overcoming of prejudice regarding the superiority
of one race and the acknowledgment of every human being as of
equal value regardless of colour, class or religion.[208]

Or perhaps Dr. Hutten's curtly dismissive criticism was based
on scepticism, his conviction that human nature, flawed as a consequence of original sin, is incapable of such an achievement. In that
case the question arises whether Jesus's admonition, 'Be ye therefore perfect, even as your Father which is in heaven is perfect'
(Matthew 5:48), is easier to realise, and whether the precepts of
the Sermon on the Mount are also 'pious hopes' or what Gerhard
Szczesny calls 'high-flown idealist ethics'.[209]

Of course everyone knows today that world peace must be
brought about if humanity is to survive. A century ago, when
Bahá'u'lláh was calling the nations to peace, the idea of world
peace was still outside the range of general consideration.[210] By

207. See below, f.n. 594.
208. Religious prejudices, too, have divided mankind for thousands of years. Unless they are overcome, the uniting of the human race cannot be achieved. On this
Bahá'u'lláh writes: 'Gird up the loins of your endeavour, O people of Bahá, that
haply the tumult of religious dissension and strife that agitateth the peoples of the
earth may be stilled, that every trace of it may be completely obliterated . . . Religious
fanaticism and hatred are a world-devouring fire, whose violence none can quench.
The Hand of Divine power can, alone, deliver mankind from this desolating affliction' (*Epistle to the Son of the Wolf*, pp. 13–14).
209. *Die Zukunft des Unglaubens*, p. 51.
210. Kant's *To Eternal Peace* (1795) neither reached nor influenced the general consciousness.

declaring this precept of Bahá'u'lláh to be a 'commonplace', Dr.
Hutten gives the impression that Bahá'u'lláh merely recognised
the task—obvious today—without pointing the way to its
achievement. He knows very well that this is not the case, that the
Bahá'í Faith offers very concrete remedies for the 'disease' of
war. But he omitted any mention of them, and so his judgment
was unfair.

The equality of men and women

Dr. Hutten called something a commonplace which was introduced in Germany by the constitution of 1949 and has only become valid in law since 1953. In many parts of the world[211]
women still do not have equality, but he ignored this as studiously
as the fact that male dominance in marriage is the rule in all the
religions of the book including Christianity (Ephesians 5:22, I
Timothy 2:12), and that Bahá'u'lláh annulled a legal premise
which has determined the structure of law for thousands of years.
This demand, revolutionary not only in the East but also in the
West at that time, has meanwhile been realised in several parts of
the world and has therefore promptly become so much taken for
granted that a Christian theologian can find it a commonplace.
Which shows that in mysterious ways the irresistible structure is
forming which the Almighty told His messenger Bahá'u'lláh to
proclaim to mankind as His will.

The Church is an institution whose theologians in the past
showed a crude contempt for women.[212] By appeal to Scripture

211. Women's equality under the law exists in all the Communist countries, in the
Scandinavian countries and in both German republics. In Britain, the United States,
South Africa and Australia equal rights for both sexes are close to being realised. In
all the other European countries—Holland, Belgium, France, Switzerland, Austria,
Italy, Spain, Greece—in the whole of Central and South America, in Canada, the
whole of Africa and non-communist Asia, marriage is still governed by patriarchal
rules.

212. The Church's anti-feminist tendencies, based on Paul (I Corinthians 7:1 et
seq.) and the Gnostic trends of his time, became more and more in evidence in the
second and third centuries. 'Woman is a sensual, sinful creature and inferior to man
in the hierarchy of creation' (I Corinthians 11:3). She is not the image of God but of
man (I Corinthians 11:7) and has therefore to remain silent in the community. She is
the 'Devil's entrance gate' because she brought God's image to the Fall and therefore
bears responsibility for the death of the Son of God (Tertullian). At the Synod of
Mâcon in the sixth century it was debated whether woman was a human being at all.
St. Thomas Aquinas described her as 'miscarried man' and spoke of the 'use of
necessary things, of woman, necessary for the preservation of the species, of food
and drink' (taken from Friedrich Heer, *Mittelalter*, p. 526). Martin Luther, too, in-

they opposed the emancipation of women as long as they possibly could, and finally, as on other points (like democracy and tolerance), they yielded to irresistible developments while masking their former demands. It is incredible to me that a representative of such an institution can presumptuously call a law of Bahá'u'lláh a 'commonplace', when it contradicts the Church's doctrine and practice for centuries. A hundred years ago women's equality did not exist anywhere in the world, and today only some of the most progressive countries have given it legal acknowledgment. Dr. Hutten must find the New Testament a veritable mine of such commonplaces. In fact the teaching of the apostle Paul on women's subordination to men brought nothing new to either Jews or pagans; it corresponded far and wide to the social reality. On the other hand, even the 'Golden Rule' (Matthew 7:12) which Buddha had proclaimed 500 years before, is to be found in all religions. So are both these teachings—Paul's and Buddha's—to be called commonplaces?

The Revelation—the Standard of all Morality

This is when Dr. Hutten made one of his basic mistakes. God did not send His messengers into the world so that they should repeatedly transform it completely and turn it upside down with new, unprecedented and unthought-of ideas, doctrines and commandments, but to impart to men according to their stage of development at each time the morality, truth and justice which would sanctify and redeem them. And in the process, because of man's self-will, it was also necessary that basic truths should be repeatedly confirmed and reinforced again. This can be illustrated by an example.

Bahá'u'lláh has declared marriage the basis of society and urges his people to marry. At first sight one could say with justice: what is the point of this platitude? But the platitude has often got lost in the course of history and is today being challenged more than ever. Since Paul, who found it 'good for a man not to touch a woman' (I Corinthians 7:1) and for whom marriage was a concession to sinful flesh, a permitted sin, Christianity has been un-

---

sisted on man's rule over women, who belong in the house and should produce as many children as possible: 'But though they labour and finally die in labour, that does not matter, just let them die in labour, that is what they are here for' (taken from Paul Althaus, *Die Ethik Martin Luthers*, p. 100, f.n. 82).

decided about marriage. Church history can show many examples of extreme hostility to marriage, like Marcion, who forbade sexual intercourse even for married couples, Origen, who castrated himself, Tertullian ('Marriage is based on that which is fornication'), Jerome ('The married live after the manner of cattle and are no different from pigs and senseless beasts'), and the Russian sect of the Skopze, who on the evidence of Matthew 19:12 thought castration was the only way of salvation willed by God and who carried out mutilations even on women and children. But apart from these and similar instances, deliberate celibacy and virginity have been recognised in the Church, especially the Catholic Church, right up to our own times, as superior to marriage. For Martin Luther also marriage was only a *remedium peccati*, a hospital for the chronically sick.[213] Bahá'u'lláh's express injunction to marry is thus to be understood as a denial of the anti-marriage and anti-sex tendencies in Christianity; it is a discouragement of every sort of celibate living, a healing of the deformities which God's religion has experienced in this respect. On the other hand it is a rebuff to the hedonists of our time, the advocates of an excessive licence, who in the immediate present declare marriage an outmoded institution and may even go in for wife and husband-swapping and for group sex. Evidently Christians are gradually straying so far from the obsolete anti-sex ethics of their Church that they are falling into the other extreme. These 'prophets of decadence'[214] include some Protestant theologians.[215]

There is thus a broad spectrum in Church ethics, from the age-old disparagement of the claims of the body, of woman and of marriage (based on Paul), to the assertion that codes of sexual morality are by no means valid for all times, permitting indulgence in extra-marital intercourse and petting. With this decay in our world order, it is for the Bahá'í a guide and not a 'commonplace' when Bahá'u'lláh says that in the new era, as in former times,

213. 'Keyn Ehepflicht on Sund geschicht' (taken from Reinhold Seeburg, 'Luthers Anschauung von dem Geschlechtsleben und der Ehe und ihre geschichtliche Stellung', in *Luther-Jahrbuch*, no. 7, 1925, p. 114).
214. Shoghi Effendi, *The World Order of Bahá'u'lláh*, p. 188.
215. For instance the Marburg theologian Siegfried Keil in an interview in the magazine *Stern*: 'Today human freedom is assured in our society. Sexuality cannot be excluded from this freedom, for it is indivisible.' In the Church monthly *Evangelische Kommentare*, Klaus Franke, a doctor who specialises in sexual ethics at the Evangelical Academy in Bad Boll, approves extra-marital affairs 'as therapy for a sick marriage'.

marriage is the place where the sexes may and should come together. In the confusions and dangers of this world the Word of God is the 'unmistakable balance' whereby 'truth shall be distinguished from error and the wisdom of every command shall be tested' (Bahá'u'lláh); it is the compass for humanity, which has lost direction and gone astray without divine guidelines and authoritative standards.[216] The statement on the equality of the sexes, like the other main principles, which Dr. Hutten called 'commonplace', is thus an authoritative norm and gauge for the new age and as such of abiding relevance, even though there is nothing *new* about it. Because Dr. Hutten overlooked this, he misjudged this whole question.

The repeal of Babel

According to the Bible, until the building of the Tower of Babel mankind was united and 'all the world' had 'a single language'. But the Lord dispersed men over the earth and confused their tongues because of their pride. The two processes were simultaneous. The unification of mankind, which Bahá'u'lláh has promised, corresponds in time to the removal of language barriers. The revelation of Bahá'u'lláh is the repeal of Babel. The introduction of a world language and script, which every child should be taught in addition to his mother-tongue, directly serves the most noble goal: the unification of the nations and their living together in peace. What is there illusory about that? Surely history shows what an integrating force a common language can be. Thus the dialect of the Qurayshites, which with Muḥammad became a world language overnight—the Arabic language and script—was, together with Islám, the bond which united many peoples of different origins. On the other hand, how far language can be a barrier to integration is shown by, for example, the quarrels over language in Belgium and India. Or think of the difficulties in the way of a rapid spread of scientific knowledge because of linguistic differences. To keep up with the latest research, a physicist or biologist should have a fair knowledge of at least English, French, German and Russian, and may soon need Chinese and Japanese as well. The only thing Dr. Hutten saw in this problem was that a world language 'would facilitate not only peaceful understanding but just as much the spreading of lies and prejudice'. He may

216. See p. 33.

meanwhile have realised the quality of his argument. For by the same reasoning one could make a *reductio ad absurdum* of Gutenberg's invention of printing, and indeed of all man's cultural achievements.

How is it that a theologian could have such a distorted view of man's cultural development and in every case could see only abuse and perversion? A world court of all states, furnished with binding authority,[217] leads (he thought) to world dictatorship, the Bahá'í model of a united world to totalitarian uniformity. If one took his way of thinking seriously, man's slogan would have to be 'Back to the Trees'!

Dr. Hutten set great store by his supposed realism. Actually he is a thorough-going pessimist—although it becomes more obvious every day that the boundaries between pacifist 'utopians' and 'realists' are progressively vanishing. Pope Paul VI himself, in his Encyclical *Populorum Progressio*, asked whether the utopians would not one day be proved to be the true realists, the so-called realists, on the other hand, to be deluded because they 'have not recognised the dynamic of a world which wants to live in a spirit of brotherhood'.[218]

The Bahá'ís and the 'Message of the Cross'

Dr. Hutten accused the Bahá'ís of 'helplessness in face of the message of the Cross'.[219] In this charge the proverbial *superbia theologorum*—the pride of the theologians—is manifested: anyone who deviates from Protestant dogma, who contradicts the central teachings of Christian theology, is 'helpless', i.e. intellectually inadequate, or—to put it quite clearly—just too stupid to understand these teachings. This favourite trick of Christian apologists, protecting themselves from undesirable criticism by charging the critic with not knowing what Christian faith is and fighting against a caricature, shows an infuriating arrogance: because the

217. Dr. Hutten was incorrect in suggesting that such a court would have more power than the super-powers. The European Court at Strasbourg has no executive power at all, and yet the Common Market countries acknowledge and obey its verdicts. It would be quite sufficient if the judgments of a future world court were to be directly valid law all over the world, comparable to the judgments of the German Federal High Court which is directly binding on the legislative, executive and judiciary in all parts of the Federal Republic.

218. A round table at Unesco on cultural co-operation ended on 25 June 1976 with a call to 'choose between Utopia and oblivion'. (Unesco press release, June 1976).

219. *Deutsches Allgemeines Sonntagsblatt*, 27 October 1968,

critic is not taken seriously, he is made out to be incapable of passing judgment.

Here is another sentence on the same level: 'The message of the Cross reveals and answers basic problems of human existence that are not even noticed, let alone answered, by the Bahá'í prophets.' So all those who do not share the Church's doctrine of redemption, all non-Christian religions and philosophies of humanity are not only wrong from the start and in their outcome, but also superficial and without depth. They do not reach the basic questions of human existence; the dimension of depth is only to be found among the Christians. It is hard to find any objectivity in such thinking.

Dr. Hutten wrote 'Throughout the Old Testament we hear of man suffering through God's justice and his own sin, and of his ending in helplessness and despair. This is why the Bible speaks of "Fallen Man", who has not the power to heal himself. It speaks of the failure of the experiments with commandments and laws.' In his book[220] he referred to the Bible's answer to the basic problems of human existence—the account of Man's enslavement to guilt and hostility to God, his bondage to sin, and his inability to redeem himself—and to the testimony of Christ's crucifixion, through which Satan's power was broken. He asked 'So what point would there be in a new revelation, while man has not abandoned his age-old state?'—and said that faced by this message of the Cross, all reformers end in helpless and embarrassed silence: that Bahá'u'lláh breaks off where Jesus is only beginning.

Whenever Christian theologians wish to prove the uniqueness, peerlessness and absolute superiority of Christianity over other religions, they all retreat to this doctrine.[221] It is the kernel of the Church's faith, which distinguishes itself from all other religions by having at its centre not just a revealed doctrine and God-fearing obedience towards the will of the Eternal, but belief in a divine figure, the Word made Flesh. Anyone who holds that the quintessence of the Christian revelation is this doctrine of the incarnate Son of God who, through his various sufferings, has reconciled God to the world, is bound to reject belief in a cyclically recurring progressive revelation of God and in the unity of all religions. To that extent I quite understand Dr. Hutten's viewpoint. But this

220. *Seher, Grübler, Enthusiasten*, p. 315.
221. e.g. Gerhard Rosenkranz, *Die Bahá'í*, p. 59.

plan of redemption proclaimed by the Church for almost nineteen
centuries, the orthodox Church doctrine which Dr. Hutten took
as his standard of judgment—is this the real message of Jesus ?

I dispute it, and find myself in the best of company, that of
many critical theologians. The question of who Jesus was and
what his message was is today wholly controversial.[222] Concerning
elementary questions of faith, especially over Christology, present-
day Protestant university theologians are engaged in an irreconcilable conflict. I cannot think that this has escaped Dr. Hutten's
notice and can only wonder at the way he fulminates from the out-
dated credal positions of his Church, as if there had been no two
hundred years of research by liberal Protestant theologians and no
modern historical criticism; as if what he presented as the message
of Jesus were not the subject of vehement dispute within the
Church.

It was no doubt very tiresome for him that this point was referred to in Huschmand Sabet's book, which, I would repeat, tried
to define the position of the world today and to offer an introduction to the Bahá'í Faith; in the limited space available it could only
deal peripherally with the Christian doctrine of redemption. Sabet
did, however, bring to light the fact that in the last decades critical
theological research has produced results 'which are irreconcilable
with the Church's teaching positions but remarkably in accord
with the teachings of the Bahá'í Faith.'[223] In his review Dr. Hutten

222. 'It is still doubtful what the content of Jesus' message was' (E. Percy, *Die
Botschaft Jesu*, p. 20).

223. *The Heavens are Cleft Asunder*, p. 110. Belief, for instance, in the Resurrection
of Christ, according to Paul the decisive factor in salvation ('. . . if Christ hath not
been raised, then is our preaching vain, your faith also is vain.' I Corinthians 15:14),
has for centuries been interpreted as the material revival of a corpse on the evidence
of the empty grave. 'Abdu'l-Bahá (*Some Answered Questions*, XXIII) offers this interpretation of the resurrection phenomenon: 'the disciples were troubled and agitated
after the martyrdom of Christ. The Reality of Christ, which signifies His teachings,
His bounties, His perfections, and His spiritual power, was hidden and concealed for
two or three days after His martyrdom, and was not resplendent and manifest. No,
rather it was lost; for the believers were few in number and were troubled and
agitated. The Cause of Christ was like a lifeless body; and when after three days the
disciples became assured and steadfast, and began to serve the Cause of Christ, and
resolved to spread the divine teachings, putting His counsels into practice, and
arising to serve Him, the Reality of Christ became resplendent and His bounty
appeared; His religion found life, His teachings and His admonitions became evident
and visible. In other words, the Cause of Christ was like a lifeless body, until the life
and the bounty of the Holy Spirit surrounded it.' This allegorical interpretation is
accepted today by some theologians as well: Dietz Lange has explained how the

rebuked Sabet by resorting to the pathetic argument that he did not know the facts, even if he had 'acquired a smattering of modern theology'—as if his view were so absurd that it was not worth discussing. But whole sections of traditional Church doctrine have been called into question to such an extent that in Germany, for instance, there is today the threat of a real schism in the Protestant Church.[224] This remarkable fact Dr. Hutten passed over as deliberately as Sabet's quotations from distinguished scholars—because they did not fit into his scheme of things. Rather than consider *them*, he faulted Sabet on his quoting Karl-Heinz Deschner,[225] instead of going by Martin Luther, and tried to give the impression thereby that Sabet's sole guarantor was Deschner, who is a free-thinker and not a theologian (and so not to be taken seriously).

Paul

This is not the place for an extensive exposition of the dubiousness of the doctrinal structure of the Protestant churches or the defectiveness of the premises from which some churchmen make their judgments. But I would like to explain as concisely as may be how the Bahá'ís, starting from their belief in the unity of religions, deal with the discrepancy between orthodox Church doctrine and Bahá'u'lláh's mission.

Resurrection is to be conceived in the light of historical criticism; 'It is nothing else but the Crucified's winning power over the hearts of His disciples' (Report in the *Süddeutsche Zeitung*, 19 May 1967).

224. On two recent '*Evangelischen Kirchentagen*' (Protestant Church Day) conflict broke out between conservatives, especially the denominational movement called '*Kein anderes Evangelium*' (No other Gospel) and the more progressive and critical theologians. The conservatives considered that disagreement on questions of theology was not in accordance with the Bible. In his militant publication *Alarm um die Bibel* (Alarm about the Bible), Gerhard Bergmann accuses modern theologians of 'betrayal of the Holy Ghost', of 'splitting up the New Testament as though it were an atom', of 'dogmatic monstrosities' and of 'atheist partisanship'. 'False teaching' is the opinion of the conservatives, 'superstition' that of the progressives, in the Protestant religious fight. Schism in the Protestant church is considered possible. Bergmann says, 'I think the day is coming when this church will split'. Präses Beckmann speaks of the 'beginning of struggle within the Church' and the Heidelberg theologian Schlink talks of 'an inner schism in the Protestant church'.

225. In large sections of his book, *Abermals krähte der Hahn*, Deschner refers to the results of historical research and with a wealth of evidence from the literature helps to overcome the state on which, according to the theologian Conzelmann, the Church lives: the ignorance of believers. For the Church no doubt a tiresome book, for the laity an extremely informative one, which no one need be ashamed to use as reference.

It is an indisputable fact that religions have always changed in the course of their long history. Religion, unless it has become a faith of the 'dead letter', is a living thing, and to be living means to assimilate, to absorb and incorporate foreign matter. All religions have done this, and the clear source of revelation has become a broad stream made up of many tributaries. In the course of their history all religions have incorporated beliefs and practices alien to them in essence and have thereby departed from their source, the revelation. The religious heritage has been constantly increased, while the revelation has been obscured by human misinterpretations and misunderstandings.

This was also something realised by the leaders of the Reformation, who saw the Catholic Church as a falling away from the essential nature of Christianity, and tried to return to the pure teaching undistorted by human additions and misunderstandings. Such understanding has been the basis for the forming of all Christian sects and indeed for all the reformations in religious history. The question is whether the Reformers of Christianity attained their objective, whether they freed the pure teaching of Christ from its incrustations.

Martin Luther thought he had rediscovered Christ in Paul (*in Paulo reperi*), and made the Pauline doctrine of man's inability to keep the law (Romans 8:2 et seq.) the centre of Reformation theology. That was a double fatality within Christianity: that in the very early days a spiritual genius such as Paul should have taken God's Cause out of the hands of the chosen heirs and executors, the simple and uneducated apostles, and transformed it into an amalgam of Christian and pagan beliefs; and that Paul, of all men, who is responsible for the shift in emphasis, thus making way for an essential change in the Christian religion, should have been the man whose teaching the Reformation leaders took as guide-line and considered to be the message of Jesus. First then, there was the work of a usurper and the split he caused at the time of Christianity's origin; second, Luther's fatal mistake (and the mistake of his Christian successors) in finding the truth where in reality there was error.

That the figure of the Nazarene, as delivered to us in Mark's Gospel, is decisively different from the pre-existent risen Christ proclaimed by Paul, is something long recognised by thinkers like Kant, Fichte, Schelling, Herder and Goethe, to mention only a few. The distinction between 'the religion of Christ' and 'the Christian religion' goes back to Lessing. Critical theological research has now disputed the idea of an uninterrupted chain of historical succession: Luther's belief that at all times a small handful of true Christians preserved the true apostolic faith. Walter Bauer[226] and Martin Werner[227] have brought evidence that there was conflict from the outset about the central questions of dogma. It has become clear that the beliefs of those who had seen and heard Jesus in the flesh—the disciples and the original community —were at odds to an extraordinary degree with the teaching of Paul, who claimed to have been not only called by a vision but instructed by the heavenly Christ. The conflict at Antioch between the apostles Peter and Paul, far more embittered as research has shown[228] than the Bible allows us to see, was the most fateful split in Christianity, which in the Acts of the Apostles was 'theologically camouflaged'.[229]

Paul, who had never seen Jesus, showed great reserve towards the Palestinian traditions regarding Jesus' life.[230] The historical Jesus and his earthly life are without significance for Paul. In all his epistles the name 'Jesus' occurs only 15 times, the title 'Christ' 378 times. In Jesus's actual teaching he shows extraordinarily little interest. It is disputed whether in all his epistles he makes two, three or four references to sayings by Jesus.[231] It is not Jesus's teaching, which he cannot himself have heard at all (short of hearing it in a vision), that is central to his own mission, but the person of the Redeemer and His death on the Cross.

Paul, however, did not pass on the revealed doctrine reflected in the glass of the intellectual categories of his time, as is often asserted; he transformed the 'Faith of Jesus' into 'Faith in Jesus'. He it was who gave baptism a mysterious significance, 'so as to connect his mission with the experience of initiates in the Hellenic mystery cults';[232] he turned the 'Last Supper' into a sacramental

226. *Rechtgläubigkeit und Ketzerei im ältesten Christentum.*
227. *Die Geschichte des christlichen Dogmas.*
228. Notably Schoeps, *Theologie und Geschichte des Judenchristentums* and Schonfield, *Those Incredible Christians.*
229. Acts 15:1 et seq.; also Galatians 2:11. See Stauffer, *Zum Kalifat des Jakobus,* p. 199.
230. Schoeps, *Paulus,* p. 50.
231. From Paul, we hear nothing, for example, of the Parables, the Sermon on the Mount or the Lord's Prayer. See Albert Schweitzer, *The Mysticism of Paul the Apostle.*
232. Schoeps, *Paulus,* p. 112.

union with the Lord of those celebrating it;[233] he was responsible for the sacramentalisation of the Christian religion, and took the phrase 'Son of God'—in the Jewish religion merely a title for the Messiah—to be an ontological reality. The idea of the Son of God, come down from Heaven to earth, hitherto inconceivable to Jewish thought,[234] was taken by Paul from the ancient religious syncretism of Asia Minor, to fit in with the need at the time for a general saviour. It is generally accepted by critical scholarship that the godparents here were the triad from the cult of Isia (Isis, Osiris and Horus) and also Attis, Adonis and Hercules. Jesus, who never claimed religious worship for himself and was not worshipped in the original community, is for Paul the pre-existent risen Christ.

The most essential and effective alteration of Jesus's message carried out by Paul was in his denying the Law's power of salvation and replacing the idea of the Covenant,[235] the objective principle of the Jewish religion, with faith in Christ and in the atoning power of his sacrificial death; the concrete Mosaic law with a mystical doctrine of salvation. Here the Cause of God was robbed of its proper centre and transformed into a mixture of Judaism, Christianity and paganism. The original community recognised the devastating effect of the 'Apostle to the Gentiles' and did not watch it passively. The Jerusalem community sent teachers ('false brethren', Paul called them) to the new communities founded by Paul; they taught the true doctrine to the believers only just won for the Faith and opposed the doctrine taught by Paul.[236] Paul was such a controversial figure that Tertullian, in his pamphlet attacking Marcion, called him 'Apostle to the Heretics', and the

233. ibid., p. 110 ff.

234. The idea that God in his essence was walking on earth is inconceivable also in Islám (*Qur'án*, súrahs 112; 2:110; 19:91–4; 5:76–8; 4:169, 170) and in the Bahá'í Faith: 'Beware, lest thou be led to join partners with the Lord, thy God. He is, and hath from everlasting been, one and alone, without peer or equal, eternal in the past, eternal in the future, detached from all things, ever-abiding, unchangeable, and self-subsisting. He hath assigned no associate unto Himself in His Kingdom, no counsellor to counsel Him, none to compare unto Him, none to rival His glory.' 'Know thou of certainty that the Unseen can in no wise incarnate His Essence and reveal it unto men' (Bahá'u'lláh, *Gleanings*, XCIV and XX).

235. So far as the idea of the 'New Covenant' is at all expressed (e.g. I Corinthians 11:26 or Ephesians 2:11 et seq.), it comes about in the 'Being in Christ'. This is the most profoundly Christian idea: 'If anyone is in Christ, he is a new creature' (II Corinthians 5:17) but that is a quite different principle, not a covenant with God.

236. E. Meyer, *Ursprung und Anfänge des Christentums*, vol. III, p. 441; Schonfield, p. 179 ff.

Pseudo-Clementine Homilies declared him a false teacher, even indeed the anti-Christ.

This was the 'Fall' of Christianity: that Paul with his 'Gospel', which became the core of Christian dogma formation, conquered the world,[237] while the historic basis of Christianity was declared a heresy, the preservers of the original branded as 'Ebionites'. As Schoeps puts it, the heresy-hunters 'accused the Ebionites of a lapse or relapse into Judaism, whereas they were really only the Conservatives who could not go along with the Pauline-cum-Hellenistic elaborations'.[238] Schonfield comes to the same conclusion: 'This Christianity in its teaching about Jesus continued in the tradition it had directly inherited, and could justifiably regard Pauline and catholic Christianity as heretical. It was not, as its opponents alleged, Jewish Christianity which debased the person of Jesus, but the Church in general which was misled into deifying him.'[239] 'Pauline heresy served as the basis for Christian orthodoxy, and the legitimate Church was outlawed as heretical'.[240] The 'small handful of true Christians' was Nazarene Christianity, which was already extinct in the fourth century.

It is worthy of note that there were striking similarities between this Christianity and Islám. Above all in Christology: in the faith of the original community Jesus was the new Moses, the Son of God as 'testified' by the adoptive act of baptism. This Christology, which corresponds completely to that of the *Qur'án*, was considered by the Pauline Church, together with obedience to the 'Jewish' law, as characteristic of the Ebionite heresy. These similarities discovered by research are ambiguous, of course. The scholar inclined towards Church dogma, who cannot see Islám as anything but a mixture of Arab paganism, Judaism and Christianity, finds them evidence that Muḥammad was 'bred' (Schlatter) on the Judaeo-Christian tradition, that he had borrowed his credal ideas from Judaeo-Christian thought. On the other hand, the

237. Not least because Paul 'the allegorising Midrash teacher expressly abolished the whole law of ritual and ceremonial . . . for the new religion' and because 'this religion with its belief in a Son of God and the atoning power of his martyr's death could link up well with the ideas held and spread in the mystery cults of the time— which was simply not possible from the premises of the Mosaic law and its ethical strictness' (H. J. Schoeps, *Jüdisch-christliches Religionsgespräch*, p. 53).

238. *Theologie und Geschichte des Judenchristentums*, p. 322, f. n .1

239. Schonfield, op. cit., p. 118.

240. ibid., p. 56.

Bahá'í, oriented towards the doctrine of cyclically recurring revelation and convinced of the mission of Islám, finds these results of
research—in the light of the unity of religions—extremely instruc-
tive, because they are a sufficient explanation for the discrepancy
between orthodox Church doctrine and the doctrine of the post-
Biblical religions, and because they show where the original truth
was preserved: not in the pagan-Christian Greater Church based
on Paul, but in the Jewish Christianity contemptuously branded
as 'Ebionism'. On this point, Islám, according to the divine plan
for salvation, was among other things the authoritative new confirmation of the credal truths preserved in Nazarene Christianity
but lost to the Greater Church.[241]

The syncretism which started in Paul's doctrine ('I have become
all things to all men'), and grew on the soil of irrationality (*credo
quia absurdum*), reached its full elaboration in the time of the
Church Fathers and became perpetuated in the hybrid dogma of
Nicea, in which—as pointed out by the Jewish thinker Salomon
Ludwig Steinheim—'with an amazing intellectual force but also
with an almost terrifying stubbornness', components of Jewish
and pagan doctrine 'were shaken together and combined to form
a homogeneous mixture'.[242] The whole of Church history there-
after was, as Steinheim rightly observes, dependent on and decided
by the conflict, continuing beneath the unity formula, between
elements of the revelation and of paganism. 'The Church took
Paul as its spiritual guide, thereby becoming involved down the
centuries in conflicts and schisms, enmity, persecution and blood-

241. On the whole subject, see also Adolf von Harnack, *Lehrbuch der Dogmengeschichte*, vol. I, p. 331 and vol. II, p. 534 ff.; A. Schlatter, *Die Entwicklung des
jüdischen Christentums zum Islám*, p. 251 ff.; Schoeps, *Theologie und Geschichte des Judenchristentums*, pp. 71 and 304 ff.; Leonhard Goppelt, *Christentum und Judentum im ersten und
zweiten Jahrhundert*, p. 175. It becomes very clear in this context how heavily Christian theology is based on Paul, not Jesus. Schlatter writes: 'We tried to understand
what the Christianity was like from which Islám grew. What kind of Christianity
is superior to Islám and can therefore help it? It must know Paul. With a Christianity based on the formula 'Not Paul but Jesus, not the Epistle to the Romans but
the Sermon on the Mount', we cannot help Islám. Legalism is not overcome by
legalism. The God of Might is eclipsed only by the God of Mercy, and the justice
which corrupts us [!] is healed only by the justice of Faith. If Christianity knows Paul,
then it partakes of the gift of Jesus redeemed from the weakness of mere dependence
on laws . . . Thus it has also risen above the opposition between the historical and the
eternal Christ, and so the historical Christ sinks into the past and into oblivion . . .'
(op. cit., p. 236).

242. *Die Offenbarung nach dem Lehrbegriff der Synagogue*, vol. III, p. 243.

shed, as Christians wrestled with the implications and interpretation of Pauline doctrines.'[243]

The centrepiece then, of Christian credal doctrine, that of Redemption, is something of which—in the judgment of the theologian E. Grimm[244]—Jesus himself knew nothing; and it goes back to Paul. This is even admitted by some Catholics: 'Christianity today mostly means Paul.'[245] And Wilhelm Nestle stated—as noted also by Sabet—'Christianity is the religion founded by Paul which replaces the Gospel of Jesus by a gospel about Jesus.'[246] So also Schonfield: 'Paul produced an amalgamation of ideas which, however unintentionally, did give rise to a new religion.'[247]

Jesus conferred authority on Peter,[248] Paul usurped it. The so-called 'throne of Peter' is in fact the throne of Paul.[249] And except for the fact that the Papacy claims Matthew 16:18 for itself, what part does the Prince of the Apostles play in Christianity today? He is the janitor at the gates of Heaven, the subject of many jokes. No one makes jokes about Paul! And who is Jesus?—the babe in the cradle and the Redeemer on the Cross! These two images, which come to the Christian's mind when he thinks of Jesus, show the subordinate part played for him by Jesus's preaching, teaching and ethics. Another sign demonstrating the deviation of the Christian religion from its Palestinian origins is that Rome, the metropolis of the pagan world at the time, became the seat of the Church; the languages of the pagans, Greek and Latin, became the languages of the Church; pagan Roman law became the basis of Church law.

The 'message of Jesus' with which conservative theologians confront the Bahá'ís is not the teaching of Jesus but the message of Paul, 'the preaching of the Cross', as he called his Gospel.[250] And if they say that the basic questions of our existence are only

243. Schonfield, op. cit., p. 89.
244. *Die Ethik Jesu*, p. 180.
245. G. Ricciotti, *Paulus*, p. 590.
246. *Krisis des Christentums*, p. 89.
247. *Those Incredible Christians*, p. 93.
248. Peter's station is also confirmed by Bahá'u'lláh: God caused 'the mysteries of wisdom and of utterance to flow out of his mouth' (Quoted by Shoghi Effendi, *The Promised Day is Come*, p. 114).
249. 'The church at Rome built on the Pauline foundation' (Schonfield, op. cit., p. 144).
250. I Corinthians 1:18; 2:2.

grasped in their true depth in 'the preaching of the Cross', I reply
with Steinheim who said: 'It may be a good philosophical idea, a
thoughtful myth, a comfortable emotional religion—that I can
accept. Only don't let it be called the teaching and revelation of
Christ, but a decline from it—its opposite, in fact. It leads to the
gods . . . of Olympus, not to Him who revealed Himself to Moses
at Sinai, of whom Christ and the apostles taught the pagans',[251]
nor—I will complete the response—to Him Who speaks in the
Qur'án and Who is proclaimed by Bahá'u'lláh.

Some may object that I have picked a few results which suit my
purpose from the vast amount of recent theological research and
have arbitrarily played these cards against the orthodox doctrine.
This objection would be a misunderstanding of the situation. The
starting-point for my discussion is not a scientific thesis, however
formed, but my conviction and faith: if, as Bahá'u'lláh teaches, all
the revealed religions are of divine origin and there is therefore an
essential unity between the religions, if the revelation of God is a
cyclically recurring, progressive process, if the purpose of revelation has always been the same, the education of the human race,[252]
then there can be no essential contradictions between the religions
on questions about the purpose of their revelations. For God does
not contradict Himself.

If religions contradict each other on questions independent of
the turn of events on earth and the development of man and
society, the contradictions go back to the individual centrifugal
developments which all religions have been through, to the
erosions of history. The criterion of judgment will always be the
most recent revelation of God. For the purification of the past
religions is one reason, among others, why whenever it has
pleased God, 'the gates of mercy have been opened' 'till the end
which has no end'. God Himself reforms, by speaking again to
mankind at the end of a cycle of revelation. That is why the revelation of Bahá'u'lláh is at the same time a judgment on the old
religions. It is, as he testifies, 'the right path' whereby 'truth shall
be distinguished from error and the wisdom of every command

---

251. op. cit., vol. II, p. xii ff.
252. 'The purpose of the one true God in manifesting Himself is to summon all
mankind to truthfulness and sincerity, to piety and trustworthiness, to resignation
and submissiveness to the Will of God, to forbearance and kindliness, to uprightness
and wisdom' (*Gleanings*, CXXXVII).

shall be tested'.[253] It separates the thorns and thistles from the grain, the true and authentic from the untrue and false, the pure divine teaching from the human additions and misunderstandings: 'Verily, the day of ingathering is come, and all things have been separated from each other. He hath stored away that which He chose in the vessels of justice, and cast into fire that which befitteth it.'[254]

Measured by the standard of Bahá'u'lláh's revelation, the Pauline doctrine of Justification, the doctrine of Original Sin, the doctrine of the Holy Trinity, the sacramentalisation of the Christian religion, the whole Church plan of salvation—which not only contradicts the Jewish understanding of God[255] but was also strongly repudiated by the revelation of God which succeeded Christianity[256]—these are a deformation of Jesus's teaching. Some critical theological scholars have confirmed that these deformations in Christianity started very early, in fact with Paul, and that the arch-apostle, without whom Marcion would not have been possible, was the arch-heretic in Christianity—as Tertullian very rightly saw.[257] * Years ago, when I became acquainted with the founder of the Christian religion in the faith of the original community through H. J. Schoeps's *Theologie und Geschichte des Judenchristentums*,[258] the standard work on the subject, I was deeply impressed. Here Jesus was not the only-begotten Son of God come down from Heaven, crucified and resurrected, nor the unique Saviour, but the messenger of God to whom the *Qur'án* testifies and who is glorified by Bahá'u'lláh.[259]

253. Bahá'u'lláh, Tablet of Aḥmad.
254. Bahá'u'lláh, Tablet to Pope Pius IX, *The Proclamation of Bahá'u'lláh*, p. 86. See also Matthew 13:24–9, 40–43.
255. It is understandable that the Jews could never accept Christianity in the completely different form produced by Paul, the form that triumphed in the greater Church.
256. See *Qur'án* 112; 19:88–94; 2:116; 5:72 et seq.; 4:171–2; 5:116; 3:58.
257. Quoted by Deschner, pp. 116 and 629.
258. *Theology and History of Jewish Christianity*.
259. 'Know thou that when the Son of Man yielded up His breath to God, the whole creation wept with a great weeping. By sacrificing Himself, however, a fresh capacity was infused into all created things' (Quoted by Shoghi Effendi, *The Promised Day is Come*, p. 114). The idea of sacrifice confronts us in every religion, for every messenger of God has 'offered up His life as a ransom for the redemption of the world' (*Gleanings*, CXLVI).
* See also note on p. 109.

The Reformation and the theological pluralism of the Church

Revelation is always reformation as well, the only true and possible reformation. All human attempts to find the origins, the true teaching, beneath the rubble of conflicting forms of Christianity and theological systems—for instance through 'demythologising' —always turn out to be defective, inadequate and doomed to failure. For every reformer is missing two vital things, a binding standard and a generally acknowledged authority. That is why the Reformation leaders did not achieve any unity either and immediately split into Lutherans and Zwinglians, then Lutherans and Calvinists, feuding violently with each other—to say nothing of the many secondary Reformation offshoots and sects. The Reformation has given Christianity, which was never a solid unity, a 'theological pluralism'[260] which is shown today in the fact that there is bitter conflict on central questions of faith (like the divinity of Christ and the Resurrection). Werner Harenberg describes the situation thus:

'On the factor which should unite its members, belief, it [the Church] lets its theologians say different and contradictory things. You can believe that God exists or that he is 'the origin of my safety with and committedness to my fellow-man' (Braun). Jesus may have been only man, or both God and man. You may believe that Jesus has been from eternity and came into the world by virgin birth. But you may also believe 'he is the Son of God because of his conduct . . . in that he fears, loves and trusts God above all things' (Zahrnt). You may believe *in* Jesus but also believe *like* Jesus . . . 'Belief is based on premises and is secured by them' or 'is unsecured and must dispense with security' (Knevels) . . . Whether it is about God or the Faith, the Holy Ghost or Eternal Life, the author of St. John's gospel or the authenticity of a saying of Jesus—there are always at least two opposing doctrines or schools . . . The church is schizophrenic, pulpit and professorial chair remain different worlds.'[261]

The Church, which does not clearly take up a position itself, has turned into a 'debating hall', in which 'unauthoritative religious declamations are presented' (Künneth), theology has 'become a maze in which even the experts . . . often lose their way' (Haren-

260. Hans Grass, *Der theologische Pluralismus und die Wahrheitsfrage*, p. 146.
261. *Jesus und die Kirchen*, p. 23.

berg). Meanwhile theological dispute has brought out such a mass of contradictions that Walter Künneth speaks of 'a high degree of confusion'[262] and Gerhard Ebeling, who deplores the 'obstinate non-understanding and misunderstanding in the discussions between theologians of the same denomination', even speaks of 'chaos'.[263] Hermann Diem sees among the Protestant university theologians 'hardly any longer a common basis for discussion . . . on which agreement could be reached'.[264] Some Protestant theologians today hold positions which make their opposing experts talk of 'the end of theology'[265] and of 'total theological sell-out'.[266]

The degrading and levelling of Christ, of which Bahá'ís are accused because they deny the doctrine of the Trinity and incorporate Jesus into the historic series of the messengers of God, has become reality in the case of many Christian theological scholars. To many of them Jesus of Nazareth has become a man like others, for whom much was unknown and who often erred[267]—an impossible concept for a Bahá'í! And what is left from the revealed Faith if, as Herbert Braun teaches, God is to be conceived only as 'an expression for the phenomenon of being able to act with courage, conscientiousness and conviction', only as 'a particular form of love for others?'[268] God would indeed have left His people on their own, if He had left it to the reformers and demythologisers to find the truth!

This state of affairs, the total confusion and utter depletion of central articles of faith,[269] is to a Bahá'í, who recognises the

---

262. *Glauben an Jesus? Die Begegnung der Christologie mit der modernen Existenz*, p. 7.

263. *Hermeneutische Theologie?*, p. 484 ff.

264. *Dogmatik*, p. 5.

265. Gerhard Petry, *Das Ende der Theologie?*, p. 17.

266. Wilhelm Andresen, *Selbstpreisgabe der Theologie?*, p. 58.

267. Walter Hartmann, for instance, stating the position that Jesus was a man and nothing but man, said: 'We should at last begin to conceive of Jesus as a real man and cease to regard him as a God changed into a man. This is really, in fact, a semantic problem. What Jesus means for us can no longer be expressed in the form of 'both God and Man'. All the situations described in the New Testament are incomprehensible for us if we say he is God. A god cannot be tempted, be hungry and thirsty, afraid, lonely, die and be buried, etc. We must come out into the open and say that Jesus was man and nothing but man. And what the Ancients meant when they said he was God, we can only express by saying that in what Jesus is and does we are shown what God has done, wishes to do and will do on earth through men who are nothing but men' (*Evangelische Unterweisung*, February 1966).

268. *Gesammelte Studien zum Neuen Testament und Seiner Umwelt*, p. 325 ff.

269. On this Bahá'u'lláh says: 'Witness how they have entangled themselves with their idle fancies and vain imaginations. By My life! They are themselves the victims

divinity of Jesus's revelation, a clear sign that the process of disintegration in Christianity is now taking place. It is also the sign of the Last Days—the end of the old era.

Man—a fallen being?

If the 'Message of the Cross' is not the centre of the Gospel but (as shown above) a Pauline addition, an amalgam, then there is basically no need to go into it further. Nevertheless, I think it is important to state the Bahá'í teachings on the matter.

The primary assumption made by Pauline and Church doctrine is the *a priori* corruption of man; for, as Pascal put it, the Christian faith 'seeks little more than to establish these two truths: the corruption of nature and its redemption through Jesus Christ'.[270] Paul's premise for recognising the complete corruption of human nature is the account of the Fall in Genesis, which has fundamental significance for him and from which the later Church, above all Augustine, derived the dogma of original sin. Man is a fallen being, by himself incapable of good and damned without the Christian work of redemption: 'Oh wretched man that I am! who shall deliver me out of the body of this death?'[271]

Against this premise, which is not shared by the Bahá'ís, the following objections can be made: the Jews, from whose Holy Book, after all, the allegory of the Fall stems, have always rejected as 'arbitrary inventions by the Christians'[272] the doctrine of original sin and the conclusion that a compulsion to sin came into the world through Adam. They have referred to the Bible, which contains many passages from the Prophets testifying to man's personal responsibility, such as this in Ezekiel 18:20: 'The soul that sinneth, it shall die: the son shall not bear the iniquity of the father, neither shall the father bear the iniquity of the son.' But Jesus too knows nothing of the total corruption of man asserted by Paul or his inability to keep the law and do good. Otherwise what would have been the sense in the rigorous ethic he called for,

of what their own hearts have devised, and yet they perceive it not. Vain and profitless is the talk of their lips, and yet they understand not' (*Gleanings*, C).

270. *Pensées*, tr. Martin Turnell, p. 106.
271. Romans 7:24.
272. Isaak Troki, quoted by H. J. Schoeps, *Jüdisch-christliches Religionsgespräch*, p. 75.

or the demand: 'Be ye therefore perfect, even as your Father which is in heaven is perfect'?[273]

If Dr. Hutten believes that the universality of human corruption, which only the atoning sufferings of Jesus can overcome, is the quintessence of the Bible and the basis for the Christians' more profound understanding of the world—well, no one can stop him believing that. But there are several things which should be said about his statement that Bahá'í teaching is inadequate because it makes light of sin.[274]

First, Christians themselves are by no means agreed on the dogma of original sin, as Huschmand Sabet observed—but unfortunately Dr. Hutten did not go into that point. He really should not expect someone outside Christianity to go exclusively by Luther. Why not by Zwingli, for instance, who is, frankly, more to my taste? He rejected the doctrine of original sin as contrary to the Gospel, and called Luther crazy and non-Christian for his deviant doctrine of the Communion. What is one to think of arguments which continually confront someone outside Christianity with dogmatic positions which are disputed within it? Further, among those who adhere to the dogma of original sin, both Catholics and Protestants, the extent of the corruption of human nature and consequently of the doctrine of justification are controversial.

Bahá'u'lláh's view of man

Secondly, Dr. Hutten failed to grasp the attitude of the Bahá'ís to this problem.

Man is not by nature evil and incapable of good, but 'the noblest and most perfect of all created things'.[275] In him 'are potentially revealed all the attributes and names of God to a degree that no other created being hath excelled or surpassed'.[276] He is the mystery of God.[277] But lack of education has 'deprived him of that which he doth inherently possess'. He is 'a mine rich in gems of inestimable value'. But 'education can, alone, cause it to reveal its treasures'.[278] Not any sort of education: what is meant

---

273. Matthew 5:48.   274. *Seher, Grübler, Enthusiasten*, p. 316.
275. Bahá'u'lláh, *Kitáb-i-Íqán*, p. 66 (Brit.), p. 102 (U.S.).
276. ibid., p. 65 (Brit.), p. 101 (U.S.).
277. 'Man is My mystery, and I am his mystery' (ibid.). 'Man is the supreme Talisman' (*Gleanings*, CXXII).
278. *Gleanings*, CXXII.

is divine education through the manifestations and according to their teachings and commandments. Just as a plant needs light to develop the perfections within it, so man needs spiritual illumination through the Sun of Truth, the Logos. Man—as is said in the daily prayer—is created 'to know and worship God'. If he fails in this duty, he has missed the purpose of his existence, and the spiritual potentialities within him will not be fully developed. Without divine guidance, and relying only on his reason, man goes astray. Bahá'u'lláh leaves no doubt that 'nothing whatsoever can exist without the revelation of the splendour of God'.[279] 'Were the Hand of Divine Power to divest of this high endowment all created things, the entire universe would become desolate and void.'[280] The whole development of the human race has been brought about by the revelations of God which have succeeded each other from time immemorial.

But, one might object, the world is in a bad state, and evil is to be seen everywhere. This is recognised well enough. 'And if God willed to punish men for their misdeeds, he would not leave a single living being on earth', it says in the *Qur'án*.[281] Bahá'u'lláh too complains that men 'have been led astray, and are truly of the heedless',[282] that there is no one who sincerely craves after truth and 'seeketh guidance', that all are 'dwellers in the land of oblivion' and 'followers of the people of wickedness and rebellion',[283] that the peoples, 'have languished, stricken and sore athirst, in the vale of idle fancy and waywardness', because they have failed 'to seek from the luminous and crystal Springs of divine knowledge the inner meaning of God's holy words'.[284] Bahá'u'lláh also warns against following 'the steps of the Evil One', who 'is lying in wait',[285] who 'hindereth the rise and obstructeth the spiritual progress of the children of men'.[286] Satan, however, is not an independent power opposed to God, but a metaphor for the lower nature of man tied to the world.[287]

279. Bahá'u'lláh, *Kitáb-i-Íqán*, p. 90 (Brit.), p. 140 (U.S.).
280. *Gleanings*, XCIII.
281. 16:62.
282. *Gleanings*, CXXXVI.
283. *Kitáb-i-Íqán*, p. 164 (Brit.), p. 256 (U.S.).
284. ibid., p. 68 (Brit.), p. 105 (U.S.).
285. *Gleanings*, LXXVI and LXXXV.
286. ibid., XLIII.
287. The allegedly deeper understanding of Christians in connection with evil, the Church's Satanology, led to exorcisms and to the witchhunts of the Middle Ages.

'Abdu'l-Bahá speaks of man's dual nature. The physical nature is inherited from Adam, the spiritual nature 'from the Reality of the Word of God'. The physical nature 'is the source of all imperfection', the spiritual nature 'of all perfection'. The low qualities of man, the sins, are the consequence of 'the power of the lusts'. The body obeys the demands of Nature: 'A man who has not had a spiritual education is a brute.'[288] Lofty as the station is 'which man, if he but choose to fulfil his high destiny, can attain'—he can also sink into the depths of degradation, 'depths which the meanest of creatures have never reached'.[289] This verse from Bahá'u'lláh is a sufficient explanation of all the evil on earth—including Auschwitz and Hiroshima. The Devil was not needed for that! But all the imperfections, all the bad qualities, 'which come from the requirements of the physical life of man', can be 'transformed into human perfections' by the Word of God, the cause of spiritual life, which 'is a quickening spirit . . . Therefore Christ was a quickening spirit, and the cause of life in all mankind.'[290]

The transformation of man—his inner deliverance and turning to God—is a precondition of his ability to partake of spiritual life. 'Repent!' cried John the Baptist of old, to those who prepared for the coming of Christ. Dr. Hutten did not recognise that the transformation of man is more than 'education, piety and brotherly love, etc.',[291] more than the naïve call, 'be kind to each other and obedient to God'.[292] The transformation of man, the 'return' demanded in the Jewish religion, is the complete turning of man to God, with whom he becomes united through the accomplishment of the law: transformation is the spiritual resurrection which Jesus demanded. Nothing can bring about this transformation except the living Word of God.

The latest covenant
God 'loveth the one that turneth towards Him'.[293] But the belief alone has no power to bring salvation. That demands responsive action, for the greater the effort, the more faithfully will man

288. *Some Answered Questions*, XXIX.
289. *Gleanings*, CI.
290. *Some Answered Questions*, XXIX.
291. *Seber, Grübler, Enthusiasten*, p. 316.
292. ibid., p. 315.
293. Bahá'u'lláh, *Gleanings*, CXXXIV.

'reflect the glory of the names and attributes of God'.[294] The
relationship between God and man is expressed in the verse:
'Love Me, that I may love thee. If thou lovest Me not, My love
can in no wise reach Thee.'[295] The idea of the Covenant got lost
in Christianity owing to Paul's misunderstanding,[296] and is not a
subject dealt with in either Catholic or Protestant theology; but,
as in Islám and Judaism, it is one of the essential factors in the
Bahá'í Faith, the latest Covenant. God's intention of the salvation
of mankind is complemented by the duty of man to obey God's
will as manifested in the Law. 'The essence of religion is to testify
unto that which the Lord hath revealed, and follow that which He
hath ordained in His mighty Book.'[297] The Bahá'í Faith is a religion of the Law. The recognition of God, a knowledge which is
'the source of all learning',[298] must be followed by realisation of
the divine will which confronts man in the Law. For 'the essence
of faith is fewness of words and abundance of deeds'.[299] From the
Law man discovers what he owes God. And only in striving to
fulfil the Law does he come into the right relationship with God.
The Bahá'í Faith is, therefore, a religion of action.[300] Divine grace
is obtained through faith[301] *and* works.[302]

Some theologians hold that man no longer needs to make himself other than he is, that he does not have to take on any form
pleasing to God but has a part in the Kingdom of Heaven 'just as
he is', because Jesus by his sacrificial death has brought the lost
world home.[303] This thesis, like the concept of man's inability to
change, is an expression of Christianity's antinomian peculiarity,
Martin Luther's *sola fide* doctrine, whereby 'man without any
action of his own or any merit is justified for Christ's sake by the

294. Bahá'u'lláh, CXXIV.
295. ibid., *The Hidden Words*, Arabic 5, which corresponds with Zachariah 1:3
and Malachi 3:7: 'Return to Me, so will I return to you, saith the Lord of Hosts.'
296. The extent to which the term 'Grace' is given a theological point is sufficiently
shown by the fact that in his epistles the word Grace comes 110 times, while it is
completely absent in Mark and Matthew
297. Bahá'u'lláh, Words of Wisdom, *Bahá'í World Faith*, p. 140.
298. ibid.
299. ibid., p. 141.
300. See p. 39 ff.; also 'Abdu'l-Bahá, *Paris Talks*, pp. 19–20, 76 ff.
301. Good works alone are not enough, if they do not result from the knowledge
and love of God. See 'Abdu'l-Bahá, *Some Answered Questions*, LXXXIV.
302. 'But believers and doers of good works, for them is mercy, and a great reward'. (*Qur'án* 35:8).
303. e.g. Gerhard Rosenkranz, *Die Bahá'í*, p. 59.

Faith'. But the prophet from Nazareth placed the accent elsewhere, as we can see from many passages in the Gospels, e.g. Matthew 7:19–23; 19:16–21; 23:2–3. These texts do not speak of 'Faith Alone' and 'Grace Alone', but of obedience to the Law and to the intention of the Law.

On Paul's polemic against the Law

On this subject Hans-Joachim Schoeps, speaking from a Jewish standpoint, has expressed basic truths so well that I cannot do better than quote at length his defence of the Law, to which as a Bahá'í I can give full agreement—thus justifying the length of this quotation:

'What is there really in the Pauline interpretation, in the Christian understanding of the Law? Judged from within Judaism, a misunderstanding of immense proportions, for all Christianity, especially the neo-Protestant polemic against the Law, misunderstands the Jewish Law as a means of obtaining justice before God (the so-called Justification by Works). Where Protestant theologians today do their best to speak in Luther's language and to take over his very often simplistic views, they confuse the claims of God's Law—which should surely in reality be the foundation of the Covenant—with the Justification by Works of the mediaeval Catholic Church in its decline. And all this because Paul, after his experience at Damascus, could no longer understand . . . what as a Pharisee he must certainly have known before, that the law of the Torah was not given to make the Jews just and pleasing to their Father in Heaven, but . . . because it makes known the holy will of this Father in Heaven. The Rabbinic glorifications of the law are to be understood only in the sense of carrying out the divine will, never in any ethic of "merit" of whatever kind. But if Paul says (in Romans 3:20) that "by the deeds of the law there shall no flesh be justified" in God's sight, then it is all very well for this great teacher of *Midrashim* to inveigh against the error made by some of his contemporary fellow-Pharisees. For Scripture, of course, does not teach *that* as the "purpose" of the Law, any more than the reason Paul adduces, "for by the law is the knowledge of sin", is its *purpose*. The Jews of his century knew as well as the Jews of all other centuries have known that man falls into sin because he does not live up to the revealed Law of God; only they have not let the living experience discoverable in daily life be petrified to an *a priori* statement which resignedly invalidates the Law because it is known from the start to be impossible of fulfilment . . .

'Paul writes to the Galatians (2:16): "Knowing that a man is not justified by the works of the law, but by the faith of Jesus Christ, even we have believed in Jesus Christ, that we might be justified by the faith of Christ, and not by the works of the law: for by the works of the law shall no flesh be justified." To this the Rabbis' answer, had it come to a dialogue, would have run something like this: We are not talking about the "works" of the Law nor about "justification"—only God is just—but about the will of God, whereby the law proclaimed by him is to be hallowed, as it says: "and ye shall be holy men unto me" (Exodus 22:31) . . .

'In Romans 7:19 Paul writes: "For the good that I would I do not; but the evil which I would not, that I do." To which the Rabbis would reply: That is to refuse to give God the honour. For in his Torah it says: "For this commandment which I command thee this day, it is not hidden from thee, neither is it far off. It is not in heaven, that thou shouldst say, Who shall go up for us to heaven, and bring it unto us, that we may hear it, and do it? Neither is it beyond the sea, that thou shouldst say, Who shall go over the sea for us, and bring it unto us, that we may hear it, and do it? But the word is very nigh unto thee, in thy mouth, and in thy heart, that thou mayest do it." (Deuteronomy, 30:11–14) . . .

'Paul might then answer (Romans 7:22–3): "I delight in the law of God after the inward man: but I see another law in my members, warring against the law of my mind, and bringing me into captivity to the law of sin, which is in my members." Whereupon the Rabbis would doubtless refer to Genesis 4:7: ". . . sin lieth at the door. And unto thee shall be his desire, and thou shalt rule over him".'[304]

Finally, Schoeps observes that the contradiction between earning salvation by faith and earning it by works, between justification by the Law and by the Gospel is 'as common as it is false'.[305] It only remains to add that Paul's assertion (in Romans 10:4) that Christ is the end of the law, contradicts Matthew 5:17–19 where Jesus says: 'Think not that I am come to destroy the law, or the prophets: I am not come to destroy, but to fulfil . . . Whosoever

304. *Jüdisch-christliches Religionsgespräch*, pp. 48–51 *passim*.
305. ibid., p. 57.

therefore shall break one of these least commandments, and shall teach men so, he shall be called least in the kingdom of heaven; but whosoever shall do and teach them, the same shall be called great in the kingdom of heaven.' How can Dr. Hutten talk, then, of 'the failure of experiments with commandments and laws'?[306]

The Bahá'í understanding of the Law

From what has been said it will be clear that the Law is not an 'obstacle, blocking the way to God', as Friedrich Gogarten puts it.[307] The Law, as Hermann Cohen states, is 'the necessary form for the carrying out of the correlation between God and Man'.[308] The laws of God are 'the breath of life unto all created things',[309] 'the lamps of My loving providence among My servants, and the keys of My mercy for My creatures',[310] 'the highest means for the maintenance of order in the world and the security of its peoples. He that turneth away from them, is accounted among the abject and foolish.'[311] Through them truth is 'separated from falsehood';[312] they embody 'the essence of justice and the source thereof' and 'the highest, the infallible standard of justice'.[313] Their purpose is 'the education of the human race'[314] and 'the happiness of all human beings'.[315] 'Whoso keepeth the commandments of God shall attain everlasting felicity.'[316]

Another word on the objection that the religion of the Law leads to man's redemption of himself which is his original sin, his fall from God, 'not what is actually demanded but what is forbidden'.[317] This polemic against the religion of the Law is shoot-

306. Isn't the idea of a God who experiments somehow blasphemous?
307. *Die Verkündigung Jesu Christi*, p. 58.
308. Quoted by H. J. Schoeps, op. cit., p. 50.
309. Bahá'u'lláh, Kitáb-i-Aqdas, quoted by Shoghi Effendi, *God Passes By*, p. 215.
310. Kitáb-i- Aqdas, quoted in *Synopsis and Codification of the Laws and Ordinances of the Kitáb-i-Aqdas*, p. 11.
311. ibid.
312. *Gleanings*, CXXXIII.
313. ibid., LXXXVIII.
314. 'Abdu'l-Bahá, *The Promulgation of Universal Peace*, p. 406.
315. ibid., *The Secret of Divine Civilization*, p. 60.
316. *Gleanings*, CXXXIII.
317. Rudolf Stählin, 'Christliche Religion'. *Fischer-Lexikon*, 1957, p. 109. In *Gott ist tot?* Stählin even speaks of 'the Law's power of Death', from whose spell man is to be delivered. This Protestant antinomianism, this harping on 'the freedom of the Christian', has had fatal effects. Anyone who in the religious sphere repudiates the Law, 'the dam against chaos', and claims freedom for himself, will in the secular sphere as well be all too easily inclined to understand binding rules as repression to

ing into the air, because it is attacking a distortion and deals with
such a religion only in its degenerate form as 'devotion to the
letter', an ethic purely of 'deserts' with legalistic observances.[318]
But the Law is not satisfied by being literally fulfilled, by a mere
external legality; it demands to be carried out from inner devotion: 'Walk in My statutes for love of Me.'[319] Merely carrying out
the Law offers no claim to God's grace, because the fulfilment of
any law needs God's acceptance: 'Nothing whatsoever shall, in
this Day, be accepted from you, though ye continue to worship
and prostrate yourselves before God . . . For all things are dependent upon His Will, and the worth of all acts is conditioned upon
His acceptance and pleasure.'[320] How seriously the Bahá'í Faith
takes the fact that no claims accrue to a man through his covenant
with God, is shown by the *Naw-Rúz* prayer[321] which says: 'For
the doings of men are all dependent upon Thy good-pleasure, and
are conditioned by Thy behest. Shouldst Thou regard him who
hath broken the fast as one who hath observed it, such a man
would be reckoned among them who from eternity had been
keeping the fast. And shouldst Thou decree that he who hath
observed the fast hath broken it, that person would be numbered
with such as have caused the Robe of Thy Revelation to be
stained with dust, and been far removed from the crystal waters
of this living Fountain.'[322]

Any 'boasting' in pious works (as suggested in Romans 2:23)
is excluded, because no believer can be sure of God's acceptance
of his works and aware of his state in God's eyes: 'He [the true
believer] should forgive the sinful, and never despise his low
estate, for none knoweth what his own end shall be. How often
hath a sinner, at the hour of death, attained to the essence of faith,
and quaffing the immortal draught, hath taken his flight unto the
celestial Concourse. And how often hath a devout believer, at the

---

be overcome. At first sight it is amazing that so many supporters of the revolutionary
left are recruited from the ranks of Protestant theological students but in fact it is
very understandable. If God's Law, as exalted by Bahá'u'lláh, is 'the highest means
for the maintenance of order in the world and the security of its peoples', the anarch-
istic tendencies of our time are not to be wondered at.

318. Romans 2:17 et seq.; Gogarten, op. cit., p. 51 et seq.
319. Bahá'u'lláh, *The Hidden Words*, Arabic 38.
320. *Gleanings*, CXXXV.
321. *Naw-Rúz* (New Year) according to the Bahá'í calendar, falls on 21 March
directly after the end of the fasting period.
322. Bahá'u'lláh, *Prayers and Meditations*, no. 46.

hour of his soul's ascension, been so changed as to fall into the nethermost fire.'[323]

God's justice and mercy

In view of the fact that every man falls short of the demands of the Law and thereby falls into sin, what happens about the 'Justification' before God? The answer is that justification does not take place—no one is just except God—because, as explained, the purpose of the Law is not to justify the individual before God, but to make him holy in carrying it out. God's forgiveness goes to the man who strives with all his might and with all his heart to obey the demands of the Law: 'Whosoever aspireth after Us, him will we surely lead on Our way.'[324] For the justice of God is surpassed by His mercy: 'The tenderness of Thy mercy, O my Lord, surpasseth the fury of Thy wrath, and Thy loving-kindness exceedeth Thy hot displeasure, and Thy grace excelleth Thy justice . . . Wert Thou to regard Thy servants according to their deserts in Thy days, they would assuredly merit naught except Thy chastisement and torment. Thou art, however, the One Who is of great bounteousness, Whose grace is immense.'[325]

In the *Qur'án*, too, we are assured: 'God will lighten your burden, for man was born weak.'[326] 'If you avoid the great sins, which are forbidden to you, We will cover your smaller sins and

---

323. Bahá'u'lláh, *Kitáb-i-Íqán*, p. 124 (Brit.), pp. 194–5 (U.S.).
324. *Qur'án* 29:69.
325. Bahá'u'lláh, *Prayers and Meditations*, no. 81. The mercy of God is a central theme which constantly recurs in the writings of Bahá'u'lláh: 'O Divine Providence! Though wicked, sinful and intemperate, we still seek from Thee a "seat of truth" and long to behold the countenance of the Omnipotent King . . . Everything Thou doest is pure justice, nay, the very essence of grace. One gleam from the splendours of Thy Name, the All-Merciful, sufficeth to banish and blot out every trace of sinfulness from the world, and a single breath from the breezes of the Day of Thy Revelation is enough to adorn all mankind with a fresh attire' (ibid., no. 160). 'I testify . . . that Thy mercy hath surpassed all created things, and Thy loving-kindness encompassed all that are in heaven and all that are on earth. From everlasting the doors of Thy generosity were open to the faces of Thy servants, and the gentle winds of Thy grace were wafted over the hearts of Thy creatures, and the overflowing rains of Thy bounty were showered upon Thy people and the dwellers of Thy realm' (ibid., no. 184). 'My God, my God! If none be found to stray from Thy path, how, then, can the ensign of Thy mercy be unfurled, or the banner of Thy bountiful favour be hoisted? And if iniquity be not committed, what is it that can proclaim Thee to be the Concealer of men's sins, the Ever-Forgiving, the Omniscient, the All-Wise?' (*Gleanings*, CXLII).
326. ibid., 4:29.

lead you in honour into Paradise.'[327] 'My mercy embraceth all
things.'[328]

God's mercy, which is great enough 'to forgive all sins and
trespasses, and to fulfil the needs of the peoples of all religions,
and to waft the fragrances of pardon over the entire creation',[329]
gives the sinner assurance that despite his failures, his falling short
of the Law's demands, he can partake of divine forgiveness and
grace. The crucial thing is his endeavour 'in the path of detachment'.[330]

Man's redemption thus comes about through steadfastness in
the Covenant, aspirations towards a 'godly way of life' lived in
humility by good thoughts, words and deeds, and deliverance
from attachment to the things of the world: deliverance (not
flight from the world and asceticism) from the finite and a turning
to the infinite, to God. The deeper spiritual foundations of the
progress of the soul to its destination have been set out in great
profundity by Bahá'u'lláh in two works written in the style and
language of Islamic mysticism, *The Seven Valleys* and *The Four
Valleys*. All men are called to travel this right path to redemption:
'The Sun of Reality hath appeared to all the world. This luminous
appearance is salvation and life; but only he who hath opened the
eye of reality and who hath seen these lights will be saved.'[331]

Theology and revelation
Dr. Hutten measured the message of Bahá'u'lláh by Christian
theology: on the face of it, a natural thing to do. By what else
should a theologian judge but his own doctrine in which he
believes and which he considers to be right? And yet the history
of Christianity itself might have made him wonder whether this
starting-point was beyond doubt the right one even when the
cause to be judged laid claim to be a revelation from God.

Jesus appeared at a time when the Jews were gripped with a
Messianic and apocalyptic excitement. The arrival of the promised
Messiah was expected, and with him the destruction of the pagan

327. *Qur'án* 4:32.
328. ibid., 7:157. There is sufficient evidence that God's mercy is the very *Leit-
motiv* of the *Qur'án* in the introductory form put before almost all the súrahs, 'In the
Name of God, the All-Merciful, the All-Compassionate'.
329. Bahá'u'lláh, *Prayers and Meditations*, no. 184.
330. ibid., *The Hidden Words*, Envoi.
331. 'Abdu'l-Bahá, *Bahá'í World Faith*, p. 390.

empires, especially Rome; and it was believed that the visions of
the prophets of the kingdom of peace would be fulfilled in the
near future under the rule of the one God. Suetonius reports in his
biography of Vespasian (4:5): 'An ancient superstition was current in the East, that out of Judea would come the rulers of the
world.' Tacitus writes in his *Histories* (5:13): 'Most of them were
convinced that according to the old writings of the priests it
would come to pass in that time that the East would grow strong
and the power which would gain world dominion should come
out of Judea.' This expectation was pitched very high: 'The end
of all things is right at the door. Only a few more decades, years,
months, perhaps only a few weeks, then the Kingdom of God
will appear with power and glory.'[332]

The Jewish theologians had quite specific ideas about the
expected Messiah: he was the anointed Prince of Peace, from
David's line, subject to the Law of Moses, equipped with earthly
power, who would ascend the throne of world dominion in Jerusalem. Jewish apocalyptics had no doubt prophesied the Messiah
of Israel at least twenty times in the New Testament age. Finally
Rabbi Akiba greeted the 'Son of the Star', the revolutionary
leader Bar Kochba, as God's Anointed and the fulfilment of the
prophecy in Numbers 24:17.

These expectations were not fulfilled, and Israel 'is still expect-
ant that the idol of her own handiwork will appear with such signs
as she herself hath conceived'.[333] Why did they repudiate the
Promised One (as accepted by Christians and Bahá'ís alike)? Because the Rabbinical exegesis of the Messianic passages was wrong.
Jesus was not the expected warrior hero bringing liberation from
the Roman yoke, and yet he sat on the throne of power. For all his
apparent powerlessness and his crucifixion—shocking to the disciples—he was the King. His dominion was a spiritual, not an
earthly one. His message has conquered and transformed men's
hearts. As expected, the power came out of Judea—only in a
different way from the interpretations of the scribes. Because the
majority of the Jews followed their religious leaders, this people
fulfilled Isaiah's prophecy,[334] echoed in Matthew (13:13): 'They

332. E. Stauffer, *Jerusalem und Rom*, p. 74.
333. Bahá'u'lláh, *Gleanings*, XIII.
334. 'Hear ye indeed, but understand not; and see ye indeed, but perceive not.
Make the heart of this people fat, and make their ears heavy, and shut their eyes; lest

seeing see not; and hearing they hear not, neither do they understand.'

The Gospels are full of complaints about man's stubbornness
and wilfulness. 'And this is the condemnation, that light is come
into the world, and men loved darkness rather than light.'[335]
'That was the true Light, which lighteth every man that cometh
into the world. He was in the world, and the world was made by
him, and the world knew him not.'[336] Jesus, who 'exploded' the
Jewish expectations of the Messiah, appealed to the testimony of
scripture, the same scripture on which the scribes based their
verdict of repudiation: 'Search the scriptures: for in them ye think
ye have eternal life: and they are they which testify of me.'[337] 'Do
not think that I will accuse you to the Father: there is one that
accuseth you, even Moses, in whom ye trust. For had ye believed
Moses, ye would have believed me: for he wrote of me. But if ye
believe not his writings, how shall ye believe my words?'[338]

The blind guides—yesterday and today

Responsibility for the people's lack of faith is attributed by Jesus
to the Jewish clergy, the 'blind guides', who keep the people from
true faith: 'But woe unto you, scribes and Pharisees, hypocrites!
for ye shut up the kingdom of heaven against men: for ye neither
go in yourselves, neither suffer ye them that are entering to go
in'.[339] 'They be blind leaders of the blind. And, if the blind lead
the blind, both shall fall into the ditch.'[340] In the same chapter of
Matthew's Gospel[341] he calls them 'blind fools', 'hypocrites',
'serpents', 'offspring of vipers', 'murderers of the prophets': 'Ye
build the tombs of the prophets, and garnish the sepulchres of the
righteous, and say, If we had been in the days of our fathers, we
would not have been partakers with them in the blood of the
prophets. Wherefore ye be witnesses unto yourselves, that ye are
the children of them which killed the prophets.'[342]

they see with their eyes, and hear with their ears, and understand with their heart,
and convert, and be healed' (6:9-10).
335. John 3:19.
336. John 1:9-10.
337. John 5:39.
338. John 5:45-7.
339. Matthew 23:13.
340. Matthew 15:14. See also Luke 6:39.
341. Matthew 23:13-24 *passim.*
342. ibid., vv. 29-31.

But how did it happen that the cultured Annas rejected God's message, while Peter, the simple fisherman, obeyed God's call? Because it was Annas's theological knowledge itself which formed the veil preventing him from recognising the truth! Because of the veil of his preconceived theological convictions he was one of those who 'seeing, see not, and hearing, hear not'. Because of the Jews' lack of faith 'the Kingdom of God shall be taken from you, and given to a nation bringing forth the fruits thereof'.[343]

The same process occurred at the appearance of Muḥammad. The acknowledged theologians of his time such as 'Abdu'lláh Ibn Ubayy, Abú-'Ámir the Hermit, Ka'b Ibn al-Ashraf and Naḍr Ibn al-Ḥárith, called him unbeliever, sorcerer, madman, deceiver, and incited the people to persecute him and banish him from their midst, while 'they who were destitute of all learning recognized and embraced His Faith'.[344] The *Qur'án*, too, is a convincing testimony to the phenomenon that the leaders of the Faith, caught in the 'subtleties'[345] of their theological systems, have always been the worst enemies of the new revelation, while the unlearned have borne witness to the truth of the words, 'Everyone that is of the truth heareth my voice'.[346] Thus Muḥammad complains: 'Hearts have ye, wherewith ye understand not; eyes have ye, wherewith ye see not; and ears have ye, wherewith ye hear not. Ye are like cattle; yea, worse than cattle have ye gone astray.'[347] They 'thrust their fingers into their ears'.[348] 'O the misery that rests upon my servants. No apostle cometh to them but they laugh him to scorn.'[349] 'So oft then as an apostle cometh to you with that which your souls desire not, swell ye with pride, and treat some as imposters, and slay others?'[350]

It was the Faith of their fathers, the traditional religion, which prevented the people from accepting the mission of Muḥammad: 'And when our distinct signs are recited to them, they say, "This is merely a man who would pervert you from your father's Worship." And they say, "This is no other than a forged falsehood"'[351] 'Verily we found our fathers with a religion, and in their tracks

343. Matthew 21:43.
344. Bahá'u'lláh, *Gleanings*, XXXV.
345. 'Let them concern themselves with their subtleties' (*Qur'án* 6:91).
346. John 18:37.   347. *Qur'án* 7:178.   348. ibid., 2:18.
349 ibid., 36:29.   350. ibid., 2:81.   351. ibid., 34:42.

we tread.'³⁵² The superseded knowledge is itself the veil which prevents the learned from recognising the new Revelation. 'Whom God causeth wilfully to err, and whose ears and whose heart he hath sealed up, and over whose sight he hath placed a veil—who, after his rejection by God, shall guide such a one? Will ye not then be warned?'³⁵³ And to the Jewish and Christian priests the *Qur'án* says: 'Say! O people of the Book! why repel believers from the way of God?'³⁵⁴

Bahá'u'lláh often gave his views on the prerequisites of faith. God is 'the Seen and the Hidden':³⁵⁵ the Seen to any that recognise and accept his revelation, the Hidden to any that reject his mission. Faith, the recognition of revelation, is conceived as an event far excelling the realm of intellectual comprehension. Religious truth is not a measurable amount of information which may be taken into possession. It cannot be demonstrated like a theorem of Euclid. The reality of religious truth is experienced in the actual encounter with it. That is why Goethe's aphorism applies:

> Niemand versteht zur rechten Zeit.
> Wenn man zur rechten Zeit verstünde,
> Dann wäre Wahrheit nah und breit,
> Und wäre lieblich und gelinde.³⁵⁶

God 'hath endowed every soul with the capacity to recognize the signs of God', and to 'ascend unto the heaven of certitude'.³⁵⁷ The prerequisite is only that a man should meditate 'with innocent and sanctified heart' on 'that which hath been sent down from the Throne on high'.³⁵⁸ and not follow the 'idle fancies and vain imaginations'³⁵⁹ of his heart: 'Then will the truth of this Cause appear unto you as manifest as the sun in its noon-tide glory.'³⁶⁰ 'For the faith of no man can be conditioned by any one except himself.'³⁶¹ Only the seeker finds the truth. And a true seeker must 'cleanse and purify his heart, which is the seat of the revelation of the inner mysteries of God, from the obscuring dust of all acquired knowledge.'³⁶² He 'must so cleanse his heart that no rem-

---

352. *Qur'án* 43:21.   353. ibid., 45:22.
354. ibid., 3:94.   355. ibid., 57:3.
356. 'No one understands at the right time. If one understood at the right time, truth would be all around us, sweet and gentle.'
357. *Gleanings*, LII.   358. ibid.   359. ibid., C.
360. ibid., LII.   361. ibid., LXXV.
362. *Kitáb-i-Íqán*, p. 123 (Brit.), p. 192 (U.S.).

nant of either love or hate may linger therein, lest that love blindly incline him to error, or that hate repel him away from the truth.363 In another place Bahá'u'lláh writes: 'In this day he who seeks the Light of the Sun of Truth must free his mind from the tales of the past.'364

The veil of learning, which stopped the Rabbis of Jesus's time from recognising Him also prevents today's divines from recognising the new Revelation, 'having weighed the testimony of God by the standard of their own knowledge, gleaned from the teachings of the leaders of their faith, and found it at variance with their limited understanding'.365 'The most grievous of all veils is the veil of knowledge.'366 It is the priests who, 'clinging unto their own learning, as fashioned by their own fancies and desires, have denounced God's divine Message and Revelation',367 who 'are wrapt in the densest veils of learning, and who, enmeshed by its obscurities, are lost in the wilds of error'368—it is they whom, in the words of the *Qur'án* God 'causeth to err through a knowledge'.369 'Satisfied with the croaking of the crow and enamoured with the visage of the raven, they have renounced the melody of the nightingale and the charm of the rose.'370

And as in the days of Jesus, when the priests shut out the kingdom of heaven and did not allow in those who wanted to enter, so it is the priests of today who keep the people from the path of God: 'Leaders of religion, in every age, have hindered their people from attaining the shores of eternal salvation, inasmuch as they held the reins of authority in their mighty grasp. Some for the lust of leadership, others through want of knowledge and understanding, have been the cause of the deprivation of the people. By their sanction and authority, every Prophet of God hath drunk from the chalice of sacrifice, and winged His flight unto the heights of glory.'371 Like Jesus, Bahá'u'lláh stands inexorably opposed to the representatives of the established reli-

---

363. ibid.
364. *The Hidden Words, Words of Wisdom and Communes*, p. 60.
365. *Kitáb-i-Íqán*, p. 10 (Brit.), p. 15 (U.S.).
366. ibid., p. 120 (Brit.), p. 188 (U.S.).
367. ibid., p. 137 (Brit.), p. 214 (U.S.).
368. ibid.
369. ibid.
370. ibid., p. 121 (Brit.), p. 189 (U.S.).
371. ibid., p. 10 (Brit.), p. 15 (U.S.).

gions, whom he repeatedly denounces and holds responsible for
the unbelief of the people.[372]

'When We observed carefully, We discovered that Our enemies
are, for the most part, the divines . . . Among the people are those
who said: He hath repudiated the divines. Say: Yea, by My Lord!
I, in very truth, was the One Who abolished the idols! . . . O concourse of divines! Fling away idle fancies and imaginings, and
turn, then, towards the Horizon of Certitude.'[373] 'We have decreed, O people, that the highest and last end of all learning be the
recognition of Him Who is the Object of all knowledge; and yet,
behold now ye have allowed your learning to shut you out, as by
a veil, from Him.'[374] 'Have ye clung unto the promptings of
your nature, and cast behind your backs the statutes of God? . . .
Reflect, and be not of them that have shut themselves out as by a
veil from Him, and were of those that are fast asleep.'[375] 'O Concourse of divines! Ye shall not henceforth behold yourselves possessed of any power, inasmuch as We have seized it from you.'[376]

Bahá'u'lláh continually makes plain that 'whatever in days gone
by hath been the cause of the denial and opposition of those
people hath now led to the perversity of the people of this age',[377]
and has caused them to dispute 'with vain words' and 'to refute
the truth'.[378] In the past, as today, the divines have not grasped
that God has manifested Himself 'in conformity with that which
He Himself hath purposed, and not according to the desires and
expectations of men.'[379] Hence Bahá'u'lláh's admonition: 'Say:

372. 'No two are found to agree on one and the same law, for they seek no God
but their own desire, and tread no path but the path of error. In leadership they have
recognized the ultimate object of their endeavour, and account pride and haughtiness
as the highest attainments of their heart's desire. They have placed their sordid
machinations above the divine decree, have renounced resignation unto the will of
God, busied themselves with selfish calculation, and walked in the way of the hypo-
crite. With all their power and strength they strive to secure themselves in their petty
pursuits, fearful lest the least discredit undermine their authority or blemish the display of their magnificence. Were the eye to be anointed and illumined with the colly-
rium of the knowledge of God, it would surely discover that a number of voracious
beasts have gathered and preyed upon the carrion of the souls of men' (*Kitáb-i-Íqán*,
p. 20 (Brit.), p. 30 (U.S.)).
373. *The Proclamation of Bahá'u'lláh*, pp. 76–7.
374. ibid., pp. 73–4.
375. *Epistle to the Son of the Wolf*, p. 49.
376. *The Proclamation of Bahá'u'lláh*, p. 80.
377. *Kitáb-i-Íqán*, p. 9 (Brit.), p. 13 (U.S.).
378. *Qur'án* 40:5.
379. *Gleanings*, XXXV.

O leaders of religion! Weigh not the Book of God with such standards and sciences as are current amongst you, for the Book itself is the unerring balance established amongst men.'[380] 'Great is the blessedness,' is Bahá'u'lláh's promise, 'of that divine that hath not allowed knowledge to become a veil between him and the One Who is the Object of all knowledge, and who, when the Self-Subsisting appeared, hath turned with a beaming face towards him. He, in truth, is numbered with the learned.'[381] And those divines 'who are truly adorned with the ornament of knowledge . . . are, verily, as a head to the body of the world, and as eyes to the nations'.[382]

The words of Bahá'u'lláh carry no weight with present-day churchmen. But what ground is there for supposing that in his invective against the Pharisees Jesus meant only the priests of his time and not a general phenomenon, the attitude of the priesthood to a new revelation? And what guarantee is there that the Christian divines of today are any less 'blind guides' than the rabbis of old? Where is the certainty that what happened in the days of Jesus could not be repeated at His second coming? Do not the Gospels contain many warnings which make one conclude that the returned Christ might also be rejected? Jesus's question, 'Nevertheless, when the Son of man cometh, shall he find faith on the earth?',[383] his parable of the wise and foolish virgins,[384] and the promise 'Behold, I come as a thief. Blessed is he that watcheth, and keepeth his garments, lest he walk naked, and they see his shame',[385] are warnings to remain vigilant. Jesus left no doubt at all as to how much faith he would find on his return: 'But as the days of Noah were, so shall also the coming of the Son of man be. For as in the days that were before the flood they were eating and drinking, marrying and giving in marriage, until the day that Noah entered into the ark, and knew not until the flood came, and took them all away; so shall also the coming of the Son of man be.'[386]

Is it likely that the Pharisees, in rejecting Jesus by appeal to Scripture, had worse grounds and were less convinced of their

---

380. ibid., XCVIII.
381. *The Proclamation of Bahá'u'lláh*, p. 79.
382. ibid.
383. Luke 18:8.
384. Matthew 25:1 ff.
385. Revelation 16:15; see also II Peter 3:10 and Matthew 24:43.
386. Matthew 24:37-9.

rightness than the Christian and Islamic priests when they pro-
nounce judgment on Bahá'u'lláh? The Jewish objections to Christ
in the Christian era almost two thousand years ago were based—
like Christian objections to Bahá'u'lláh—on scripture. Yet these
apparently compelling theological grounds were false, because
God had revealed Himself otherwise than men expected. Had Dr.
Hutten been a Jew at the time of Jesus, is he sure that he would
have been on the side of the 'small handful', the 'tiny band' (his
terms for the Bahá'í communities), of the despised and obscure
sect of Christians, and not on the side of those who 'occupied the
seats of authority and learning?'[387]

The failure of theology

No doubt Dr. Hutten will not care for these questions. But they
contribute to a clarification of the situation. The theologians fail
because they have taken possession of God, because He is at their
disposal. This applies, of course, not only to Christian theologians.
It was this attitude with which Muḥammad reproached the Jewish
divines: '"The hand of God," say the Jews, "is chained up."
Their own hands shall be chained up . . . Nay! outstretched are
both His hands!'[388] 'The hand of God was over their hands!'[389]
From Paul Tillich comes the remarkable judgment: 'Nothing
characterises our religious life so much as these self-created
images of God. I think of the theologian who does not wait for
God because he possesses him, shut up in a lecture hall. I think of
the theological student who does not wait for God because he
possesses him, shut up in a book. I think of the man of the Church
who does not wait for God because he possesses Him, shut up in
an institution. I think of the believer who does not wait for God
because he possesses Him, shut up in his own experience.'[390]
Because the theologians are not ready to surrender 'their whole
knowledge of God, which they think they possess, and to wait
upon Him',[391] they are deaf to the voice which is now proclaiming
to mankind 'the glad-tidings of the nearness of God'.[392] That is
why, in this age also, 'they seeing see not, and hearing they hear

387. *Kitáb-i-Íqán*, p. 10 (Brit.), p. 15 (U.S.).
388. *Qur'án* 5:69.
389. ibid., 48:10.
390. 'In der Tiefe ist Wahrheit', *Religiöse Reden*, vol. I, p. 165.
391. Heinz Zahrnt, *Die Sache mit Gott*, p. 465.
392. Bahá'u'lláh, Tablet of Aḥmad.

not, neither do they understand'.[393] That is why, at the very time that the Lord has spoken, they have the 'experience of a void', the experience 'of the absence of God'.[394] We cannot but agree with the theologian Zahrnt who says: 'God must also forgive us our theology, perhaps there is nothing for which we need His forgiveness so much as our theology.'[395]

393. Matthew 13:13.
394. 'We live in a period in which God is for us the absent God' (Paul Tillich, quoted by Zahrnt, op. cit., p. 463).
395. Zahrnt, op. cit., p. 467.

[In Bahá'í teaching 'the primacy of Peter, the Prince of the Apostles, is upheld and defended' (Shoghi Effendi, *The Promised Day is Come*, p. 113). Paul was described by 'Abdu'l-Bahá as 'Saint Paul, the great Apostle', and both Bahá'u'lláh and 'Abdu'l-Bahá sometimes quoted verses from the Epistles of Paul (e.g., *Epistle to the Son of the Wolf*, p.91; *Some Answered Questions*, chs. XX, XXIX). See also Balyuzi, '*Abdu'l-Bahá*, pp. 148, 354. ED.]

And thy Lord shall come and the angels rank on rank.

Qur'án 89:24

The Bahá'í Faith and Islám

The religion of the Bahá'ís is often dismissed either as a 'sect' or as a 'syncretism'. Are these reproaches well-founded? Since the background of the Bahá'í Faith is to be found in Islamic culture, is it not simply an offshoot of Islám?

The Bahá'í Faith and Islám are closely related in their history, phenomenology and theology. Because of the common factors in their teachings and terminology, the superficial onlooker quickly comes to the conclusion that the Bahá'í Faith is only a special school of thought of Islám. If he is ready to apply the religious-sociological notion of the 'sect' to relatively small communities because they are small, and without considering their constituent elements, he will call the Bahá'í Faith an Islamic sect without taking into account its self-interpretation and its sociological structure. Thus in earlier literature, especially in reference works and textbooks by Islamic scholars, the Bahá'í Faith is more often than not described as a sect of Islám, and even—in the case of Roemer, a Jesuit—as an order of dervishes. [396] But the more recent scholars[397] have come to understand that the Bahá'í Faith is an original and independent religion. Irrespective of the fact that the criteria of the sect-concept worked out by Max Weber, Ernst Troeltsch[398] and Gustav Mensching[399] are without exception absent in the Bahá'í Faith,[400] its original character can be deduced

396. Hermann Roemer, *Die Babi-Behai*, pp. 175–6.
397. Here the following are to be noted: Gerhard Rosenkranz, *Die Bahá'í*, pp. 7 and 56; Alessandro Bausani in *Enzyklopedia Cattolica*, vol. II, pp. 640 and 692 and *Chambers's Encyclopaedia*, New revised edition, 1966; Rudolf Jockel, *Die Lehren der Bahá'í-Religion*, p. 104; Joachim Wach, *Religionssoziologie*, p. 149; see also Glasenapp in a report of 3 October 1961 published in *Bahá'í-Briefe*, vol. 14, October 1963.
398. *Die Soziallehren der christlichen Kirchen und Gruppen*, p. 366 ff., 794 ff.
399. *Soziologie der Religion*, p. 193 ff.
400. The criteria of the sect are its particularistic and individualistic character, 'the fact that the religious community and its dogmatic foundations are based upon a part

from the fact that the *Qur'án*, the revealed book of Islám, is not
for Bahá'ís the foundation of their faith or of their law.

Since the Bada<u>sh</u>t Conference of 1848, Islamic religious law has
been considered by Bahá'ís as no longer valid. The Bahá'í Faith,
according to its own interpretation, does not aim to be a reform
or a restoration of Islám, but rather claims its origin in a new act
of God, in a new outpouring of the divine spirit and in a new
divine covenant. The foundation of belief and of law is the new
divine word revealed by Bahá'u'lláh. This is why the Bahá'í is not
a Muslim. For the law of the *Qur'án* and the unalterable creed of
orthodox Islám, such as the finality of Muḥammad's revelation,
have no validity for him. The Bahá'í Faith has sprung from Islám
in the same way as Christianity did from Judaism: Islám is the
mother-religion of the Bahá'í Faith. The old covenant established
by Muḥammad is replaced by the new divine covenant revealed
by Bahá'u'lláh. Therefore the *Qur'án* is to the Bahá'í what the Old
Testament is to the Christians: a document of the past history of
the salvation of man which also points towards the future to the
'appointed hour', the 'great Announcement', which the Muslims
are still expecting and which, for the Bahá'í, has already made its
appearance.

Similarities of both religions

One cannot deny that the two religions present important similarities in their teachings, their ideas and their terminology. In
view of their kinship, this is not surprising. Close relatives re-
semble one another. Religions do not appear in a religious or
cultural vacuum, in a space free of a historical background. Each
and every manifestation of God has taken up the prevailing social
conditions, the existing doctrines, trends of thought and termi-
nologies, and has sanctioned them, or thrown new light upon

---

of the original religion' (Mensching), the narrowness and one-sidedness of its
thinking, its inimical attitude to culture and its ethical rigorism. None of these
criteria can be applied to the Bahá'í Faith. Its essential character is not individualistic
but universal in the way it embraces the whole of mankind and shapes all the realms
of life, especially as far as social life is concerned. Its exclusion of any kind of charismatic authority and the fact that the legal guidance of the believers is bound to objective institutions show how little individualistic it is. The attitude of the Bahá'í Faith
is one of openness to the world and of affirmation of culture; moreover it traces back
the cause of the different cultures of mankind to the creative impulses of the divine
revelations.

them, or changed, or rejected them. One cannot but agree with Goldziher's opinion: 'Religion never confronts us in the form of a world of ideas detached from definite historical conditions; it lives in deeper and higher states and manifests itself in definite forms which differ from one another on account of the varying prevailing social conditions.'[401] Christianity, too, is inconceivable without the Jewish Faith. What the Church maintains to be her essential mystery is God's covenant which, in the history of Israel, was fulfilled in Jesus Christ. She feels herself 'spiritually linked to the line of Abraham'.[402] Jesus is not the only figure to refer everywhere to Moses and the prophets; the apostle of the Gentiles, Paul, who 'hellenised' the young Faith of God and implanted in it pagan beliefs derived from former syncretisms, based his whole argument on Jewish scripture. To the whole of ecclesiastical Christianity, which until the middle of the second century had no holy book of its own, the Book of the Jews was above all the decisive written authority.[403] It is therefore astonishing to read what Rosenkranz writes: 'Bahá'ism is an Islamic movement, not only in its origin but also in its essence. This is proved for example by its concept of God, its belief in prophets, its veneration of the book . . . ; it even shares with Islam, with all the objections which must be raised against it, the claim that it is a rational, scientific, social and anticlerical religion.'[404] 'The one God it proclaims—and all the word-plays and thought-plays which the Bahá'ís make about it cannot disguise this fact—is the God of Islam: Allah. The Muslim teaching of the Tawhid, of the unity of Allah forms the basis of its concept of God.'[405] This peculiar statement reveals a regrettable lack of understanding of religious history and an obvious inability to acknowledge the analogies evident in the history of the Christian Faith. Moreover, it is not clear as to when the Bahá'ís ever tried to disguise with 'word-plays' and 'thought-plays' the fact that the Islamic teaching of the unity of God and along with it the teaching of the equality of rank of His messengers[406] are religious truths which were reaffirmed by Bahá'u'-

---

401. Ignaz Goldziher, *Vorlesungen über den Islám*, p. 1.
402. *Declaration of the Second Vatican Ecumenical Council on the Relation of the Church to the non-Christian religions*, no. 4.
403. J. Klausner, *Jesus von Nazareth, seine Zeit, sein Leben und seine Lehre*, p. 534.
404. *Die Bahá'í*, p. 58.   405. ibid., p. 52.
406. 'We believe in God, and that which hath been sent down to us, and that which hath been sent down to Abraham and Ismael and Isaac and Jacob and the tribes: and

lláh and stated by him in great detail. They are unalterable consti-
tuents of the Bahá'í Faith.

A further essential feature common to both religions is that they
are both endowed with laws and with a book.

A religion of law

Hereby the reciprocity of the relationship with God is expressed.
Man cannot attain salvation through the grace of God alone nor
through faith alone. What is necessary is the active response of the
believing individual.[407] The grace of God will be granted to him
through faith and deeds: 'But believers and doers of good works, for
them is mercy, and a great reward!'[408] Thus salvation is achieved
in a covenant between God and man. The concept of the covenant,[409] which we know from the Old Testament and which is
the principle of both Islám and the Bahá'í Faith, means that on the
one hand there is God's redemptive plan and on the other man's
duty to submit to the will of God manifested in the revealed
divine Law: 'The essence of religion is to testify unto that which
the Lord hath revealed, and follow that which He hath ordained
in His mighty Book.'[410] To the Bahá'í and the Muslim as to the
Jew, the Law is no restraining chain, no 'curse',[411] but the basis of
a life worthy of a human being. The aim of the Law is not—as Paul
and with him the whole Protestant Church misunderstand it—to
make man righteous before God, but to bring about an interrela-
tion between God and man. It is 'the necessary form for the accomplishment of the correlation between God and man'.[412] Man must
fulfil the Law not in order to become righteous before God but
in order to do God's will and thus to be made holy. The Law is

that which hath been given to Moses and to Jesus, and that which was given to the
prophets from their Lord. No difference do we make between any of them' (*Qur'án*
2:130; also 2:285). 'God, the Creator saith: There is no distinction whatsoever
among the Bearers of My Message . . . To prefer one in honour to another, to exalt
certain ones above the rest, is in no wise to be permitted' (Bahá'u'lláh, *Gleanings*,
XXXIV).

407. 'O Son of Being! Love Me that I may love thee. If thou lovest Me not, My
love can in no wise reach thee' (Bahá'u'lláh, *The Hidden Words*, Arabic 5). Compare
also Zachariah 1:3 and Malachi 3:7.

408. *Qur'án* 35:8.

409. Genesis 9:11–17.

410. Bahá'u'lláh, Words of Wisdom, *Bahá'í World Faith*, p. 140.

411. Galatians 3:13.

412. Hermann Cohen, *Religion der Vernunft aus den Quellen des Judentums*, quoted by
H. J. Schoeps, *Jüdisch-christliches Religionsgespräch in neunzehn Jahrhunderten*, p. 50.

given to men for their salvation, not their justification;[413] and for the sanctification of mankind, not only the individual but also the whole of humanity. The universality of both Islám and the Bahá'í Faith, their engagement in the things of this world and their rejection of any kind of ascetic escapism,[414] are shown in their theocratic aims: the world is accepted, but not in its present form. On the contrary it must be transformed in accordance with the revealed divine Law. God's will must be carried out in all realms of life, especially on the social level. Both religions agree in their understanding that this sanctification of society cannot be brought about when only the individual treads the path of virtue. Both realise that from the social point of view objective measures of sanctification are necessary: the establishment of law. That is why in both, religious law and therefore justice occupy a high rank: 'The Great Being saith: The structure of world stability and order hath been reared upon, and will continue to be sustained by, the twin pillars of reward and punishment.'[415] 'As forgiveness is one of the attributes of the Merciful One, so also justice is one of the attributes of the Lord. The tent of existence is upheld upon the pillar of justice, and not upon forgiveness.'[416]

The idea that justice, compared to love, is something inferior and that a fundamental conflict exists between the two; that the Law is—as Luther said—a 'makeshift' only necessary to protect

413. See also pp. 97–9.

414. 'We gave him (Jesus) the Evangel, and we put into the hearts of those who followed him kindness and compassion: but as to the monastic life, they invented it themselves' (*Qur'án* 57:27). The fact that ascetic tendencies appeared later in Islám, too, does not contradict the fact that Islám in its basic structure is not ascetic. In fact, Bahá'u'lláh bids the believer to free himself from all the ties of the world but adds immediately afterwards how this is to be understood: 'Know ye that by "the world" is meant your unawareness of Him Who is your Maker, and your absorption in aught else but him. The "life to come", on the other hand. signifieth the things that give you a safe approach to God, the All-Glorious, the Incomparable. Whatsoever deterreth you, in this Day, from loving God is nothing but the world. Flee it, that ye may be numbered with the blest. Should a man wish to adorn himself with the ornaments of the earth, to wear its apparels, or partake of the benefits it can bestow, no harm can befall him, if he alloweth nothing whatever to intervene between him and God, for God hath ordained every good thing, whether created in the heavens or in the earth, for such of His servants as truly believe in Him. Eat ye, O people, of the good things which God hath allowed you, and deprive not yourselves from His wondrous bounties. Render thanks and praise unto Him, and be of them that are truly thankful' (*Gleanings*, CXXVIII). Man is summoned not to flee the world but to reach an inner detachment from material things.

415. Bahá'u'lláh, *Gleanings*, CXII.

416. 'Abdu'l-Bahá, *Some Answered Questions*, LXXVII.

the righteous against the unrighteous, but which could be dispensed with once the world were entirely inhabited by Christians;[417] or even the extreme concept of Tolstoy that law is ungodly and that human society should be based on the commandments of the Sermon on the Mount alone[418]—these ideas are foreign to both Islám and the Bahá'í Faith. In both religions law and justice are immanent: they are the foundation for the order of the world. In fact, in the Bahá'í Faith, justice is the main virtue: 'Tell, O 'Alí, the loved ones of God that equity is the most fundamental among human virtues. The evaluation of all things must needs depend upon it.'[419] 'The light of men is justice; quench it not with the contrary winds of oppression and tyranny. The purpose of justice is the appearance of unity among people.'[420] This is why it becomes an inner necessity that the community of the believers should have a legal framework.[421] Rudolf Sohm's thesis of the incompatibility of spirit and law and his conclusion that a spiritual community—here the Church—should have no legal system for 'the spirit bloweth where it listeth', and that only a charismatic organisation is appropriate to the essence of the cause, that the bond of faith and love but not that of law should bind the believers together,[422] and Gustav Mensching's similar conception that spirit and form are in a reciprocal but opposite relationship to one another[423] are acceptable neither to Islám nor to the Bahá'í teachings. Both religions agree, however, in their exclusion of any form of legal control from the sphere of personal conscience. There is no *forum internum sacramentale* as in the Catholic Church, nor does either religion have any sacraments,[424] sacramentals,[425]

417. Martin Luther, *Von der weltlichen Obrigkeit, wie weit man ihr Gehorsam schuldig sei*, 1523.

418. cf. W. A. Hauck, *Rudolf Sohm und Leo Tolstoi*, p. 157 ff., 233, 257 ff.

419. Bahá'u'lláh, *Gleanings*, C.

420. Bahá'u'lláh, 'Kalimát-i-Firdawsíyyih' (Words of Paradise), *Bahá'í World Faith*, p. 182.

421. For more detail on the question of 'Law and Religion' see my thesis, 'Die Grundlagen der Verwaltungsordnung der Bahá'í', pp. 38–60.

422. Rudolf Sohm, *Kirchenrecht*, vol. I, p. 1.

423. *Soziologie der Religion*, p. 257. Compare notes 168 and 200 of my thesis.

424. In the Tablet of Bishárát Bahá'u'lláh has strictly forbidden confession.

425. According to Catholic dogma the difference between sacraments and sacramentals is as follows: sacraments are acts of worship taking place between a person entitled to administer them and a receiver, through which the receiver partakes of divine grace. The visible rite itself and the act of faith involved guarantee the promised grace. Sacraments therefore work '*ex opere operato*'. Since the twelfth century the Catholic Church has known seven sacraments: baptism, confirmation,

benedictions, consecrations or exorcisms, or—especially—priest-hood.[426] This is why neither of them is a 'church'.[427]

A further consequence of their being religions of law is that, in both, the moral act stands in the foreground. As important as right belief is right action, and more important than the dogmas are the ethics. Thus we read in the *Qur'án*: 'There is no piety in turning your faces toward the east or the west, but he is pious who believeth in God, and the last day, and the angels, and the Scriptures, and the prophets; who for the love of God disburseth his wealth to his kindred, and to the orphans, and the needy, and the wayfarer, and those who ask, and for ransoming; who ob-serveth prayer, and payeth the legal alms, and who is of those who are faithful to their engagements when they have engaged in them, and patient under ills and hardships, and in time of trouble: these are they who are just, and these are they who fear the Lord.'[428] And Bahá'u'lláh revealed these words: 'O Son of My Handmaid! Guidance hath ever been given by words, and now it is given by deeds. Every one must show forth deeds that are pure and holy, for words are the property of all alike, whereas such deeds as these belong only to Our loved ones. Strive then with heart and soul to distinguish yourselves by your deeds. In this wise We counsel you in this holy and resplendent tablet.'[429] 'The essence of faith is fewness of words and abundance of deeds; he whose words exceed his deeds, know verily his death is better than his life.'[430]

---

penance, the anointing of the sick, marriage, ordination and the eucharist. The Reformation only kept the sacraments of baptism and holy communion.

In Catholicism there are also religious acts which do not bestow grace of them-selves (*ex opere operato*) but through the intercession of the Church, like benediction, consecration, anointing, blessing. To this category belong also the things made sacred through such acts: the altar, the church, the chalice, the holy water, etc. Protestant churches reject sacramentals.

426. The 'ulamás of Islám are not priests but religious scholars who have no func-tion as intermediaries for redemption. The Bahá'í Faith has no official ecclesiastics in this sense of the word either.

427. Next to the interpretative administration the sacramental administration is a fundamental element of the notion of 'church': 'Wherever word and sacrament exist, the church institution exists' (Ernst Troeltsch, *Die Soziallehren der christlichen Kirchen und Gruppen*, p. 449).

428. *Qur'án* 2:172.   429. *The Hidden Words*, Persian 76.

430. Bahá'u'lláh, Words of Wisdom, *Bahá'í World Faith*, p. 141. This is reminiscent of Matthew 7:19–23: 'Every tree that bringeth not forth good fruit is hewn down, and cast into the fire. Wherefore by their fruits ye shall know them. Not every one that saith unto me, Lord, Lord, shall enter into the kingdom of heaven; but he that doeth the will of my Father which is in heaven. Many will say to me in that day, Lord,

'Abdu'l-Bahá has made it clear that, according to the Bahá'í
teachings, the essential aim of the Manifestation of God is to exalt
and perfect man: 'The corner-stone of the religion of God is the
acquisition of the Divine perfections and the sharing in His manifold bestowals. The essential purpose of Faith and Belief is to
ennoble the inner being of man with the outpourings of grace
from on high . . . Wherefore it is incumbent upon all Bahá'ís to
ponder this very delicate and vital matter in their hearts, that, unlike other religions, they may not content themselves with the
noise, the clamour, the hollowness of religious doctrine. Nay,
rather, they should exemplify in every aspect of their lives those
attributes and virtues that are born of God . . . They should justify
their claim to be Bahá'ís by deeds and not by name. He is a true
Bahá'í who strives by day and by night to progress and advance
along the path of human endeavour . . . Only when he attains unto
such perfect gifts can it be said of him that he is a true Bahá'í. For
in this holy Dispensation, the crowning glory of bygone ages, and
cycles, true Faith is no mere acknowledgment of the Unity of God,
but rather the living of a life that will manifest all the perfections
and virtues implied in such belief . . .'[431]

A religion of the Book
This means that the central element of the Faith is the Book of
God[432] and not—as in ecclesiastical Christianity—a God-like figure.
According to Islamic understanding and the Bahá'í teachings, a
revelation is God's message to humanity. This is why belief in the
message and obedience to the commandments and laws, after one
has recognised the messenger's authority, are the decisive factors.

This principle is of even greater consequence in the Bahá'í
Faith, inasmuch as the oral tradition as a source of revelation is
excluded. Whereas in Christianity—especially in Catholicism—
the real source of the Faith is tradition, and the Scriptures are only
an expression of the apostolic traditions,[433] and whereas in Islám

---

Lord, have we not prophesied in thy name? and in thy name have cast out devils?
and in thy name done many wonderful works? And then will I profess unto them, I
never knew you: depart from me, ye that work iniquity.'

431. *The Divine Art of Living*, pp. 24–5.

432. 'No doubt is there about this Book. It is a guidance to the Godfearing, who
believe in the unseen'(*Qur'án* 2:1).

433. Karl Adam, *Das Wesen des Katholizismus*, p. 161; Renft, in *Lexikon für Theologie und Kirche*, vol. X, p. 243; 'The scriptures are indeed the most valuable but not
the oldest witnesses of tradition.'

and Judaism an oral tradition has developed in each and been given the same importance as the Scripture, the Bahá'í Faith is a religion exclusively based on the writings themselves. In it the postulate of the old Protestant *sola scriptura* is radically carried out. This does not mean that the Bahá'í Faith does not possess an oral, second-hand tradition but only that the latter is given no authority. Shoghi Effendi's secretary, on his behalf, explains the reason for Bahá'u'lláh's rejection of this principle of tradition: 'Bahá'u'-lláh has made it clear enough that only those things that have been revealed in form of Tablets have a binding power over the friends. Hearsays may be matters of interest, but can in no way claim authority. This basic teaching of Bahá'u'lláh was to preserve the Faith from being corrupted like Islám which attributes binding authority to all the reported sayings of Muḥammad.'[434] Shoghi Effendi alludes to the important consequences in the development of early Islám, when the collected sayings and customs (sunnah) attributed to the Prophet took on an ever-growing importance, as the memory of them really should have faded. During dogmatic, legal and political discussions, some traditions were devised in all naïvety and attributed to the Prophet, when it seemed certain that he would have said or done such-and-such a thing in a special case. This gradually led to self-contradictory 'words of the Prophet' being handed down to posterity. When the critique of the Ḥadíth was later established, it could no longer abolish this abuse and explain which of the traditions were authentic.[435] The oral tradition, the weakest source of all historical traditions, is— according to the Bahá'í teachings—one of the main causes of the mistaken development of past religions, because it leads to a constant increase in religious assets and through the ensuing infiltration of essentially foreign and incompatible ideas finally leads to a radical transformation of the original religion.

The Bahá'í Faith is different to Islám in its attitude to tradition. But the most fundamental difference between orthodox Islám and the Bahá'í teachings is seen in the question of the period for which the revelation is valid, and along with it the question of the essence of revelation itself.

---

434. *Principles of Bahá'í Administration*, p. 45.

435. From among the traditions gathered and critically selected in the second and third centuries A.H. six collections achieved canonic recognition in the seventh century A.H. See Richard Hartmann, *Die Religion des Islám*, p. 56; Goldziher, p. 33; Arnold, *The Caliphate*, p. 12.

Differences in the concept of revelation

According to Islamic teaching (and as the *Qur'án* testifies), God has from time immemorial sent his prophets and messengers to the peoples of the world to teach them the right path and to inform them of his will and his intentions. Through Muḥammad, Muslims believe, he proclaimed his final message to the whole of mankind. With him, revelation to mankind as a whole is ended. He is the last of God's messengers, the 'Seal of the Prophets'.[436] Islamic theologians have made the same claim to absolute excellence, immutability and finality as the Jewish and Christian religious scholars did. It is therefore not surprising that the claim that a new divine revelation has come, replacing the former one, is looked upon as heretical and is violently attacked.[437]

There is no room in the Bahá'í Faith for the concept of revelation as a unique event[438] once and for all completed in the past and attached to a certain historical figure. Bahá'u'lláh has rejected the belief 'that all Revelation is ended, that the portals of Divine mercy are closed' as idle assertions of 'small-minded, contemptible people'[439] and he announces that God who, in the past, has manifested himself to mankind through his manifestations, to 'safeguard the interests and promote the unity of the human race, and to foster the spirit of love and fellowship amongst men',[440] 'will continue to do so, until "the end that hath no end"; so that His grace may, from the heaven of Divine bounty, be continually vouchsafed to mankind'.[441] This cyclic return of the manifestation is made necessary by the change of the times[442] and the alteration

436. *Qur'án* 33:40. Cf. Bahá'u'lláh, *Kitáb-i-Íqán*, pp. 106–12 (Brit.), pp. 165–73 (U.S.).

437. On 10 May, 1925, the Appellate religious Court of Beba, Egypt, subsequently sanctioned by the highest ecclesiastical authorities in Cairo, described the Bahá'ís in a verdict as believers of heretical teachings which attack and offend Islám and are quite incompatible with the recognised dogmas and the practice of Islám's orthodox believers. This verdict declares in the most unequivocal terms, 'The Bahá'í Faith is a new religion, entirely independent, with beliefs, principles and laws of its own, which differ from, and are utterly in conflict with, the beliefs, principles and laws of Islám. No Bahá'í, therefore, can be regarded a Muslim or vice versa, even as no Buddhist, Brahmin, or Christian can be regarded a Muslim or vice versa' (Quoted by Shoghi Effendi, *God Passes By*, p. 365).

438. This idea and the accompanying doctrine of exclusivity also found its expression in Christianity.

439. *Kitáb-i-Íqán*, p. 88 (Brit.), p. 137 (U.S.).   440. *Gleanings*, CX.

441. Quoted by Shoghi Effendi, 'The Dispensation of Bahá'u'lláh', in *The World Order of Bahá'u'lláh*, p. 116.

442. 'Nothing alive can escape the transforming influence of time' (Adolf v. Harnack, *Kirchenverfassung*, p. 87). This is why all religions have, in their individual

of conditions on earth. Revelation, which is the education of humanity by God, is related to mankind's cultural, spiritual and social development at the time: 'Words are revealed according to capacity.'[443] 'For every age requireth a fresh measure of the light of God. Every Divine Revelation hath been sent down in a manner that befitted the circumstances of the age in which it hath appeared.'[444] 'Every Prophet Whom the Almighty and Peerless Creator hath purposed to send to the peoples of the earth hath been entrusted with a Message, and charged to act in a manner that would best meet the requirements of the age in which He appeared.'[445] 'The Prophets of God should be regarded as physicians whose task is to foster the well-being of the world and its peoples, that, through the spirit of oneness, they may heal the sickness of a divided humanity ... Little wonder, then, if the

---

historical developments taking place under different conditions, moved further and further away from their origin, from the pure source of revelation. They have wasted their original spiritual impulse and, today, have lost their vitality. Hans-Joachim Schoeps (*Jüdisch-christliches Religionsgespräch in neunzehn Jahrhunderten*, p. 154) has characterised our present spiritual situation, which is different in quality to the situation of past ages, as the 'state of affairs of non-belief': 'Jews and Christians are today in much the same situation: one of non-belief. The great break of the ages, the real change in the times which, as is well known, took place in the last 150 years, compared to the incredulity of past ages, which always remained on the periphery of positive faith and until Kierkegaard and Nietzsche still had the dialectic tendency to change into positive faith, has brought about an entirely new state of affairs in the last few decades: that of non-belief which refuses all discussion—even a polemic one —with the witnesses and bearers of faith, which adopts towards the history of the salvation of man witnessed throughout the centuries, an attitude no longer of incredulity and doubt but much more one of disbelief and indifference ... This is a catastrophic process which has not remained unnoticed either, but which today is becoming increasingly clear and more threatening ... There is no sense in shutting our eyes to the post-Christian world situation of the present, and in credulously believing that the modern powers of technology and of the industrial environment, of co-operative movements and national interests can still be christianised by the Church. This age is no longer one of Jewish-Christian belief; as regards its qualitative nature, it is already something quite different.' This condition, noted by many thinkers of our age (Radhakrishnan should be mentioned here), cannot be altered by human means—by a reformation—but only by God, i.e. through a new revelation. All human attempts to breathe new life into the old religions will fail: 'The vitality of men's belief in God is dying out in every land; nothing short of His wholesome medicine can ever restore it. The corrosion of ungodliness is eating into the vitals of human society; what else but the Elixir of His potent Revelation can cleanse and revive it?' (Bahá'u'lláh, *Gleanings*, XCIX).

443. Bahá'u'lláh, quoted by J. Esslemont, *Bahá'u'lláh and the New Era*, p. 131.

444. *Gleanings*, XXXIV; compare also XLIV and LXXXIX. John 16:12 is also to be understood in this sense.

445. ibid., XXXIV.

treatment prescribed by the physician in this day should not be found to be identical with that which he prescribed before.'[446]

As the development of humanity has no end, revelation, too, cannot be final. In this sense religious truth is not absolute but relative. The phenomenon of religions is created by these divine acts of revelation which are progressive and recur in cycles:[447] all the great religions of humanity are divine in their origin and are reflections of the one truth, however little their present form may testify to this. In the common heart[448] of all the religions their unity can be seen. Having grasped this fact, one can see its consequence: Bahá'u'lláh is not the last of God's messengers. In the new age introduced by him the 'Gates of Mercy' will be opened, whenever it pleases God to do so, until 'the end that hath no end'.

The Bahá'í Faith and the Messianic expectations in Islám

The concept of a redeeming event to come is not foreign to Islám either. It is a religion with distinct eschatological expectations. In addition to the beliefs that there is only one God, that the duty of

446. *Gleanings*, XXXIV.

447. Rudolf Stählin ('Christliche Religion', *Fischer-Lexikon*, p. 231) is absolutely right in emphasising that there is no direct way of man to God but that only the way from God to us exists and that it is only when God comes to us that we attain to him. Bahá'u'lláh, too, denies the possibility of man saving himself without a revelation: 'The way is barred, and all seeking rejected!' (*Kitáb-i-Íqán*, p. 91 (Brit.), p. 141 (U.S.)). But Stählin's belief is that only in Jesus does God reveal himself to man. His opinion, based on this, is that the phenomenon of the religions demonstrates nothing more than 'man's seeking of God and his attempts to provide this seeking with fulfilment'. He declares that all non-Christian religions—according to K. Barth (*Kirchliche Dogmatik* I.2, p. 356) the 'religions of deceit'!—are man's incompetent attempts to save himself. These statements can only be understood in the light of Christian claim to exclusiveness, and blindness towards the realisation, which to be sure cannot be conclusively proved by rational means, that God has also spoken outside the Bible and that his word 'is one word, even if the speakers were many' ('Abdu'l-Bahá).

448. Of course scientifically this unity can be neither proved nor refuted. It is evident for those who want to see it. Nikolaus von Cues (Cusanus) spoke of the one religion in the diversity of religious customs (*una religio in rituum varietate*) and theologians like Söderblom and Heiler have effectively testified to this unity in religious history. The teachings, laws and customs of different religions which are incompatible with one another are partly based on the differing conditions and circumstances in which they were revealed. The extent to which these contrasts can be traced back to the obscuring and the changing of religion by human actions and misinterpretations and to the historical wear and tear of time is shown by the development of Christianity, which has expressed itself in such different forms as Catholicism and the Salvation Army. When such developments were possible within the one and the same religion, how much more then with divine revelations taking place at different ages under different conditions!

man is to be righteous and that he will have to answer for his deeds in the next world, a future event is also part of the proclamation of the Arabian Prophet: the 'coming of the Hour', 'the meeting with God', 'the great Day of God', the 'Day of Judgment', of which he warns his followers.[449] Of this day it is said: 'And Thy Lord shall come, and the angels rank on rank.'[450] Both Sunní and Shí'ah Islám expect, at the last days, the coming of a great world teacher whom God will some day awaken and send to mankind. He, who will be preceded by a forerunner from the family of the Prophet, will restore his destroyed work and 'fill the world with justice, just as it is filled with injustice',[451] will set up a kingdom of peace and justice and assist Islám towards its final victory. Sunní Islám awaits the 'Mahdí' (The One Who is Guided) and the return of Jesus Christ, Shí'ah Islám the 'Qá'im' (He Who arises) and the Qayyúm (the Self-Subsisting) who is the return of Imám Ḥusayn. These Messianic expectations of the followers of Islám do not in their view contradict in any way the fundamental ideas of the orthodox teaching—that Muḥammad ends the line of the prophets for ever, that he fulfils for eternity what his predecessors had paved the way for, that he is the bearer of the last message of God to mankind.[452] In Muslim thought the expected 'Mahdí' is

449. 'In the Name of God, the Compassionate, the Merciful. The Blow! what is the Blow? Who shall teach thee what the Blow is? The Day when men shall be like scattered moths. And the mountains shall be like flocks of carded wool, then as to him whose balances are heavy—his shall be a life that shall please him well: And as to him whose balances are light—his dwelling-place shall be the pit. And who shall teach thee what the pit (El-Hawiya) is? A raging fire!' (*Qur'án*, súrah 101).

450. *Qur'án* 89:23.

451. Quoted by Goldziher, p. 227.

452. In the *Qur'án* Muḥammad is described as 'Khátamu-n-nabíyin' (Seal of the Prophets): 'Muḥammad is the Messenger of God and the Seal of the Prophets' (33:40). From this verse the Muslims have inferred the end of all revelation through Muḥammad and the eternal validity of Qur'ánic law. They believe Muḥammad to have been the last messenger from God and that with His appearance divine revelation was ended and completed (compare Sayyed Abul A'la Maudoodi, *Towards Understanding Islam*, translated by Khurshid Ahmad, Islamic Publications Ltd., Karachi, 1960, pp. 84 ff.: 'The Finality of Prophethood').

But the Qur'ánic verse quoted is in no way a conclusive proof of the finality of all revelation as postulated by orthodox Islamic theology. The *Qur'án* uses two concepts describing the Prophet Muḥammad: *'nabí'* and *'rasúl'*. *Nabí* is a prophet who foresees and foretells the future. *Rasúl*, on the other hand, is the Messenger, the One sent by God. Had Muḥammad wanted to mark his revelation as the end of all revelation he would not have used in this context the concept *nabí* but the concept *rasúl*. The reasons Maudoodi gives to prove that Muḥammad ends the cycle of divine revelation are in no way logical. They are the weakest point of this otherwise excellent work.

The description 'Seal of the Prophets' is to be understood in this way: with the

only the restorer of the last prophet's work, a work which had been dissipated by the corruption of humanity. He himself is not a prophet or the proclaimer of a development surpassing the achievements of Muḥammad. He is not the bearer of a new re-deeming teaching or of a new law.

The Bahá'í Faith is the fruit, the fulfilment of these Messianic expectations in Islám. The history of these expectations is at the same time the background history of the Bahá'í Faith.

When Muḥammad died in 632, his will as to who should lead the community after his death was not clearly and legally estab-lished. Lying on his death-bed, he had asked for writing-material: 'Bring ink and paper so that I may lay down in writing for you that which will always guard you from error.' But 'Umar said: 'The pain is confusing him, we have God's Book; this is suffici-ent.' Thus his companions quarrelled at his death-bed as to whether they should fetch the writing-material, and Muḥammad sent them away. As the *Qur'án* contains no ruling about who was to succeed him, the Prophet's father-in-law, Abú-Bakr, was chosen to be the first Caliph at the instigation of the mighty 'Umar during a stormy community gathering.[453] From the beginning protests were raised by influential Muslims against this way of bestowing the Caliphate and it was recalled that Muḥammad had on different occasions publicly designated his cousin and son-in-law 'Alí as his successor. According to tradition, on the way back from his last pilgrimage to Mecca the Prophet had stopped the caravan by the water-hole of Khumm and had had a platform erected out of saddles on which 'Alí had to sit. Muḥammad had then addressed his people: 'Whoever has me as a master has 'Alí as a master'. He announced his approaching end and spoke of the two treasures which he was leaving behind for them: 'The greatest treasure is the Book of God . . . Hold fast unto it, do not relax its laws or falsify it! The other treasure is the line of my successors.' According to the Shí'ah[454] interpretation, the Caliphate was

---

message of Muḥammad the universal prophetic cycle which started with Adam—the cycle of prophecy or the Adamic cycle—ended and, with the coming of Bahá'u'lláh, a new era of fulfilment has dawned. Muḥammad was the last of God's messengers to have announced the 'Day of Judgement', the 'Day of Resurrection'. These redemp-tive events promised by all the prophets are fulfilled in the advent of Bahá'u'lláh (compare Bahá'u'lláh, *Kitáb-i-Íqán*, p. 103 (Brit.), p. 161 (U.S.)).

453. a *Khlífa*: representative (of the Prophet).

454. Shí'ah: the party of 'Alí, thus Shí'ah Islám, in opposition to Sunní Islám which regards Abú-Bakr as legitimate successor.

usurped by Abú-Bakr and 'Umar and taken away from the real chosen ones, the descendants of the Prophet.[455] With the exception of 'Alí who was Caliph from A.D. 656 to the year he was murdered, 661, Muḥammad's descendants were excluded from the Caliphate and exposed to violent persecutions by the ruling dynasties. However, the Shí'ah have never ceased to claim that the Caliphate is a hereditary office and belongs to the natural descendants of the Prophet. According to the so-called Shí'ah Twelvers (the state religion of Persia since 1572), twelve descendants of Muḥammad exercised their office as 'Imám',[456] an office which apart from 'Alí's five years as Caliph lacked all worldly power and was therefore a vestige of what it should have been.[457]

All the Imáms, with perhaps the exception of the last one, were murdered. The third Imám, 'Alí's youngest son Ḥusayn, whose brother and predecessor Ḥasan had been poisoned, died on the

455. From the union of his daughter Fáṭimih with 'Alí.

456. This is what the Shí'ah religious leaders are called.

457. The following must be said to clarify the institutions 'Caliphate' and 'Imámate'. The Caliph and the Imám were worldly sovereigns. Both were the rulers of all Muslim believers, a theoretical sovereignty as far as the Imám was concerned. They bore the title 'Amíra'l-Mu'minín' (Commander of the Faithful). Moreover, the Imám held a spiritual post. He had an infallible doctrinal authority, *auctoritas interpretativa*. According to Shí'ah theology, he possessed complete and infallible knowledge. He was in possession of a mysterious knowledge surpassing the spiritual treasures accessible to all Muslims and which extended to truths about religion and the secular events. '"Alí knew not only the real meaning of the *Qur'án* which is hidden from the common intelligence but all that which will come to pass until the time of resurrection' (Goldziher, p. 213). Thus, in theory, all spiritual and worldly power was concentrated in the hand of the Imám, to whom sinlessness was attributed. Hence Donaldson writes: 'It may be remarked, however, that if the theoretical Imámate of the Shí'ites had ever come to its own in secular and spiritual authority, it would have outstripped the Papacy in its most golden age' (*The Shí'ite Religion*, p. xxiv). In contrast to this, the Caliph was only 'the representative of the judicial, administrative and military state power' (Goldziher, p. 265). This, however, does not mean that Sunní Islám did not possess any binding doctrinal authority. It had in the *ijamá'* (the consensus), a principle which produced an authoritative elucidation of both the spiritual and legal problems. According to a tradition attributed to Muḥammad, the Prophet was supposed to have said that his community could never be of one mind when in error. It was deduced from this that the truth would always be at the root of a consensus about a problem and that the will of God would be directly expressed in it. Accordingly all that had been sanctioned by the collective consciousness of the Muslims was looked upon as right and true and had binding authority. As the interpretation of the *Qur'án* and that of the *'sunnah'* was only considered as the right one when the consensus had established it as such, the door to free investigation regarding such questions (about which a consensus already existed) was closed. Whatever had been decided by the *ijamá'* was forever binding. (About the whole question cf. my thesis p. 151, notes 497–501). The Imámate died out in 260 A.H.; the Caliphate was abolished by Kemal Pasha in 1924.

plain of Karbilá on 10 October 680. The band of his followers, nearly dying of thirst, was massacred by the troops of the 'Umay-yad Caliph Yazid I. His head was severed from his dead body and placed on a spear. The martyrdom of Imám Ḥusayn at Karbilá, as well as the sufferings inflicted on the whole family of the Prophet, carry a special significance[458] in the Shí'ah world. The twelfth Imám, known by the name 'Abu'l-Qásim, is said to have disappeared in mysterious circumstances at the age of eight in the year 260 A.H. According to Shí'ah teachings, he was withdrawn from the earth and has been living ever since as the hidden Imám in 'gháiba' (absence), in order to appear[459] at some future date, as the world's saviour. He is the 'Lord of the Age' who, living in the mysterious towns of Jábulqá and Jábulsá, will return at the time of the end and inaugurate the millennium.

In the thirteenth century A.H. (the nineteenth century of the Christian Era) an adventist reform sect, the Shaykhí movement, was formed in Persia under the leadership first of the Arab Shaykh Aḥmad-i-Aḥsá'í (1743–1826) and then, after his death, of Siyyid Kázim. Their main teaching, apart from the call for the general spiritualisation of one's religious life, was the imminent coming of the 'end' prophesied by Muḥammad and the advent of the Qá'im. Just as some Jewish theologians and mystics calculated[460] the exact time of the Messiah's appearance, in the same way Ṣúfí and Shí'ah thinkers had been devoting all their efforts to reckoning the time of the hidden Imám's appearance,[461] on the basis of the cabbalistic use of Qur'ánic verses and letter-number relationships. From obscure indications in the *Qur'án*, especially from the súrah of Worship[462] and the oral traditions concerning this subject, the Shaykhís had calculated the year to be 1260 A.H. Acting on the belief that the legal leadership of the believers had come to an end with the expiration of the Imámate in 260 A.H., they established the date of the end of the thousand years absence

458. About this Bahá'u'lláh writes: 'Should We wish to impart unto thee a glim-mer of the mysteries of Ḥusayn's martyrdom, and reveal unto thee the fruits thereof, these pages could never suffice, nor exhaust their meaning' (*Kitáb-i-Íqán*, p. 83 (Brit.), p. 129 (U.S.)).

459. On the whole question, see: Hartmann, *Die Religion des Islám*, p. 29; Gold-ziher, p. 190 f.; Balyuzi, *Muḥammad and the Course of Islám*, pp. 254–62.

460. Mostly on the basis of the Book of Daniel.   461. Goldziher, p. 219.

462. 'From the Heaven to the Earth He governeth all things: hereafter shall they come up to him on a day whose length shall be a thousand of such years as ye reckon' (*Qur'án* 32:4); compare *Qur'án* 22:47.

of legal guidance foretold by Muḥammad as the year 1260 A.H., i.e. the year 1844 of the Christian era. This same year was calculated on the basis of Biblical prophecy by the Christian Adventist sect in the U.S.A. as the date of Christ's return.[463] Siyyid Kázim, just before he died in 1843, sent his followers to Arabia and Persia to seek the expected divine messengers. On 23 May 1844, the Persian Siyyid 'Alí Muḥammad, a descendant of the Prophet, declared to one of these Shaykhís, Mullá Ḥusayn, that he was the Promised One. This was the hour of birth of the Bahá'í Faith.[464] The Báb, gradually unveiling the magnitude of his prophetic office, announced his claim to be the fulfilment of the prophecies of the Mahdí and the Qá'im, and, beyond that, to be the bearer of an independent revelation superseding that of Muḥammad. This proclamation, which went far beyond the expectations of Islamic orthodoxy, cut the umbilical cord joining the religion of the Báb to its mother-religion, Islám; since then it has suffered from the latter every defamation and persecution of which an intolerant fanaticism is capable.[465]

Now how is the accomplishment of Islám's eschatological expectation to be understood? According to Bahá'u'lláh's teaching, the history of mankind runs in universal cycles within which God reveals himself through His manifestations. The universal prophetic cycle introduced by Adam[466] and preceded by other cycles[467] was sealed by Muḥammad who, as the last of the Pro-

463. The number 1260 (42 months = 3½ 'times') appears a number of times in The Revelation of St. John (11:2; 11:9; 11:11; 12:6; 12:14; 13:5). It is, as 'Abdu'l-Bahá has shown (*Some Answered Questions*, XI and XIII) a reference to the period of validity of Muḥammad's mission.

464. To the question asked by the President of the assembly of ecclesiastics and worldly dignitaries in Tabriz as to who he was, the Báb answered: 'I am, I am, I am the Promised One! I am the One Whose name you have for a thousand years invoked, at Whose mention you have risen, Whose advent you have longed to witness, and the hour of Whose Revelation you have prayed God to hasten' (*God Passes By*, p. 21).

465. During the lifetime of the Báb and shortly after his martyrdom (1850) in Persia, the cradle of the Faith, 20,000 followers met their death in a monstrous bloodbath which caused horror even in Europe. In Persia there were open persecutions as recently as 1955.

466. He is not literally the first man, but the first man in the modern sense and at the same time the first bearer of a revelation of which we have a record.

467. The fact that we know nothing about them 'should be attributed to their extreme remoteness, as well as to the vast changes which the earth hath undergone since their time' (Bahá'u'lláh, *Gleanings*, LXXXVII). Moreover, God had already manifested Himself to the world in the ages before Adam: 'The Manifestations of His Divine glory . . . have been sent down from time immemorial, and been commissioned to summon mankind to the one true God. That the names of some of

phets ('Seal of the Prophets') foretold the great radical change mankind would experience on the 'Day of Judgment'.[468] 'The end',[469] when the sun shall be darkened and the stars fall from heaven, is not understood as the end of life on our planet, as the destruction of the cosmos and the annihilation of mankind, as God's mechanical intervention in our form of existence, but rather as the end of the Adamic age, as the collapse of past traditional ways of life and the breaking up of recognised value-concepts—an upheaval we are witnessing today—and as a universal historical process brought about by the spiritual forces released by the new manifestation through which man and the social order are transformed. This transformation is visible today only to the believers but, when the time is ripe, it will be acknowledged by all. The end of the old is also the beginning of the new, the time of the end is also a turning-point of the ages, just as the Apocalypse not only predicts the passing away of the old order but also promises a 'new heaven' and a 'new earth'. Bahá'u'lláh, in whom the Bahá'ís see the fulfilment of Messianic expectations—not only those of Islám but of all religions[470]—has introduced a new era in which mankind, which has now come of age and been brought under a new law, will experience the complete fulfilment of its potentialities. The age of prophecy is thus followed by the age of fulfilment. The 'new heaven' and the 'new earth' are to become realities through the establishment of the unity of mankind and the lasting guarantee of world peace. Not by the efforts of the politicians alone will this unity of peoples be brought about, but above all by the transforming power of Bahá'u'lláh's revealed Word through which a new energy was instilled into all things, by the heeding of his laws and adherence to his counsels. This is the *sine qua non* for world peace: 'That which the Lord hath ordained as the sovereign remedy and mightiest instrument for the healing of all the world is the union of all its peoples in one universal Cause, one common Faith.'[471] 'The well-being of mankind, its

---

them are forgotten and the records of their lives lost is to be attributed to the disturbances and changes that have overtaken the world' (ibid.).

468. The concepts of 'Day of Judgment', 'Resurrection' and 'Return' have been explained by Bahá'u'lláh in their allegorical sense in the *Kitáb-i-Íqán*.

469. Matthew 24:14.

470. For the Biblical prophecies concerning the time of the end and their fulfilment in Bahá'u'lláh, see W. Sears, *Thief in the Night*, George Ronald, Oxford, 1976.

471. Bahá'u'lláh, *Gleanings*, CXX.

peace and security, are unattainable unless and until its unity is firmly established. This unity can never be achieved so long as the counsels which the Pen of the Most High hath revealed are suffered to pass unheeded.'[472]

The establishment of world peace will take place in two stages: the 'Lesser Peace' which, based on international agreements, will banish and abolish war, and has as a spiritual motive the people's fear of war; and the 'Most Great Peace', which will come about as the result of Bahá'u'lláh's revelation, and means the complete harmony of the peoples, races and religions of the world, spiritual unity and the establishment of a just and universal order. The Lesser Peace will be preceded by violent confusion and terrible chaos: 'The time for the destruction of the world and its people hath arrived.' 'The hour is approaching when the most great convulsion will have appeared.' 'The promised day is come, the day when tormenting trials will have surged above your heads, and beneath your feet, saying: "Taste ye what your hands have wrought!"' 'The day will soon come whereupon they will cry out for help and receive no answer' . . . 'When the wrathful anger of the Almighty will have taken hold of them . . . He shall cleanse the earth from the defilement of their corruption, and shall give it for an heritage unto such of his servants as are nigh unto Him.'[473] 'The world is in travail, and its agitation waxeth day by day. Its face is turned towards waywardness and unbelief. Such shall be its plight, that to disclose it now would not be meet and seemly. Its perversity will long continue. And when the appointed hour is come, there shall suddenly appear that which shall cause

472. Bahá'u'lláh, *Gleanings*, CXXXI.
473. Bahá'u'lláh, quoted by Shoghi Effendi, *The Promised Day is Come*, pp. 1–2. In this work, Shoghi Effendi has described our present stage from a religious point of view: 'We are indeed living in an age which, if we would correctly appraise it, should be regarded as one which is witnessing a dual phenomenon. The first signalizes the death-pangs of an order, effete and godless, that has stubbornly refused, despite the signs and portents of a century-old Revelation, to attune its processes to the precepts and ideals which that Heaven-sent Faith proffered it. The second proclaims the birth-pangs of an Order, divine and redemptive, that will inevitably supplant the former, and within Whose administrative structure an embryonic civilisation, incomparable and world-embracing, is imperceptibly maturing. The one is being rolled up, and is crashing in oppression, bloodshed, and ruin. The other opens up vistas of a justice, a unity, a peace, a culture, such as no age has ever seen. The former has spent its force, demonstrated its falsity and barrenness, lost irretrievably its opportunity, and is hurrying to its doom. The latter, virile and unconquerable, is plucking asunder its chains, and is vindicating its title to be the one refuge within which a sore-tried humanity, purged from its dross, can attain its destiny' (p. 16).

the limbs of mankind to quake. Then, and only then, will the Divine Standard be unfurled, and the Nightingale of Paradise warble its melody.'[474]

From this world catastrophe mankind will emerge chastised and purified; through the vivifying forces of the new revelation, it will experience a spiritual rebirth. The kingdom of peace promised and sung by the prophets, when the swords will be beaten into ploughshares—God's kingdom on earth as promised by Jesus Christ—will appear on earth through the power of the Holy Spirit and through the world order revealed by Bahá'u'lláh. Its model is the legal structure of the Bahá'í community and the functional role played by its parts.[475] It is not a transcendental but rather an immanent kingdom, not a Utopian anarchy of love, as Tolstoy understood it, but rather a 'world federal system, ruling the whole earth, . . . blending and embodying the ideals of both the East and the West, liberated from the curse of war and its miseries, . . . a system in which Force is made the servant of Justice, whose life is sustained by its universal recognition of one God and by its allegiance to one common Revelation.'[476] The promise that God himself will rule his people, that there will be 'one fold and one shepherd'[477] will then be fulfilled: 'This is the Day whereon the unseen world crieth out: "Great is thy blessedness, O earth, for thou hast been made the foot-stool of thy God, and been chosen as the seat of His mighty throne!"'[478]

474. Bahá'u'lláh, *Gleanings*, LXI.
475. See p. 46 above and Shoghi Effendi, *The World Order of Bahá'u'lláh*.
476. Shoghi Effendi, 'The Unfoldment of World Civilization', in *The World Order of Bahá'u'lláh*, p. 204.
477. John 10:16.
478. Bahá'u'lláh, *vide* Shoghi Effendi, op. cit., p. 206.

Blessed are they that judge with fairness.

Bahá'u'lláh

Muḥammad and the West

To the Bahá'í who seeks a deeper understanding of the Bahá'í Faith, a thorough knowledge of Islám is as indispensable as the study of the Old Testament for the Christian theologian. Shoghi Effendi has urged the believers 'to approach reverently and with a mind purged from pre-conceived ideas the study of the Qur'án' and to acquire a sound knowledge of the history and teachings of Islám which 'is the source and background of their Faith'.[479] But knowledge of this religion to which a considerable part of human-ity[480] belongs and to which culture—including Western culture, which from a very narrow-minded attitude is called Christian—owes a great deal, is profitable not only to the Bahá'í believer but also to anyone interested in world cultural and historical events. The cultural and historical importance of Islám can scarcely be overrated even for the Western world. The recent world political events in the Middle East and the awakening of Arab nationalism in particular make the unbiased analysis of the world of Islamic thought especially topical. The knowledge Westerners have in this domain, even among the learned, is astonishingly limited. The concept the European has of Islám is tarnished by century-old prejudices and misunderstandings, partly also by spiteful defama-tory descriptions delivered by certain confessions which look with fear and aversion on this sister-religion of Christianity and Judaism.[481]

479. *The Advent of Divine Justice*, p. 41.
480. About 450 million people.
481. Recently a greater restraint may be noted here too, as the Second Vatican Ecumenical Council has, for the first time in the history of religion, adopted a more conciliatory position in its explanation of the attitude of the Church to the non-Christian religions. One can only hope that this attitude will also be adopted by the believers and the Catholic clergy. A special section is devoted to Islám: 'The Church also regards with esteem the Muslims who worship the one, subsistent, merciful and

Western polemics flared up, above all, around the person and the life of Muḥammad, the founder of this religion. To the Christian Middle Ages he was what he still is to some Christian theologians: the deceitful heretic, the false prophet. One of the Fathers of the Church, the Greek John of Damascus, saw Muḥammad as the Anti-Christ; Dante called him the '*seminator di scandalo e di scisma*'.[482] Muḥammad is described as the first of the accursed ones:

> Whilst eagerly I fix on him my gaze,
> He eyed me, with his hands laid his breast bare,
> And cried, 'Now mark how I do rip me: lo!
> How is Mohammed mangled: before me
> Walks Ali weeping, from the chin his face
> Cleft to the forelock; and the others all,
> Whom here thou seest, while they lived, did sow
> Scandal and schism, and therefore thus are rent.'

Luther saw in the 'Turk' a creation of the Devil. 'The difference in belief is surely insufficient', writes the orientalist Fück, 'to explain the raging hatred which the Christian Middle Ages harboured against Muḥammad. The reason for this hatred is rather to be found in all the bitterness, fear and misery which the Western world, threatened in its existence by this unexpected rival, felt against the man who, by his appearance, had set such a revolution in motion.'[483] For the thinkers of the Age of Enlightenment who were hostile to religion, Muḥammad was a deceiver and his religion—as Voltaire said—'a web of charlatanism and stupidity'. In his drama 'Mahomet', he makes the prophet commit the most horrifying atrocities. That a camel-driver should cause a

---

almighty God, the Creator of heaven and earth, who has spoken to man. Islám willingly traces its descent back to Abraham, and just as he submitted himself to God, the Muslims endeavour to submit themselves to his mysterious decrees. They venerate Jesus as a prophet, without, however, recognising him as God, and they pay honour to his virgin mother Mary and sometimes also invoke her with devotion. Further, they expect a day of judgment when God will raise all men from the dead and reward them. For this reason they attach importance to the moral life and worship God, mainly by prayer, alms-giving and fasting. If in the course of the centuries there has arisen not infrequent dissension and hostility between Christian and Muslim, this sacred Council now urges everyone to forget the past, to make sincere efforts at mutual understanding and to work together in protecting and promoting for the benefit of all men, social justice, good morals as well as peace and freedom' (*Declaration on the relation of the Church to non-Christian religions*, no. 3).

482. *Inferno*, Canto 28, Verses 10–12. Translated by the Rev. Henry Francis Cary.
483. In the magazine *Saeculum*, vol. III, part 1, p. 71.

tumult and claim to have received an incomprehensible book, each page of which 'makes Reason shudder', is something which one 'who is not a born Turk' could not defend, wrote the great scoffer who, to be sure, wrote in a similar way about Christ and Moses.

However, at that time, there were already thinkers who did more justice to Muḥammad. Even if they refused to call him a prophet, they saw in him one of the greatest men who had ever lived. He is described as a wise and enlightened law-giver who created a sensible religion to replace the doubtful dogmas of the Jewish and Christian Faiths. Savary saw in Muḥammad's religion a universal teaching which only contains what is reasonable: the belief in one God, in the rewarding of virtue and the punishment of crime. That Muḥammad made his appearance as 'Messenger of God' seemed to him to be a pious fraud dictated by reasons of prudence. The nineteenth-century Scottish writer Thomas Carlyle, too, opposed the interpretation according to which Muḥammad was an impostor[484] and in the last century the historian Heinrich Leo expressed the following opinion: 'But those who call a man like Muḥammad a deceiver have a very paltry inner experience and poor understanding. They know nothing of that power of the spirit which motivates communities, and raises the leader of true communities to heights which have been inaccessible at all times to the common mind.'[485]

Whereas representatives of Christian orthodoxy still describe Muḥammad as a 'liar-prophet' and the religion founded by him as an 'abortion from hell' and 'opium of the people'[486] a more objec-

484. 'For innumerable people Muḥammad's words have been as the guiding star of their life. Can one imagine that so many of God's creatures have lived and died for something that must be described as a miserable fraud? What should we think of this world anyway, if charlatanry should wield such power over men?' (*Heroes and Hero-Worship*).

485. *Lehrbuch der Geschichte des Mittelalters*, p. 204.

486. The theologian Blank writes in the *Evangelisches Missionsmagazin* (1936, p. 375): 'One thing is certain and that is that in Islam we are dealing with a particularly dangerous hellish monstrosity', and A. Spindeler, Professor of Catholic moral theology and homiletics in Hildesheim writes concerning Muḥammad in *Katholische Glaubenskorrespondenz*, which appeared in 1966 (Letter I) and which aims at giving generally comprehensible information about the essential branches of Catholic doctrine: 'When someone passes himself off as messenger of God and prophet and as such spreads "divine revelations" or imposes his belief upon people with violence, he is then nothing but a liar-prophet, even if he had great success or was able through his teaching to bring about a certain improvement in the existing social or religious order, or rather disorder. Thus Muḥammad is and remains a false prophet, who, to

tive historical outlook, which considers the prophet of Arabia in the light of and with the methods of general religious history, does him more justice. His uprightness, the self-denial with which he struggled to carry out his mission in the face of a hostile world, his genuine conviction that he was an instrument in the hand of the Almighty, the depth of his belief are fully recognised today: 'A man of unusual quality, a fearless and selfless champion of a great Cause who led his people out of the darkness of barbarism to the light of civilization and of higher moral consciousness'; this is what the Roman orientalist Francesco Gabrieli writes about him.[487]

Islamic research in the West

However, it must be said that even today theological publications about Islám are far from being unbiased about this religion and its founder or truly appreciative of them. In fact this is not surprising, because research into Islám has emerged mainly from Christian missionary research. Missionary scholars, who had mainly had an Evangelical or Catholic education, looked at Islám from a teleological point of view, and were not able to consider it outside the Judeo-Christian framework or to grasp its essence. A method which mainly depends on finding points of contact for the Christian mission and on unmasking the subject-matter as an amalgam of Arabic, heathen, Jewish and Christian elements is, from the start, incapable of achieving any kind of insight into the subject. Even modern authors not affected by denominational considerations nevertheless frequently—and usually quite unconsciously—subsume the result they have obtained from historical and phenomenological research under the religious concepts acquired from Christianity and Judaism, and thus obstruct their own way to a proper understanding of the religion under study. Very often they lack sympathy, sensitivity and understanding for the originally

---

be sure, brought about a higher culture, a deeper devotion and political successes to several peoples, mainly because he stole from Judaism and Christianity a few essential teachings which he presented as his own revealed teachings like the notions of a personal God, of the Day of Judgment, and of Christ's messianic act. But through his usurped prophethood which was not real, the true teachings are so mixed with so many and such untrue assertions like that of the fatalistic predestination of man, of the 'joys of Heaven', of the depravity of all non-Muslims, of the non-human nature of woman, etc. . . . that the whole work is unacceptable because it is false and unworthy.'

487. 'Muhammad und der Islam als weltgeschichtliche Erscheinungen', p. 348.

religious element which lies in the sphere of the numinous or irrational and which does not reveal itself to purely intellectual research. Religion is a subject which can only partly be explored by science in the same way as the natural world with its cause and effect. Basically, the science of the study of religions is only possible as religious history, religious phenomenology and religious sociology. However, religious life is far from being exhausted in these branches of the study of religion. This is why the presentation of a religion is also always dependent on the intellectual attitude of the one presenting it. For in the sphere of the religious, in the domain of cultural values, a completely objective intellectual attitude does not exist. From the start, different conclusions are to be expected when Islám is presented by a convinced Christian, a staunch atheist, or a Muslim. The attitude adopted towards the subject—the conviction that after Christ a divine manifestation is impossible, or that a divine manifestation is not possible at all, or that the Arabian Prophet revealed the Word of God—will be clearly visible in the presentation. For it is of crucial importance whether a religion is described from within or without.[488] He who is not satisfied with a pure recording of religious phenomena and of their interpretation according to subjective standards which from the start are taken as absolute criteria, but who wants to learn something about the essential mystery of a religion, should acquaint himself with a believer's own interpretation of his Faith.[489]

The critique of the *Qur'án*

The holy book of Islám, the *Qur'án*, which according to the Orientalist von Hammer 'is as unmistakably the word of Muhammad as the Muslims believe that it is the Word of God',[490] is often

488. The religious philosopher Martin Buber once formulated this idea in the following way: 'The mystery of the other is always immanent and cannot be understood from the outside. No one outside Israel knows about the mystery of Israel. And no one outside Christianity knows about the mystery of Christianity' (Quoted in Hans-Joachim Schoeps, *Jüdisch-christliche Religionsgespräch in neunzehn Jahrhunderten*, p. 154).

489. For all those who evaluate the religion of others according to subjective standards, the words of the theologian A. Poisy are intended: 'One can say about all religions that they have an absolute value for their followers but only a relative one in the eyes of the philosopher and of the critic' (*Revue critique et litteraire*, 1906, p. 307).

490. Quoted by William Muir, *The Life of Mahomet*, p. xxxiii. The authenticity of the *Qur'án* is indisputable. Shoghi Effendi, too, emphasises that the *Qur'án* 'apart from the sacred scriptures of the Bábí and Bahá'í Revelations, constitutes the only

treated by the critical non-Muslim reader with lack of appreciation and often with arrogance. This is why he reaches a conclusion about the book which is often subjective, unjust and presumptuous. Whoever decides to read this book should do so with the understanding that it is a holy book—for centuries a guiding-star for countless human beings. The reader should approach this work if not with a feeling of awe, then at least with respect, and mindful of the warning given by the eighteenth-century scientist Lichtenberg about one's approach to reading a book,[491] should remember the following points.

The judgment passed on a holy writing depends to a great extent on the religious concepts and the emotional values held by the one judging it. The European's ideas, even if he is an agnostic, are shaped by Christianity. To the Christian, the Gospel is the essence of the Word of God. He has known and loved this work since his childhood. He understands it, or thinks he does. He considers it to be *a priori* different from every other writing. He adopts it as a standard by which he judges unfamiliar revealed writings like the *Qur'án*, with which he only becomes familiar through the veil of inadequate translations since he has no command of Arabic, and is without any knowledge of the ideas, situation and conditions of that period of history, which are occasionally referred to in the *Qur'án* itself. And after a superficial reading of it he lays this book aside, disappointed and convinced of the unsurpassable and matchless quality of the Gospel. In doing so he fails to realise that the language of the Word of God is very varied. The divine truth has been expressed at different periods, in different places, in very different forms of human thought and language. To say nothing of the holy writings more removed from us like the Bhagavad Gita and the Dhammapada, even the writings of the Old Testament are very different in content and stylistic form. The gospels, too, show differences in their stylistic characteristics: the Gospel of St. John differs from the synoptic gospels to a great degree by its adoption of Hellenistic ways of thinking and speak-

---

Book which can be regarded as an absolutely authenticated Repository of the Word of God' (*The Advent of Divine Justice*, p. 41).

491. 'When a head and a book collide and a hollow sound results, is it always the fault of the book?' and 'Such works are mirrors; when a monkey looks into them, the reflection cannot be that of an apostle.' Also compare in this context Schopenhauer's valuable remarks about man's intellectual incapacity to recognise perfection, in *Aphorismen zur Lebensweisheit*, chapter 4.

ing. The *Qur'án* which, for the first time, preserves for mankind the pure, directly spoken and undistorted word of the Almighty, cannot be compared in its literary quality to any of the books of the Old and New Testaments. Apart from the philological aspect of the work, namely the extraordinarily expressive Arabic language which is capable of the finest nuances, and which has been, since Muḥammad's advent, the language of revelation,[492] this uniqueness lies in the singular way the book is presented and in the overpowering spirit of its prophetic parts. Thus the *Qur'án* is described by non-Muslim experts of the Arabic language as a great masterpiece of literature. Of course, to the superficial reader who remains aloof, its original character, its poetic expression and the hidden, symbolic meaning of its verses disclose themselves just as little as the 'Art of Fugue' would to the man who does not understand Bach's polyphony.

Another fact should be considered: Islám claims—like Judaism and the Bahá'í Faith—to be not only the rule of conduct and the guide to God for the individual in need of salvation but also the remedy and guidance for a lamentably sick human society. The social order is also an object of divine solicitude. Therefore in Muḥammad's proclamation man as a whole is addressed, as an individual as well as a social, political body. This is why the *Qur'án* also contains ordinances and laws; this is why it is also—like the Pentateuch—a book of laws. But by no means a systematic code of laws in the sense of our modern codification! Bahá'u'lláh's warning about the *Kitáb-i-Aqdas*, the book of laws which he revealed, applies also to the *Qur'án*: 'Think not that we have revealed unto you a mere code of laws. Nay, rather we have unsealed the choice Wine with the fingers of might and power.'[493] 'Say: O leaders of religion! Weigh not the Book of God with such standards and sciences as are current amongst you, for the Book itself is the unerring balance established amongst men.'[494]

With what inadequate criteria the *Qur'án* is evaluated is shown by Gabrieli's arrogant verdict: 'That he was no outstanding thinker is testified by his obscure and confused holy Book in which the revelations he believed to have received from his God and Lord throughout two decades are faithfully collected. More-

---

492. The Báb and Bahá'u'lláh, too, wrote mainly in Arabic.
493. *Synopsis and Codification of the Laws and Ordinances of the Kitáb-i-Aqdas*, p. 12.
494. *Gleanings*, XCVIII.

over, the initial demoniac inspiration gradually decreased more and more, finally losing itself in homily and in admonitions of a very banal nature.'[495]

What should one think of such a critique coming from a renowned scholar? This is not a unique case. Rosenkranz reasoned in the same way when describing the *Kitáb-i-Aqdas*, the book of laws revealed by Bahá'u'lláh's pen, as a 'confusion of commandments'.[496] As if a revealed book had ever appeared as an alphabetical work of reference classified under different subjects, or a religion as a methodical punctilious system! It is unfortunately not known how and according to what criteria Gabrieli judged other revealed writings and with what he would have reproached Islám had the *Qur'án* been a book systematically worked out in the manner of a philosophical textbook. It is surprising how easily even theologians forget essential facts when they turn their eyes with suspicion towards the religious world unfamiliar to them. The whole of religious history teaches that the founders of religions are not systematic thinkers, that the prophets are not theologians,[497] that their teachings may not be understood in the sense of a logically developed system of rational enlightenment. As Rosenkranz himself emphasises in the same work, the essence of religion lies in the numinous, in the suprarational. Theologians and lawyers have always provided a systematic order for the revealed teachings and laws. The reproach that the *Qur'án* is obscure and inconsistent shows an utter failure to grasp the essence of religion. Coming from Christians this reproach is all the more unacceptable. For no book from the start has caused so many varied interpretations as the New Testament. It is indeed impossible to maintain that the verses of the *Qur'án*, which claims as a proof of its divine origin to be free from contradictions,[498] can always be easily brought into agreement. Those looking for contradictions will certainly be satisfied. For them are intended these verses: 'He it is who hath sent down to thee "the Book". Some of its signs are of themselves perspicuous—these are the basis of the Book—and others are figurative. But they whose hearts are given to err, follow its figures, craving discord, craving an interpretation.'[499] 'Hearts have they with which they under-

495. op. cit., p. 347.   496. *Die Bahá'í*, p. 32.
497. Goldziher rightly emphasises this, p. 71.   498. *Qur'án* 4:83.
499. ibid. 3:5. Bahá'u'lláh writes: 'It is evident unto thee that the Birds of Heaven and Doves of Eternity speak a twofold language. One language, the outward

stand not, and eyes have they with which they see not, and ears have they with which they hearken not. They are like the brutes: Yea, they go more astray: these are the heedless.'[500] 'Leave them in their pastime of cavillings.'[501]

The critic sometimes finds one feature of the *Qur'án* unusual and wearisome: the frequent repetitions of the same topics.[502] Varied as the *Qur'án* is, giving in many places an account of the earlier divine messengers and of the life and sufferings of Christ, the following points recur time and again as *Leitmotive* of the revelation: the testimony to the unity and awe-inspiring omnipotence of God, to the reward for the ones devoted to doing the will of God and to the chastisement of those denying his signs. Above all the *Qur'án* proclaims God's mercifulness: 'My mercy embraceth all things.'[503] 'In the Name of God, the Compassionate, the Merciful' thus reads the introductory formula which opens each súrah. Goethe's verdict upon these passages, which repeat the central themes in new contexts and which are obviously founded in the Prophet's educative purpose was: 'Unlimited tautologies and repetitions form the body of this Holy Book which, every time we take it up, revolts us anew, fills us with amazement and finally commands our veneration.'[504] Understanding this book depends, as Bahá'u'lláh continually reminds us, on 'purity of heart, chastity of soul, and freedom of spirit'.[505] Whoever calls it a confused, obscure and muddled work is like the blind of whom Bahá'u'lláh writes: 'Yea, the blind can perceive naught from the sun except its heat, and the arid soil hath no share of the showers of mercy. "Marvel not if in the Qur'án the unbeliever perceiveth naught but

---

language, is devoid of allusions, is unconcealed and unveiled; that it may be a guiding lamp and a beaconing light whereby wayfarers may attain the heights of holiness, and seekers may advance into the realm of eternal reunion. Such are the unveiled traditions and the evident verses already mentioned. The other language is veiled and concealed, so that whatever lieth hidden in the heart of the malevolent may be made manifest and their innermost being be disclosed. Thus hath Ṣádiq, son of Muḥammad, spoken: "God verily will test them and sift them." This is the divine standard, this is the Touchstone of God, wherewith he proveth his servants. None apprehendeth the meaning of these utterances except them whose hearts are assured, whose souls have found favour with God, and whose minds are detached from all else but Him' (*Kitáb-i-Íqán*, p. 162 (Brit.), p. 254 (U.S.)).

500. *Qur'án* 7:178.   501. ibid., 6:91.
502. Thus Glasenapp, 'Die Nichtchristlichen Religionen', p. 180.
503. *Qur'án* 7:155.
504. *Noten und Abhandlungen zum Westöstlischen Diwan.*
505. *Kitáb-i-Íqán*, p. 135 (Brit.), p. 211 (U.S.).

the trace of letters, for in the sun, the blind findeth naught but heat.'''[506]

The image of Islám in theological studies

Now, how does Islám appear in the theological field of research? Almost without exception it is presented as an amalgam of Heathen–Jewish–Christian ideas and teachings. Generations of scholars have considered it the task of their life assiduously to investigate the alleged origins of the principles of these teachings and to demonstrate the syncretic character of Islám.[507] Just as Christian controversialists never saw in Islám anything but the product of an act of spiritual theft, modern scholars themselves maintain that the basic ideas of Islám are borrowed from the Biblical religions and describe this 'a fact which requires no further discussion'.[508] 'When one examines each of the elements of Mohammad's system of belief,' Tor Andrae writes, 'it seems impossible to decide to which of these religions he is most indebted.'[509] Goldziher asserts 'that the assimilative character of Islám was already stamped on its brow at its birth. Its founder Muḥammad proclaims no new ideas. He has not enriched the ideas about man's relationship with the transcendental and the infinite.

'The proclamation of the Arabic prophet', he continues, 'is an eclectic composition of religious ideas which he was inspired to reveal through his contacts with Jewish, Christian and still other[510] ideologies by which he himself was deeply affected, and which he considered suitable for the awakening of a truly religious spirit among his fellow-men; ordinances which he also drew from foreign sources, and which he recognised as necessary for the establishment of a pattern of life in accordance with the divine will.'[511] Goldziher, like Tor Andrae, thinks that the Christian

506. *Kitáb-i-Íqán*, p. 133 (Brit.), p. 209 (U.S.).

507. In the nineteenth century an essay by Geiger appeared which today is still occasionally quoted: 'What Muhammad has taken over from Judaism.'

508. Tor Andrae, *Mohammed: The Man and His Faith*, p. 11.

509. ibid., p. 113.

510. Karl Vollers (*Archiv fur Religionswissenschaft*, XII, 1909, p. 277) and Richard Hartmann (*Preussisches Jahrbuch*, CXLIII, p. 92 ff., 1911) too, thought they had found late reminiscences of Babylonian and Hellenistic mythology; Hubert Grimme thought influences from the Southern-Arabian world of ideas were visible (*Nöldeke-Festschrift*, 1906, p. 453 ff.).

511. Goldziher, op. cit., pp. 3–4.

elements of the *Qur'án* have reached Muḥammad mostly 'through the channel of apocryphal traditions and of the heresies scattered in Eastern Christianity[512] ... Muhammad absorbed everything he came across in his superficial contacts in the circle of his associates and he utilised most of it without any fixed plan at all.'[513] Gabrieli comes to the same conclusion: 'He had only a vague and fragmentary knowledge of the two monotheistic religions preceding his own. He borrowed from the former the idea of the one God, the creator, as well as the cosmology and view of mankind's early history, and also the distorted and somewhat misunderstood story of the old patriarchs, generals and kings whom he fused together one and all in the category of "prophets"; finally as the last and most questionable element he borrowed the crippling ritualism. From Christianity he took over the figure of Jesus, not as the Son of God but merely as a prophet of miraculous birth, a miracle-worker, and as his own [Muḥammad's] immediate predecessor. On the other hand, a closer knowledge not only of the dogma of the Trinity, the concept of salvation and of the Eucharist but also of the deeper ethical content of Christianity, eluded him. After all, he had only a vague oral information of its sources, the apocryphal gospels; still, wandering Christian preachers in the desert might have influenced his dialectic reasoning and the whole style of his proclamation.'[514] Glasenapp, too, considers Islám as an assimilated mixture of Christianity and Judaism.[515] He maintains that the Jewish and Christian legends have been partly distorted in the *Qur'án* as 'the prophet had no biblical texts at hand, but only got to hear oral reports'.[516] Frank Thiess also believes Muḥammad has produced the irrefutable proof 'that new, significant, effective structures can be erected out of the stones of old buildings, like churches out of heathen temples'.[517]

So this is the way the non-Muslim religious scholar conceives the birth of a religion which has lasted for centuries and has

512. Tor Andrae: Nestorian, Ebionite and Manichean teachings.

513. Goldziher, p. 13; by this Goldziher means that it is not his duty 'to trace back the pathological factors which awakened and strengthened in him [Muḥammad] the consciousness that he was the bearer of a revelation' (p. 4). C. H. Becker, too, thinks that the knowledge Muḥammad had about Jesus and which he reported in the *Qur'án* came from 'pseudo-epigraphic cancerous growths' (*Islamstudien* I, p. 389).

514. op. cit., pp. 347–8.

515. op. cit., p. 180.

516. ibid.

517. *Die griechischen Kaiser*, p. 521 ff.

changed the world. But how strange that the amalgam of such disparate elements became so characteristic, peerless and full of vitality as to be capable of transforming its followers into such a specific and homogeneous type of people. In this context, let it be noted that the Bahá'í Faith, too, when it is not bluntly dismissed as a reformed sect of Islám, is looked upon by religious historians as a syncretic formation. Rosenkranz has earnestly endeavoured to trace its alleged Greek–Neoplatonic–Islamic–Ṣúfí origins.[518] The theologian Willem Visser't Hooft regards the Bahá'í Faith as the outcome of an artificial synthesis which in the end leaves nothing but an insignificant common denominator of all religions: 'Baha'i is therefore a new, religious mixture which replaces the old religions.'[519]

The limits of theological knowledge

This criticism levelled at Islám by theologians shows the correctness of the assertion that the appreciation of the truth of a religion largely depends on the mental, subjective attitude one holds towards the subject. It proves the inadequate understanding of the theologian who approaches a subject only from the outside and can no more refute the truth of a religion than he can prove it. And if the scholar is Muslim, then his presentation proceeds from his inner religious conviction which is not accessible to Christian theologians. Someone who believes that the message of Muḥammad was a revelation from God no longer wonders about the origin of the message he proclaimed. Similarities with the ideological world of other religions do not worry him in the least. They are—the revealed Truth being taken as the criterion—the remains of former religious truths, the authority of which is being reaffirmed in the new revelation. From this angle, similarities between the religious world of Islám and that of Ebionite or Nestorian Christianity are explained by the fact that it was precisely in those Christian fractional groups, which had been accused of heresy by the High Church, that religious truths from which orthodox teaching had digressed were preserved. It is not Church orthodoxy, therefore, which is the criterion by which Islám is to be judged, but rather the other way round. If, on the other hand, the scholar does not believe in Islám, and does not accept the fact that God has revealed himself through Muḥammad or that divine

518. *Die Bahá'í*, p. 50 ff.   519. Visser't Hooft, *No Other Name*, p. 45.

revelation is at all possible,[520] Islám cannot but appear to him as an eclectic conglomeration of heterogeneous ideas and teachings, as a syncretism. Then, of course, to investigate the origins of the borrowed ideas and to prove the lack of originality of the Prophet appears as an exciting task to the scholar.

This analytical method is to be criticised in so far as it fails to understand the essence of religion. In no way does the originality of a religion merely consist of the proclamation of new ideas never thought of before; it also consists to a great extent of new moral and religious impulses for existing ideas and values. The revelation is, as Bahá'u'lláh says, the 'Unerring Balance', the 'Straight Path'[521] through which 'truth shall be distinguished from error and the wisdom of every command shall be tested'.[522] It is the compass for a humanity deprived of divine guidance and authoritative values and which, aimless, is going astray. Mankind does not suffer from a lack of ideas, especially today, but rather from a lack of generally accepted authority and direction. Were it only a question of creating new and entirely original ideas,[523] each religion should be denied its originality. For religious ideas can always be traced back to ideas which already exist and have been thought of before. Thus Jodl, for example, writes in his history of ethics:[524] 'When compared to these Roman stoics, Christianity has hardly a moral idea which does not have its parallel among these thinkers.' And Herbert Preisker[525] sees the only contribution

---

520. This is true, for instance, of the biography of Muḥammad by Maxime Rodinson (*Mahomet*, Editions du Seuil, Paris, 1961; English edition: *Mohammad*, translated by Anne Carter, The Penguin Press, 1971). The author, who used to be a member of the French Communist party and now works as a theorist and writer for the Marxist left, openly admits in his foreword that he considers the figure of Muḥammad from an atheist point of view. He agrees that a religious person would naturally understand Muḥammad in a different way: 'But better? I am not so sure.' This biography, so much praised for its 'unbiased objectivity', by its German publisher, conveys a Marxist interpretation of Islám which is essentially wrong.

521. Quoted by Shoghi Effendi, *God Passes By*, p. 215.

522. Tablet of Aḥmad.

523. Tor Andrae himself acknowledges that 'a new form of religious life like that of Islam is not merely a body of doctrine or a system of ritual. It is, when profoundly regarded, a form of spiritual energy, a living seed. It develops its own life and attracts other spiritual life to itself, according to a law whose significance and purpose is completely revealed only after an extended development. There is originality enough in Mohammed's achievement in catching up into a vital and adaptable personal synthesis the spiritual potentialities of his age' (*Mohammed: The Man and His Faith*, p. 11).

524. Vol. I, p. 27.

525. *Christentum und Ehe in den ersten drei Jahrhunderten*, p. 11.

made by Christianity towards the history of marriage in 'the moral seriousness and the new energy which is released in views already known to the Jews and the Pagans'.

With this method used by scholars of Islám, one can apply the scalpel to every religion and 'prove' where the founder of the religion draws his ideas from and even that he never existed at all.[526] It is possible, for instance, to trace back the whole message of Jesus to the different influences of Judaism (especially of the Essenes) of the Hellenistic philosophy, of the mystery cults, of Buddhism and Hinduism and to dispute the originality of Jesus.[527] The socialist Karl Kautsky did not find in Christianity 'one single idea which could not be traced in the "pagan" or Jewish literature from before Jesus'.[528] Moreover, the concept of being God's children, of having a 'Father in Heaven' was very current in Judaism,[529] and the command to love one's enemy was prevalent

526. The theologian David Friedrich Strauss rejected in his *Leben Jesu*, written in 1835-6, the authenticity of the gospels. The theologian Bruno Bauer questioned openly for the first time the historical existence of Jesus (*Christus und Cäsaren, Der Ursprung des Christentums aus dem römischen Griechentum*, 1877). In the twentieth century many scholars have questioned that Jesus actually lived (Arthur Drews, *Die Christusmythe*, 1909, *Die Leugnung der Geschichtlichkeit Jesu in Vergangenheit und Gegenwart*, 1926; Georg Brandes, *Die Jesussage*, 1925).

527. A few examples must be given here; many more could be quoted: 'All that which is true in Christianity can also be found in Brahmanism and in Buddhism' (Artur Schopenhauer, *Sämtliche Werke*, ed. N. Kohler, V, p. 331). 'If a person initiated into one of the mystery cults could be called back to life today, he would confirm to us that the figure of the Saviour, Jesus, from his birth to his ascension reminds him scene for scene of the two redeemers Dionysus and Heracles' (H. Raschke, *Das Christusmysterium*, p. 117). 'Whatever was beautiful and elevated in the myth of the Sun (cult of Mithras) was taken over by Christianity; Helios became Christ' (Karl Schneider, *Geistesgeschichte des antiken Christentums*, I, p. 258). 'Thus the Pythagoras of history and legend has become from a religious-historical point of view the most eminent forerunner and rival of the two gods on whose proclamation and work Christianity is founded, Jesus and Paul' (H. Windisch, *Paulus und Christus*, p. 62). 'Before Christianity spoke of its saviour in these terms, the Emperor in Rome was celebrated in this manner and in him the hearts which knew nothing of Jesus were edified' (H. Weinel, *Die Stellung des Urchristentums zum Staat*, p. 20 ff.). 'The great significance of the Dead Sea scrolls lies above all in the fact that they have unveiled to us the cult of the Essenes, which until now was so intriguing and mysterious, and which offered us the first outline of the Christian teachings' (André Dupont-Sommer, *Die essenischen Schriften vom Toten Meer*, p. 399). 'Two great Greek mythical creations have, above all, influenced Christianity most profoundly, the myth of the God who has become man who suffers and dies with men and the myth of the imprisoned soul liberated by a divine redeemer' (Karl Schneider, *Geistesgeschichte* I, p. 236). 'Nothing, only the arrangement, is new' (William Durant, *Caesar and Christus*, p. 644).

528. *Der Ursprung des Christentums*, p. 342.

529. Malachi 2:10; on this whole subject see J. Schneewind, *Das Gleichnis vom verlorenen Sohn*, 1940, p. 27.

both among the Stoics[530] and the Jews.[531] The saying of Jesus: 'Therefore all things whatsoever ye would that men should do to you, do ye even so to them'[532] corresponds to the maxim of Buddha: 'Act in such a way, as if it were happening to yourself' and 'One overcomes anger by not getting angry; one overcomes evil with good; one overcomes the miser with gifts; one overcomes the liar with truth.'[533]

But what purpose does this serve? The essence of Moses's Torah can be as little derived from Hammurabi's codex as Jesus's ethics from the parallels of the Rabbinic writings, or the teachings and laws of the *Qur'án* from analogies in Judaism and Christianity. It is just as vain to look for the genetic origins of the Bahá'í Faith in the previous religions or even in the Age of Enlightenment in the West. For it is as difficult for the religious historians to prove that such influences were in fact present as for the believers to prove their faith in the revealed quality of the message received.[534] H. J. Schoeps' opinion is penetrating: 'If a new relevant trend of thinking teaches anything, then it is this: that historic results can only proceed from historic reality. It is a sign of prejudice when one wants to interpret an event—particularly a holy one—in a different way from the way it explains itself.'[535] And the Catholic Romano Guardini gave the decisive answer to the question of the originality of a religion—in this case Christianity: 'Only a faith based on reality has the world-subduing power which was and still is characteristic of the Christian conviction.'[536]

530. Seneca, *De Beneficiis*, IV: 26, a sentence reminiscent of Matthew 5:44: 'When thou wantest to imitate the gods, do good to the ungrateful also! For the sun rises even for criminals and the seas are open to the pirates.'

531. Exodus 23:4-5: 'If you meet thine enemy's ox or his ass going astray, thou shalt surely bring it back to him again. If you see the ass of him that hateth thee lying under his burden, and wouldest forbear to help him, thou shalt surely help with him.'

532. Matthew 7:12.

533. Quoted by Deschner, *Abermals krähte der Hahn*, p. 137.

534. Or what could one say in this context about Bahá'u'lláh's law according to which—for the first time in religious history—the education of the daughter takes precedence over that of the son, when one discovers for instance that the Greek philosophers Musonius and Plutarch already advocated this idea? (see Herbert Preisker, *Christentum und Ehe*, p. 26).

535. *Jüdisch-christliches Religionsgespräch neunzehn Jahrhunderten*, p. 148.

536. *Das Bild von Jesus dem Christus im Neuen Testament*, p. 32.

The world-subduing power of Islám

For that same power which was characteristic of Islám, the scholars have no explanation to offer. That an uneducated man should leave a book which has attracted and influenced the most enlightened minds for many centuries and who has 'like hardly any other educated his followers to a special type of person',[537] that he should be able to create a religion sparkling with life, a religion which spread all over the world in a few years, influenced millions of people throughout the centuries and gave rise to a culture equal to Western culture—this is a mysterious phenomenon for scholars. The orientalist Fück broke with the hitherto prevailing image of Islám: 'Finally the inadequate results reached with this method of research led to the conclusion that there must be a fault at the very beginning of this approach ... In fact, all narrow-minded attempts to attribute Muḥammad's appearance to Christian or Jewish influence have failed.'[538]

The theme of tolerance in Islám

When conversing with Christians, even the educated among them, one experiences again and again that however ready they may be to admit that their knowledge of Islám is poor, there is still one thing they are certain about: that Islám is an intolerant religion which was propagated with fire and sword by its fanatical followers. The European's view of Islám mostly comprises this concept and the one already examined, i.e. that Muḥammad stole his teachings from the Jewish and Christian faiths. This traditional assertion, that Islám was spread by the sword, which has been propounded time and again and is as false as it is popular, has long since been refuted by historical research. Today not one single scholar supports this theory[539] which is based on a complete ignorance of the factual circumstances and conditions of the Prophet's epoch.[540]

In reality Islám in its very essence has tolerance written on its

---

537. Glasenapp, op. cit., p. 193.

538. In the magazine *Saeculum*, vol. III, part 1, p. 73.

539. The orientalist Weil still expressed this belief as recently as in the middle of last century: 'But as soon as he [Muḥammad] ceases to be tolerant, as soon as he tries to make truth triumph by the sword ... he sets the stamp of human frailty and transience on his word and on himself' (Quoted in E. Diez, *Glaube und Welt des Islam*, p. 21).

540. Spindeler, who spreads this idea in *Katholische Glaubenskorrespondenz*, can hardly be granted bona fides, for his defamatory intention is obvious.

brow: 'Let there be no compulsion in religion'[541]; 'But if thy Lord had pleased, verily all who are in the earth would have believed together. What! wilt thou compel men to become believers? No soul can believe but by the permission of God.'[542] 'We know best what the infidels say: and thou art not to compel them. Warn then by the Qur'án those who fear my menace.'[543] Thus did Muḥammad teach his people, to whom he himself was also an example[544] of gentleness and forbearance in the manner he treated his defeated opponents. 'On the triumphal march to Mecca, leading an army of believers intoxicated by the consciousness of a power now irresistible, the Prophet was riding with bowed head in humble thankfulness for the grace Allah had granted to him, and whenever he was victorious he was able to show humane and magnanimous qualities'; this is Gabrieli's[545] opinion, and Tor Andrae himself admits that 'it is rarely that a victor has exploited his victory with greater self-restraint and forbearance than did Mohammed'.[546] The followers of other revealed religions were not forced to become Muslims. The Qur'án contains the following instruction as to how to treat them: 'Verily, they who believe, and the Jews, and the Sabeites, and the Christians—whoever of them believeth in God and in the last day, and doth what is right, on them shall come no fear, neither shall they be put to grief.'[547]

The peoples of the Book (dhimmí)[548]—those possessing scriptures—the Christians and the Jews, are placed under the protection of Islám and forbearance towards them was ordained by Muḥammad: 'Whoever kills one of the dhimmí will not inhale the fragrance of Paradise.'[549] Even the mere act of discriminating against the non-Muslims living under Islamic protection was considered a sinful transgression and the cause of crisis in affairs of empire: 'When the dhimmí are oppressed, power goes into the hands of the enemy', 'Whoever oppresses one of the dhimmí and lays upon him burdens that are too heavy, to him will I myself

541. *Qur'án* 2:257.   542. ibid., 10:99–100.   543. ibid., 50:45–6.
544. 'A noble pattern had ye in God's Apostle' (*Qur'án* 33:22).
545. op. cit., p. 347.   546. op. cit., p. 233.
547. *Qur'án* 5:73; very similar is 2:59.
548. *Dhimmí*: a non-Muslim, but follower of another religion, who is living as a subject in an Islamic state and who is commended to the responsibility which the theocratic Islamic state takes upon itself.
549. Thus reads one of Muḥammad's oft-cited oral traditions (Goldziher, op. cit., p. 34).

appear as an accuser on the Day of Judgment', 'Whoever does any
wrong to a Jew or a Christian will have me as accuser': thus reads
the oral traditional teaching of the Prophet.[550] The Christian
community of Nadjran was under Muḥammad's protection: 'If
anyone encroaches upon their rights, I myself shall be his enemy
and shall accuse him before God's countenance.'[551] Islám was not
interested in making proselytes. The saying of the old Arab writer
Ibn Sa'd is characteristic of the magnanimity of Islám: 'If they
become converted to Islám, this is good; if they do not, let them
remain (in their former faith); Islám is indeed spacious.'[552]

A Muslim's attitude to non-Muslims is determined by two concepts: '*jihád*' and '*jizyah*'. *Jihád* means something like effort for the
Cause, religious struggle, religious war. *Jizyah* is the poll-tax
which the conquered Christians and Jews had to pay.

Muḥammad and war

Muḥammad had allowed religious war when his community was
being threatened by extermination: 'And fight for the cause of
God against those who fight against you: but commit not the injustice of attacking them first: God loveth not such injustice: And
kill them wherever ye shall find them, and eject them from whatever place they have ejected you; for civil discord is worse than
carnage . . . But if they desist, then verily God is Gracious, Merciful. Fight therefore against them until there be no more civil discord, and the only worship be that of God: but if they desist, then
let there be no hostility.'[553]

It is incomprehensible that it should be precisely Christianity—
which since Augustine[554] has known the concept of the 'just war'
and which has also developed the concept of 'holy war' in which
even attack was allowed, which led the crusades, and still blessed
guns in the twentieth century and implored God to help its wars—
which should be so persistently critical of Muḥammad's attitude
in this matter. 'Abdu'l-Bahá has opposed this biased polemic with
the following consideration: 'If Christ himself had been placed in
such circumstances among such tyrannical and barbarous tribes,
and if for thirteen years He with His disciples had endured all

---

550. Quoted in Emile Dermenghem, *The Life of Mahomet*, p. 331.
551. Goldziher, p. 33.   552. ibid., p. 309.   553. *Qur'án* 2:186–9.
554. 'What have people got against war? Merely that people who, after all must
die one day should perish?' (*Ep. 205 ad Bonif*).

these trials with patience, culminating in flight from His native land—if in spite of this these lawless tribes continued to pursue Him, to slaughter the men, to pillage their property, and to capture their women and children, how would Christ have acted towards them? If this oppression had fallen only upon Himself He would have forgiven them, and such an act of forgiveness would have been most praiseworthy; but if He had seen that these cruel and bloodthirsty murderers wished to kill, to pillage and to injure all these oppressed ones, and to take captive the women and children, it is certain that He would have protected them and would have resisted the tyrants. What objection then, can be taken to Muḥammad's action? Is it this, that He did not with His followers, and their women and children, submit to these savage tribes? To free these tribes from their bloodthirstiness was the greatest kindness, and to coerce and restrain them was a true mercy.'555 This opinion is also shared by Fück: 'The fact that Muḥammad tolerated war has already given rise to sharp criticism. But one should not forget that he lived in a world where, to a great extent, the law of the jungle ruled and where robbery was considered an honest trade. At that time in Arabia there was no state which guaranteed through its institutions a secure existence to its citizens and which would have protected them against injustice within the country by its laws and against the outside world by its army. Under such circumstances Muhammad could not renounce the right of self-defence if he did not want to abandon to certain destruction the fruit of his efforts.'556

Now it is right to point out that after Muḥammad's death, the Arabs conquered Persia, Syria, Palestine and the whole of North Africa and—having gone as far as the Loire—established an empire in which Islám was the ruling religion, and that this expansion of Islám took place at the cost of Christianity which, especially in North Africa, lost its most flourishing communities. But this historic event was not caused by the religious zeal and the proselytism of the Muslims. The rise of the Arabs in the seventh century was a national event comparable to the migration of nations, the migration to the south of the Germanic tribes in quest of land. It was not a religious war. It is true that Islám was spread thereby, but not by a planned or even a forced conversion of the subdued peoples: 'Apart from exceptions' the orientalist C. H.

555. *Some Answered Questions*, VII.   556. *Saeculum*, vol. III, part 1, p. 89.

Becker emphasises, 'it did not occur to the Arabs at all in the beginning to convert the subjected peoples. In the manner of modern colonizers they wanted to have control over the mass of paying zealots.'[557] Scholars like Hugo Winkler,[558] Leone Caetani[559] and C. H. Becker[560] have convincingly proved that the motivating force underlying the expansion of Islamic dominion is to be sought not in religious but in economic causes. Becker writes: 'The expansion of Islam as a state can in no way be mainly attributed to religious enthusiasm. The redeeming idea elucidating for us the whole reorganisation of the Orient in the 7th century is that of mass migration . . . The Arab migration is . . . the last large Semitic migration of people who, coming from the Arab peninsula, the cradle of the Semites, poured into the civilised countries.' This migration was caused 'by a climate which has been altering throughout centuries and by the gradual desiccation of the land . . . It is not religious enthusiasm but hunger which drives the Arabs over the limits of their peninsula.'[561] Islám had no greater part in this event than the following: because of the teachings and work of Muḥammad, the Arabs, who had been carrying on numerous tribal feuds with each other, overcame the tribal jealousy which had made every joint venture impossible, attained unity as a nation and, by means of the enormous impulse of the new divine revelation, developed powers which enabled them to conquer a large part of the ancient world. Becker thinks that it is superfluous 'to enter into the particulars of the old nursery tale according to which the Arabs had forced their religion by the sword onto the Middle East'—the convenient main weapon of Christian polemics, for 'everywhere the subjected peoples enjoyed the free exercise of their religion, as long as they placed themselves politically under the supreme authority of the Arabic–Islamic state'.[562] 'At any rate, there was nothing to be seen of an urge to convert.'[563]

Christians and Jews in the Islamic state

The *Qur'án* gave binding instruction for the treatment of the subjected *dhimmís*, the Christians and the Jews: 'Make war upon such of those to whom the Scriptures have been given as believe not in

557. *Islamstudien*, vol. I, p. 6 ff.
558. *Arabisch–Semitisch–Orientalisch*, p. 52 ff.
559. *Annali dell'Islam*, II, A.H. 12, para. 105–17.
560. *Islamstudien*, vol. I, p. 6.
561. ibid., p. 7.   562. ibid., p. 6.   563. ibid., p. 69.

God, or in the last day . . . and who profess not the profession of the truth, until they pay tribute out of hand, and they be humbled.'[564] For payment of a moderate poll-tax (*jizyah*) which exempted them from military service and to which only men fit for service and able to pay were liable,[565] and for the payment of $2\frac{1}{2}$ per cent of their annual income instead of the alms-tax binding on the Muslims, they were entitled to protection against any enemy.[566] Otherwise they were in every respect equal to the Muslims who did not have to pay any poll-tax but had, instead, to do military service. In particular, they were allowed to practise their religion as they pleased. Never did Islám want—like the Church—to convert the world, but 'only to be the ruling religion and to be acknowledged as such. Wherever this is the case, it tolerates believers of other religions.'[567] Becker stresses the fact that it is 'impossible to talk of fanaticism against Christianity'. 'Religious war against the Christians does not therefore carry the catchword "death or Islam" but it merely wants to achieve the recognition of Islamic authority, whilst freedom in religious practice is granted.'[568] There is an obvious financial reason why the Arab Muslims did not force the conversion of the subjected Christians and Jews, but even impeded it:[569] the Muslims did not have to pay any tax apart from the alms-tax in the first few centuries. Therefore the basis of the Arab financial administration was first and foremost the poll-tax imposed on the non-Muslims. With each able-bodied Jew or Christian who converted to Islám, a tax-payer was lost.[570] Financial reasons have always wielded great power! According to Becker: 'In the territories first conquered by the Arabs, recognition of the Islamic state was enforced by the sword; but the acceptance of the Islamic religion was totally voluntary; it was even not wished for, because the Islamic state economically presupposed a large number of non-Islamic subjects. Only in a very small measure can one therefore talk of the expansion of the religion by the sword. The conquest of the old world by the Arabs

564. *Qur'án* 9:29.

565. Women, children and old people were excluded, as they were not fought against.

566. Only those who had not voluntarily surrendered were deprived of this mild treatment. Their landed property was shared out among the Muslims.

567. E. Giese, *Die Toleranz im Islam*, p. 10.

568. C. H. Becker, *Islamstudien*, vol. I, p. 397.

569. Sigrid Hunke, *Allahs Sonne über dem Abendland*, p. 199.

570. Becker, *Islamstudien*, pp. 108–109.

was not the same as converting it to Islam.'[571] Thus in Egypt after 500 years of Islamic rule the Muslims formed only 50 per cent of the whole population.[572] The fact that the Christians of Syria and Egypt, and those of the Coptic and Monophysite churches, joyfully welcomed the invasion of the Muslim conquerors is due to the century-long persecutions of these minority groups by the orthodox Church,[573] especially under the Emperor Heraclius, who had sent an army against Muḥammad and had thus caused the Arab campaign of conquest.[574] The treaty which Caliph 'Umar entered into with the city of Jerusalem is an example of the manner in which Christians were treated by their Islamic rulers. It reads:

> In the name of God, the Merciful, the Compassionate. This treaty is valid for all Christian subjects, priests, monks and nuns. It guarantees them security and protection wherever they may be. As Caliph we are bound by our duty to secure protection for ourselves and our followers and for all Christian subjects discharging their duties. Suitable protection is assured to their [Christian] churches, houses and places of pilgrimage as well as to those who visit these places: the Georgians, Abyssinians, Jacobites, Nestorians and all those who recognise the Prophet Jesus. All these deserve respect, as they have been formerly honoured in a writ from the Prophet Muhammad under which he placed his seal and which emphatically commanded us to be benevolent to them and to grant them protection. Accordingly it is our duty as head of all true believers to show benevolence, and this as a sign of devotion towards him who already showed his graciousness and grace to you. Accordingly as pilgrims in all Muslim lands, by sea and on land they are exempt from the payment of all duties, taxes and of the poll-tax. When they enter the Church of the Holy Sepulchre and during their entire pilgrimage no manner of tax is to be levied against them . . . Whoever has read this treaty and acts against it or deals with them in defiance of this treaty between today and the Day of Judgment breaks the Covenant with God, and that of his well-loved Prophet . . .'[575]

571. Becker, *Islamstudien*, p. 332.
572. Sir Abdullah Suhrawardy, *The Sayings of Muḥammad*, pp. 47–8.
573. Becker, *Islamstudien*, p. 399.
574. Fück in the magazine *Saeculum*, vol. III, part 1, p. 93.
575. Quoted by Rudolf Jockel, *Islamische Geisteswelt*, p. 75.

When Jerusalem was taken, 'Umar had marched in by the side of
Patriarch Sophronius and had left all shrines and churches un-
touched, whereas the Christian Heraclius had massacred the Jews
during the former invasion of the city. The same scene repeated
itself in the Crusades. In 1099 when Jerusalem was taken, the
crusaders caused a terrible slaughter among the native population
during which Jews and Muslims were killed and burnt. When in
1187 Saladin wrested the city from the crusaders, he shamed the
Christian world by allowing the Christian priests to take away
with them all their church property. In an instruction left by
'Umar in his will 'nothing is more emphatically recommended to
his successor than that he should refrain from violence towards
his non-Muslim charges, indeed, rather should he, himself, take
up arms to ensure their protection'.[576] As recently as the last
century people pointed to the site of the 'Jew's house' near Bostra
of which legend reports that in its place a mosque had been stand-
ing which 'Umar had pulled down because its governor had
seized the house of a Jew by force in order to build a mosque in
its stead.[577] Later Islamic theology, too, places injury of a *dhimmi*
on the same level as that of a Muslim. The Meccan teacher of law
Ibn Ḥadschar al-Hejtamí (d. 973 A.H.) includes it among the capital sins.[578]

The fact that adherents of other faiths were treated by the
Muslims according to these legal and religious instructions inspired by the spirit of tolerance, was also acknowledged by contemporary Christians and was widely testified: 'What we believe
concerning the Muslims', Eliyya, Bishop of Nasibin (1008–49)
writes, 'is that their obedience and love impresses us more than
the obedience of all other religions and kingdoms that are opposed
to us, whether we are in their land or not and whether they treat
us well or not. And that is because the Muslims regard it as a
matter of religion and duty to protect us, to honour us, and to
treat us well. And whosoever of them oppresses us, their Master,
i.e. their Prophet, will be his adversary on the Day of Resurrection.'[579] A Syrian source from the end of the seventh century,
commonly known as the Chronicle of Arbela, reports the victories

576. Goldziher, op. cit., pp. 34 and 312, note 16.
577. J. L. Porter, *Five Years in Damasus*, London, 1870, p. 235.
578. Goldziher, p. 34.
579. M. Searle Bates, *Religious Liberty*, p. 263.

of the Arabs over the Persians and the Romans and offers interesting details about the events and conditions of that epoch. It emphasises that freedom of belief existed under the reign of the Umayyad Caliph Mu'áwíyah, and that unfortunately the 'damned heretics'—by which term the Monophysites were meant—'had used that freedom to gain power'.[580] 'They are just', writes the Patriarch of Jerusalem to the Patriarch of Constantinople in the ninth century, 'and do not treat us with any injustice or any kind of violence.'[581]

The good relationship existing between Muslims and Christians in the Islamic state is proved by the fact that in the first decades Muslims did not hesitate to hold a religious service with Christians in the same building, and that at all times, especially in the first few centuries, the Christians rose to the highest political positions —even to the viziership—without having to recant their faith. Even during the crusades, as religious antagonism intensified exceedingly, Christian officials were not a rarity.[582] In Egypt, Christian festivals were partly days of rejoicing for the Islamic population, too. Even in the eleventh century, ecclesiastical funeral processions could circulate through the streets with all the emblems of a Christian religious service, disturbances being an exception, as the chroniclers record.[583] The historian Laurence Browne writes: 'The few instances we have been able to quote of Muslims and Christians joining in each other's festivals are probably significant of a great deal of daily contact . . . Christians and Muslims probably lived on fairly friendly terms up to the time of the Turkish invasion of the eleventh century, and even on into the thirteenth century.'[584]

The Jews received the same treatment. It was under Islamic rule in Spain that medieval Judaism—against which an unscrupulous war of extermination had been previously waged by Christian orthodoxy[585]—experienced its greatest flowering and where its greatest philosopher Rabbi Moshe Ben Maimon (Maimonides) taught. When at the end of the fifteenth century Spain once more

580. Nöldeke in *Zeitschrift für Assyrologie*, vol. 30, 1915, p. 120.
581. Quoted by Hunke, *Allahs Sonne über dem Abendland*, p. 199.
582. Becker, *Islamstudien*, p. 398.
583. Becker, op. cit.
584. Laurence E. Browne, *The Eclipse of Christianity in Asia*, p. 136, quoted by Bates, *Religious Liberty*, p. 263.
585. Becker, *Islamstudien*, p. 121.

came under Catholic dominion, the spirit of tolerance and indulgence was over. Now the government no longer operated according to Muḥammad's command: 'Let there be no compulsion in religion', but after the motto which the Curia Cardinal Ottaviani still defended in the Second Vatican Ecumenical Council: 'No freedom for error.' Sigrid Hunke describes the change in the spiritual atmosphere which ensued with the end of Arab dominion in Spain: 'When on the 2nd of January Cardinal D. Pedro Gonzalez de Mendoza planted the cross on the Alhambra, the red royal castle of the Nasrids, it was not only Arab dominion in Spain that ended ... Under Archbishop Juan Ximenez the Muslims and the rest of their flowering culture sank in a sea of terror, in which waves of religious fanaticism devoured everything: every time they expressed their faith, every time they used their language, at every word, every song, every time they played their instruments, used their surname, their national costume, or visited the baths, they were sent to the galleys, imprisoned, persecuted, even burnt alive. Whatever the conquering Christians or Berbers had not yet destroyed among the treasures of Arabic science and poetry was dragged out of all the libraries and hiding-places by the Archbishop's bailiffs and huge piles were thrown to the flames ... Through mass-expulsions and the fury of the *autodafé*[586] the most flourishing land of that part of the world was depopulated and in a short time had once more become a desert.'[587]

The Ottoman Turks who had conquered extensive Christian dominions also followed the principles of the *Qur'án*. After the flight of the Spanish Jews to Constantinople the chief Rabbi was recognised as the head of the Jewish community. The Greek Orthodox Church was politically recognised. In spiritual matters the non-Islamic religious communities were autonomous and all had their own jurisdiction.[588] Giese writes about the situation in the Ottoman state: 'The Christians could freely pursue their affairs and practise their religion without the Ottoman state bothering about it, as long as they paid their taxes ... and did not cause any trouble ... the situation which was brought about, was really satisfactory for the subjected peoples. They enjoyed a tolerance which, in those days, was far from existing in any Christian state

586. Literally 'act of faith'!
587. Hunke, *Allahs Sonne über dem Abendland*, pp. 345–6.
588. Giese, *Die Toleranz im Islam*, p. 22.

and were much happier than before when under Byzantine or Catholic dominion.'[589]

It is therefore not surprising that Jews and Christians fled to Islamic countries during the Middle Ages and even in modern times in order to escape the persecutions of the Church, as for example in 714 when Emperor Leo had the Jews baptised by force. Spanish Jews sought protection in Turkey at the end of the fifteenth century. For a long time the Calvinists preferred the domination of the Turks to that of the Catholic Habsburgs. In the seventeenth century Protestants from Silesia fled to countries under Turkish rule.[590] Also in the seventeenth century, Makarios, the Patriarch of Antioch, publicly denounced the cruelties suffered by Orthodox Russians at the hand of Catholic Poles: 'May God render the rule of the Turks eternal! For they collect their taxes and do not meddle with the religious affairs of their Christian and Jewish subjects.'[591]

These peaceful mutual relationships created a flourishing culture. Sigrid Hunke writes about the outstanding fecundity of this spiritual world: 'Scholars of all confessions now work together and help cultivate Arabic learning, in the same way as the scriptures of the Muslims, Christians, Jews and Sabeans stand next to each other in Arab libraries. And the same spirit of tolerance which does not despise the Christian as a teacher[592] is ready also to turn to the heathens and to draw from the mighty fountains of Greek and Indian wisdom.'[593]

In view of the cultural, religious and political history of many European countries right up to the present day, the conditions in the medieval Islamic state seem to us amazing. But the immense significance of the tolerance towards other religions ordained by Muḥammad and practised by the Muslims only becomes fully clear to us when we contrast it with the attitude of the Church to tolerance and with the treatment of non-Christians in the Christian West.[594]

589. Giese, *Die Toleranz im Islam*, p. 22.
590. Bates, *Religious Liberty*, p. 266.
591. Quoted by Giese, op. cit., p. 24.
592. Whereas in the second third of the twentieth century the Church was still fighting by all legal means possible to retain denominational schools!
593. op. cit., p. 102; compare also p. 231.
594. Unlike the *Qur'án*, the *Bible* does not contain any directions about the treatment of the followers of other revealed religions. With the exception of Judaism which according to Christian understanding is part of the story of the Salvation of

Footnote 594 *continued.*

Man, all non-Christian religions were looked upon as human usurpation until the twentieth century. The Protestant theologian Karl Barth describes them as 'religions of deceit'. This attitude affected the way Christians treated members of these religions, especially followers of Judaism and Islám. The Muslims, by their claim to be in possession of a post-Christian revelation, were a particular provocation to Christians. The Jews, who had bloodily persecuted the new Christian community, were themselves persecuted once Christianity became the state religion, on account of their having rejected and killed Christ. Until the nineteenth century it was hardly possible to live as a Muslim under Christian rule and openly profess Islám. With the reconquest of Spain by the Catholics at the end of the fifteenth century Islám was driven out of Spain root and branch.

The persecutions of the Jews from the early Middle Ages until the twentieth century were in no wise attacks from individuals but actions which had their root in the teachings of the Church. St. Justin in the *Dialogue with the Jew Tryphon* calls the Jews terrible people, spiritually ill, idolaters, cunning and sly, unjust, lacking in reason, hard-hearted and devoid of understanding. He maintains that they fornicate, that they are completely wicked, that their wickedness goes beyond all bounds, that all the water of the sea would not suffice to purify them; that they incite other peoples against the Christians and are not only guilty of the wrong which they themselves commit 'but also of that done by all other men' (quoted by Deschner, *Abermals krähte der Hahn*, p. 446). St. Cyprian taught the Christians to say the Lord's Prayer against the Jews: 'When he says "Father", the Christian should remember that the Jews do not have God, but the devil as their father' (quoted by Schneider, *Das Frühchristentum als antisemitische Bewegung*, 1940, p. 16). The Father of the Church St. Chrysostom accused the Jews of robbery and stealing, called the synagogue a brothel, a den of cut-throats, a refuge for vile animals, and described the Jews as 'pigs and goats' (quoted by Deschner, *Abermals krähte der Hahn*, p. 447). During the whole of the Middle Ages the Jews were suppressed by order of the synods. At the end of the sixth century in Merovingian Franconia, even compulsory baptism, mass deportations and burning down of synagogues became normal. The sixth synod of Toledo ordered in 638 that all Jews living in Spain should be baptized. The Archbishop Agobart of Lyon (d. 840), a Catholic saint, already anticipated the ill-famed Nazi slogan 'do not buy at any Jew's' (Deschner, *Abermals krähte der Hahn*, p. 453). The seventeenth synod of Toledo declared in 694 that, because of the abuse of Christ's blood, all Jews were slaves. Their possessions were confiscated, and their children taken away from them as soon as they were seven years old.

In Germany the persecutions of the Jews began with the crusades. 'What use is it to seek out the enemies of Christianity in far-away regions, when the blasphemous Jews, who are far worse than the Saracens, are allowed in our midst to abuse Christ and the sacraments', the crusaders argued (quoted by Deschner, *Abermals krähte der Hahn*, p. 454). Over the centuries it came to banishments, bloody persecutions and burnings alive.

Legal history shows what the Christians thought of non-Christians. The lawyer Doepler posed the question: 'When a Christian has sexual intercourse with a Jewess or a Jew with a Christian woman, whether this is also to be considered an act of sodomy and is therefore to be punished by death?' (Hans Berkenhoff, *Tierstrafe, Tierbannung und rechtsrituelle Tiertötung im Mittelalter*, p. 43). He was of the opinion that although the case was different (in nature), the act was still to be looked upon as sodomy like the familiar association with Turks and Saracens 'as such people cannot in any way be differentiated from animals in the eyes of the Law and of the holy Faith' (H. v. Hentig, *Soziologie der zoophilen Neigung*, p. 38). The intercourse of a Christian with a Jew was punished as an act of sodomy. The Dutch scholars De

Footnote 594 *continued.*
Damhouder and Wielant, too, put the intimate association with Turks, Saracens and Jews on a par with that of dogs or of a dead woman (H. v. Hentig, ibid.), an act which was punished by the death sentence for the Christian partner as well.

This was the fruit of century-long defamations by the Fathers of the Church and Popes against the Jews who were not willing to be converted. Pope Leo the Great had called them 'abominable and detestable', Pope Stephen 'dogs', and Innocent III in 1205 called them 'slaves accursed in the eyes of God'.

The Reformation did not bring about any change either. Luther, who believed the Jews to be 'worse than a sow' (Quoted in W. Maurer, *Kirche und Synagoge*, p. 103 ff.) was a raving antisemite who used a language which Julius Streicher's *Stürmer* (a notorious Nazi agitation-paper of anti-semitic character) drew from: 'These Jews are such a desperate, utterly wicked and corrupted and bedevilled sort that for these last 1,400 years they have been and still are our torment, pestilence and all our misfortune. *Summa* they are proper devils' (*Erlanger Ausgabe*, XXXII, p. 242). 'Here in Wittenberg in our parish church there is a sow carved in stone; under it lie young piglets and Jews, which are sucking; behind the sow stands a rabbi who lifts up the right leg of the sow and with his left hand pulls the tail over himself, he bends down and with eagerness looks under the tail of the sow into the Talmud as if he wanted to read and observe something exact and important . . . The Germans say of a person who, for no apparent reason, pretends great intelligence: where did he get it from? To talk bluntly, from the backside of the sow' (*Erlanger Ausgabe*, XXXII, p. 298). In his essay 'About the Jews and their lies', he wrote: 'I want to give a piece of sincere advice. First that their synagogues be set on fire . . . Second that their houses be pulled down and destroyed, too . . . Third that all their prayer-booklets be taken away from them . . . Fourth that their rabbis be forbidden to teach any more at the risk of losing their life. Fifth that freedom of movement and the right to go out in the streets be completely removed from the Jews . . . Sixth that they be forbidden to practise usury and that all ready money and valuables in gold and silver be taken away from them . . . Seventh that the young, strong Jews and Jewesses be given axes, picks, shovels and spindles in the hand and be made to earn their bread by the .sweat of their noses . . . But if we fear that they could do us some harm if they have to work and serve us . . . let us get back from them what they have extorted from us by usury and then drive them out of the land for ever' (*Erlanger Ausgabe*, XXXII, p. 233 ff.). These are the words of one of the men who had a lasting influence on the way of thinking and the character of the Germans. 'What Hitler did, Luther had recommended' is Karl Jaspers' opinion (*Die grossen nichtchristlichen Religionen unserer Zeit in Einzeldarstellungen*, p. 123).

The persecutions of the Jews by the Christians lasted until the nineteenth century and continued in Russia until the twentieth century. Equality of rights in the state came into being only under the influence of the Enlightenment. The Christian anti-semitism of the Middle Ages which had its root in Christian theology was followed in the nineteenth century by the racially-founded philosophy (Maurer *Kirche und Synagoge*, p. 9) that, in the recent past, with the annihilation of six million Jews, has demonstrated that it is an explosive force which has outlived centuries.

Even during the persecutions of the Jews under Hitler Protestant Churches in Germany renounced their baptized Jewish members. On 17 December 1941 the bishops and presidents of the Synods of Saxony, Mecklenburg, Schleswig-Holstein, Anhalt, Thüringen and Lübeck published a declaration in which, with reference to Martin Luther, they defined the Jews as the 'born enemies of the world and of the empire' and demanded the strictest measures to be taken against them: 'Christian baptism will change nothing of the racial character, the national membership and biological nature of the Jew. A German Protestant church has the duty to look after

Intolerance in the period of decadence

As we draw nearer the period of decadence in Islám we find complaints being raised about the treatment of Christians and Jews. In the first few centuries restrictions such as the interdiction against the ringing of church bells or the building of churches higher than the mosque, etc. were temporary occurrences under narrow-minded rulers such as 'Umar II or the 'Abbasid Caliph al-Mutawakkil, a 'repulsive bigot, who knew well how to reconcile a wine-bibbing drunkard's life, immoderate sensuality and the encouraging of obscene literature with dogmatic orthodoxy'.[595] As proselytism and religious hatred[596] began to emerge in Islám,

---

and promote the religious life of fellow Germans. Christians of the Jewish race have no place and no right in it. This is why the undersigned Protestant churches and church-leaders have cleared every community of Jewish Christians' (Evidence by J. Kahl, *Das Elend des Christentums*, p. 41).

Tolerance is the fruit of the Enlightenment so reviled by the Church. Erhard put the question first in 1604: *an diversae religiones in bene constituta republica tolerandae*. In 1602 the jurist Burckhardt in his work *De Autonomia* had answered in the negative the question whether 'the freedom to choose among the different religions and faiths . . . should be granted and allowed by the Christian authorities'. It was only when the Peace of Westphalia was signed that the various Christian confessions were equally tolerated. Frederick the Great, who was the first monarch to abolish torture from the very beginning of his reign and who, for this act alone, has earned the title 'the Great', is the first authoritative representative of a policy of tolerance. From him comes the famous marginal note: 'All religions must be tolerated and the state must only watch that none of them injures the other for, in this matter, each one must find salvation in his own way.' In his treatise *De la Religion de Brandenburg*, he writes: 'False religious zeal is a tyrant that depopulates the provinces; tolerance is a loving mother who cares for them and promotes their prosperity.' Tolerance has gradually been enforced since 1848.

The Catholic Church abandoned its traditional standpoint (in spite of the embittered opposition of an influential minority) in the Second Vatican Ecumenical Council and accepted the principle of religious freedom. The Vatican Council studied 'the sacred tradition and teaching of the Church—the treasury, from which she brings forth new things ever in harmony with the old' (*Declaration on Religious Liberty*, no. 1), and declared 'that the individual has the right to religious liberty. This type of liberty means that every man should be immune from coercion from individuals, from social groups or any human authority: in religious matters no one should be forced to act against his conscience or prevented from acting according to his conscience privately or in public, whether alone or in company with others, within due limits' (ibid., no. 2). Not only the individual but also the communities 'have a right to immunity in order that they may organize their lives in their own way. They are entitled to honour the supreme Godhead with public worship' (ibid., no. 4). This right, as the Church acknowledges, 'is based on the dignity of the individual' (ibid., no. 9).

595. Goldziher, op. cit., p. 111; about this question see also p. 33; Becker, *Islam-studien*, p. 398.

596. Hunke, op. cit., p. 199.

the cause of oppression[597] was mostly to be found in acts of violence by minor governors who, on account of the weakness of the central government, were not punished for their crimes. In connection with this, Becker's statement 'that Christian influence was the first to call forth opposition against Christianity' is interesting. Becker is of the opinion that intolerance towards believers of other religions had never been so great in the Christian world as at that time, and that Christianity taught this attitude to Islám.[598] This opinion is shared by the outstanding Islamic scholar Leone Caetani who wrote: 'In the initial period the Arabs were not fanatical, but associated in an almost brotherly manner with their Christian semitic cousins; but, however, after these had rapidly become Muslims too, they brought into the new religion that implacability, that blind hostility against the Byzantine faith in which they had previously left Eastern Christianity to languish.'[599]

The Bahá'ís do not have much reason to intercede for the idea of the tolerance of Islám, after the bitter experience which they have undergone in the cradle of their Faith through the fanaticism of the Islamic clergy who stirred up the Muslim believers. But Muḥammad can be held as little responsible for these actions as Jesus for the inquisition and the witch-burnings of the Church. Fanaticism, proselytism and religious hatred are defective human attitudes and sure signs that the living spirit of the Faith has left the body of the religion and that nothing is left but the dead letter. It is not surprising, therefore, that in Shí'ah Persia,[600] the most backward of all Islamic countries in the nineteenth century, Muḥammad's command to let no compulsion be used in religion was so grievously neglected.

Faith, necessary for salvation

According to the *Qur'án*, man's acceptance or rejection of the message of God is a matter of great import. 'Believe in God and

597. Giese, op. cit., p. 29.
598. op. cit., p. 398.
599. *Das historische Studium des Islams*, p. 9.
600. Goldziher emphasises that Shí'ah Islám was much narrower in the interconfessional interpretation of law than Sunní Islám: 'When we further recognize that the broad- or narrow-mindedness of religious view-points are evaluated mainly by the degree of tolerance shown towards followers of other doctrines, the Shí'ah branch of Islám must be placed on a lower rank in comparison with the Sunní branch' (p. 234).

his apostle, and bestow in alms of that whereof God hath made you heirs: for whoever among you believe and give alms—theirs shall be a great recompense.'[601] Faith is a necessary condition for salvation. In this respect there is no difference from the Gospels, which state: 'He that believeth and is baptised shall be saved; but he that believeth not shall be damned'[602] and 'For God sent not his Son into the world to condemn the world; but that the world through him might be saved. He that believeth in him is not condemned: but he that believeth not is condemned already, because he hath not believed in the name of the only begotten Son of God.'[603]

But there is a difference in the consequences which can be drawn from this. According to the concept of the Church, salvation is granted only to the believer who is a member of the institution of the Church as the mystical reality of Christ. Therefore not only are the Jews and the heathen condemned and, according to the dogma expressly proclaimed at the Council of Florence, will all go to hell,[604] but so are all heretics and schism-mongers. For the Church alone can lead to salvation. 'He cannot have God as father who does not have the Church as mother'; 'He is not a Christian, who does not belong to the Church of Christ'; 'Outside the Church there is no salvation'. This is what St. Cyprian, the Father of the Church, used to teach. And St. Augustine taught: 'When thou standest outside the Church and art cut off from the bond of unity and the ties of love, thou succumbest to the eternal punishment of hell, even shouldst thou let thyself be burnt for the sake of Christ.'[605] Boniface VIII decreed *ex cathedra* that it is necessary for every human being who would be saved to put himself under the protection of the Roman pontiff.

The *Qur'án* teaches that the godless who 'know the outward shews of this life present' but who 'of the next life are careless',[606] who talk, joke, play and are full of gay heedlessness, obeying whatever their senses dictate, are condemned. This is why the hour of judgment will take them by surprise as they carry on living, heedless and unaware.[607]

601. *Qur'án* 57:7; compare also 48:29.
602. Mark 16:16.   603. John 3:17–18.
604. See Friedrich Heiler, *Der Katholizismus, Seine Idee und seine Erscheinung*, p. 316, note 33.
605. *Epistulae* 173:6.   606. *Qur'án* 30:6.
607. 'In the name of God, the Compassionate, the Merciful. The desire of increasing riches occupieth you, till ye come to the grave. Nay! but in the end ye shall

But the verdict of damnation is not delivered upon the members of the other revealed religions.[608] They belong to the greater community of believers and have their share of eternal life. This is why the name 'Muslim' in the *Qur'án* does not apply solely to the followers of Muḥammad and his revelation but in general to those who were devoted believers in one of God's revealed religions.[609] Islám never claimed to be the unique source of salvation for man. It only claims to be God's last and most perfect revelation to mankind.

The symbolism of concepts about life after death

The 'joys of heaven', those (apparently) grossly sensual descriptions given in the *Qur'án* about heaven, are looked upon with suspicion by Christian believers. In Islám, heaven is the garden of Eden where the servants of the Almighty shall hear no vain discourse 'but only "Peace"', where 'their food shall be given them at morn and even'[610] where they will dwell in the company of the prophets, the righteous, the martyrs and the pious, the garden ''neath which the rivers flow',[611] where the believers are well protected, 'therein no weariness shall reach them, nor forth from it shall they be cast for ever',[612] the garden wherein they shall 'have wives of perfect purity'.[613] It is obviously the dark-eyed heavenly companions, the '*houris*', who arouse the suspicions of the Christians about the joys of heaven promised in the *Qur'án*. But the *Qur'án* does not promise a dissolute life after death, for the black-eyed beauties are virgins and behave modestly in a chaste manner.

---

know—Nay, once more, in the end ye shall know your folly. Nay! Would that ye knew it with knowledge of certainty! Surely ye shall see hell-fire. Then shall ye surely see it with the eye of certainty; then shall ye on that day be taken to task concerning pleasures' (*Qur'án*, súrah 102). 'Shall he then who is a believer be as he who sinneth grossly? They shall not be held alike. As to those who believe and do that which is right, they shall have gardens of eternal abode as the meed of their works: but as for those who grossly sin, their abode shall be the fire' (32:19–21). 'In the name of God, the Compassionate, the Merciful. I swear by the declining day! Verily, man's lot is cast amid destruction, save those who believe and do the things which are right, and enjoin truth and enjoin steadfastness on each other' (súrah 103).

608. 'Verily, they who believe (Muslims), and they who follow the Jewish religion, and the Christians, and the Sabeites—whoever of these believeth in God and the last day, and doeth that which is right, shall have their reward with their Lord: fear shall not come upon them, neither shall they be grieved' (*Qur'án* 2:59).

609. Rudolf Jockel, *Islamische Geisteswelt*, p. 315; so for instance Abraham is called a Muslim (*Qur'án* 3:68).

610. *Qur'án* 19:62.   611. ibid., 9:73 and 2:23.
612. ibid., 15:48.   613. ibid., 2:23.

In many passages the *Qur'án* enjoins believers of both sexes to obey the law of chastity and exhorts them to shun an incontinent life. Of course in some ways the joys of heaven appear to be sensual. But they are all allegories by which Muḥammad seeks to familiarise his people—inhabitants of the desert!—with the concept of paradise. In contrast to the Jews, Greeks and Romans, the people addressed by Muḥammad were uncivilised, barbaric and unaware of spiritual truth. How could he make these people understand the believer's life in 'heaven' other than through symbols which reflected their ideals: meadows, streams, springs and the like? Muḥammad himself calls this sensual description of heaven and hell an allegory: 'A picture of the Paradise which is promised to the God-fearing!'[614] Ṣúfism is an example of the heights later reached by Islamic mystics in their understanding of God. They, too, have expressed the metaphysical, spiritual realities by means of sensual allegories; for instance, the famous lovers Laylí and Majnún were symbols of the mystic journey and the search for truth.

Revelation is indeed dependent upon the conditions prevalent in the period of history in which it appears. Revealed truths are clothed in a mantle suitable to the period concerned. This fact is duly stressed by modern Christian theologians. In Christianity, too, the modern concept which regards heaven and hell as spiritual states was the result of a development approaching our modern understanding of life. As long as heaven and hell were considered to be places—that is until very recently—statements concerning them often included traits of primitive mythology. And while the torments of the sinner were painted in vivid colours, allusions made to the spiritual joys bestowed upon the dweller of Paradise were less abundant. A special joy for the saved—and this could be taken as an objection against the Christian concept of the celestial joys—is to observe the torments and misery of the damned, heaven's 'greatest attraction', as Karl-Heinz Deschner sarcastically observes.[615] Tertullian,[616] Cyprian and Lactantius depicted these 'joys' in glowing colours and Thomas Aquinas taught: 'In order that they better appreciate sal-

614. *Qur'án* 47:16.

615. *Abermals krähte der Hahn*, p. 110.

616. 'What kind of spectacle will be there?' he said referring to hell, 'What will be the object of my astonishment, of my laughter? Where is the place of my rejoicing, my exultance?' (Deschner, op. cit.).

vation and that they be more thankful to God for it, the saved
ones may watch the punishments suffered by the damned ones.'[617]
In comparison, the heaven described by the *Qur'án* can easily be
accepted.

The status of women in Islám

Another subject criticised and attacked by Christian theologians
was the position of woman in Islám. A closer look at the conditions prevailing in Muḥammad's time leads to a different conclusion.

One cannot deny that, according to Qur'ánic law, marriage
reflects a patriarchal system. In this respect, Islám is different
neither from Judaism nor from Christianity. The *Qur'án* indubit-
ably gives more rights to men than to women as far as inheritance,
witness-deposition, polygamy and divorce are concerned. But this
was only a 'concession made to the hard-heartedness and brutality
of the male who was still emerging out of the pagan way of life'.[618]
This concession must be understood as the Prophet's struggle
against ancient Arab paganism reflected in his legislation. Any
kind of legislation is dependent upon the prevailing structures and
must take them into account. Muḥammad could not at a stroke
lead his people out of the barbarism of the past ages into the way
of thinking and living which are appropriate today. In the context
of ancient Arabic paganism, the Qur'ánic prescriptions (which
also forbade the barbaric pagan practice of burying new-born baby
girls alive) meant a significant improvement of the social and legal
position of women. This is also true of the polygamy permitted by
Muḥammad which has caused so much consternation in the West
where monogamy is legally the rule.[619] To critics one may answer
that Muḥammad did not introduce polygamy but rather greatly
restricted it by limiting the number of wives to four: 'Of women
who seem good in your eyes, marry but two, or three or four; and
if ye still fear that ye shall not act equitably, then one only . . . this
will make justice on your part easier.'[620] From the early days,

617. See Deschner, ibid.

618. Al-Anisa Nazira Zainaddin, *Al-fatáh wásh-shnyúkh*, Beirut, 1348/1929 (quoted
by Rudi Paret, *Zur Frauenfrage in der arabisch-islamischen Welt*, p. 31). Compare also
Matthew 19:8.

619. From the beginning the actual situation here has amounted to illegal polygamy.

620. *Qur'án* 4:3.

there have been Islamic commentators who, from this exhortation to marry only one wife in order to protect oneself against injustice, drew the conclusion that, in fact, Muḥammad had encouraged union with one woman only, as it is impossible to treat several wives justly. The following verse supports this interpretation: 'And ye will not have it at all in your power to treat your wives alike, even though you fain would do so.'[621] The representatives of the Islamic women's rights movement refer to these passages of the Scriptures in their discussions with conservative theologians.[622] In view of the conditions of that time Muḥammad could not abolish polygamy any more than he could do away with slavery. The time was not yet ripe for that action. For, as Georg Christoph Lichtenberg once remarked: 'To want to do everything all at once is to destroy everything all at once.' Muḥammad could only mitigate both institutions and eliminate their abuses. And this he did.

However antiquated it may appear to us today, the right of divorce granted by the *Qur'án* was also a great step forward in relation to the state of affairs found by Muḥammad. The woman was no longer prey to man's despotism but attained a secure legal position. Limits were imposed on the male's power, his right of repudiation was checked, his responsibilities to support the woman he had divorced were stipulated and the right of divorce by means of legal action was introduced for women. Like Moses,[623] Muḥammad too, taking into consideration the 'hard-heartedness' of men,[624] allowed divorce in the form of a one-sided repudiation. But on the other hand, according to the Islamic concept, divorce is heinous to God. As Muḥammad once said, of all that is legally permitted, divorce is the institution God abhors most.[625]

One cannot deny that to a certain extent the legal practice led to grave abuses, but it was Islamic lawyers who were responsible for these abuses as they tightened up the laws on divorce in favour of the man by means of an exegesis which was often inclined to split hairs. On the whole, divorce is looked upon as a necessary evil which should be avoided as far as possible. Besides it is a fact that in Islamic countries divorce is less frequent than in European states or in the U.S.A.

---

621. *Qur'án* 4:128.   622. Rudi Paret, op. cit., p. 29 ff.
623. Deuteronomy 24:1 ff.   624. Matthew 19:8.
625. N. Zainaddin, quoted by Rudi Paret, op. cit., p. 59.

The fact that men and women receive different legal treatment in the *Qur'án* does not in the least mean that they are not equal before God. The authority of men is relevant to the external circumstances of this earthly life only. Before God, men and women are equal. In the Scriptures women are not spiritually or intellectually inferior. In rank they are men's equals.[626] Muḥammad enjoins upon the believers a moral concept of marriage and commands men to treat women with 'kindness, friendliness and justice'.[627]

History provides plenty of evidence to show that Muslim women were often not treated with justice. There are two institutions in particular which have oppressed Muslim women for centuries and which have been rightly criticised by Europeans: the inhuman obligation for women to wear the veil and their confinement within the home. Women must leave the house as little as possible and must remain confined in their apartments as long as there are male visitors in the house. If they go out they must cover not only their arms and neck but also their face with a veil which falls down from their forehead and leaves only two holes for the eyes. But all Islamic scholars agree that neither the wearing of the veil nor confinement were desired by Muḥammad. These institutions cannot be traced back to the *Qur'án*, to the traditions or to the consensus.[628] There are four passages in the *Qur'án* which at a superficial glance seem to urge the wearing of the veil and confinement. They are súrahs 33:32 ff., 33:53, 33:59 and 24:31. Apart from the fact that the obligation to wear the veil cannot be derived from the verses of súrah 33, it is out of the question that they should be taken as the basis of this institution because according to their wording they refer to the prophet's

626. 'And one of his signs it is, that He hath created wives for you of your own species, that ye may dwell with them and hath put love and tenderness between you. Herein truly are signs for those who reflect' (*Qur'án* 30:20); compare also 4:3. 'I will not suffer the work of him among you that worketh, whether of male or female, to be lost' (3:193). 'Truly the men who resign themselves to God, and the women who resign themselves, and the believing men and the believing women and the devout men and the devout women, and the men of truth and the women of truth, and the patient men and the patient women, and the humble men and the humble women, and the men who give alms and the women who give alms, and the men who fast and the women who fast, and the chaste men and the chaste women, and the men and the women who oft remember God: for them hath God prepared forgiveness and a rich recompense' (33:35).

627. Tor Andrae, op. cit., p. 268.

628. See p. 151, note 455.

wives only. Súrah 24, verse 31 reads: 'And speak to the believing women that they refrain their eyes, and observe continence; and that they display not their ornaments, except those which are external and that they throw their veils over their bosoms, and display not their ornaments, except to their husbands or their fathers, or their husbands' fathers, or their sons; ... or male domestics, who have no natural force, or to children who note not women's nakedness ...'. The question was to know where the feminine charms which have to be covered up begin. Muḥammad spoke of the bosom, so the Muslim woman did not originally wear a veil. The Arab woman of the first centuries was in no way repressed or in bondage. Muḥammad's wife, the confident, quick-witted, intelligent Khadíjah, who took part in public life, was a leading example of the Arab aristocracy. In conformity with the Prophet's exhortations that women, too, should seek education and knowledge, important lawyers demanded that women be granted the permission to exercise the office of judge. Sigrid Hunke writes on this subject: 'Women lawyers are seen appearing in the mosques to hold public lectures and expound laws. Among them there is a political lawyer, the much-appraised "champion of the women lawyers". The erudite Schochda was honoured as "Scheicha", "lady professor" and as the "pride of women". After having studied under the different lights of science, she received permission to teach and ignited her own little lamp. Poetesses still vie with poets just as they always did and no one finds this peculiar.'[629]

Veils and harems must be traced back to Persian and Byzantine influences during the time of the 'Abbasid caliphs, especially during the regency of the narrow-minded al-Qádir. 'What had started so harmlessly as a fashion became religious compulsion under their gloomy influence. And seclusion in the harem which, in the Persian manner, was carried out with the help of eunuchs in accordance with the traditional Byzantine custom, and which started as the elegant fashion of the distinguished, the rich and the indulgent, took on daemonic proportions under the "stay-at-home" appeal addressed by the Prophet to his own wives and led to the compulsory banishment of women and the exclusion of anything feminine from public life.'[630] From then on the theologians decided that even the female face should be considered as one of

629. op. cit., pp. 278–9.   630. ibid., p. 279.

the forbidden attractions. And thus even today the wearing of the veil and confinement are still customary in large circles in the Islamic world, especially in cities. The bedouin woman never wore the veil nor did she ever live in the seclusion of the harem. 'Economical and practical reasons would never have allowed the simple inhabitants of the steppes and desert such luxury, any more than they would have made possible the luxury of marrying four wives as allowed by the Prophet . . . And this is why the bedouin woman of the first Islamic centuries is even freer, more independent and influential than the very respected, distinguished women of the highest court circles of Damascus.'[631] The suppression of the Islamic woman is therefore not rooted in the law of the Prophet. It is a manifestation of corruption and decadence for which Muḥammad cannot be held responsible.

On the whole it should be noted that it is unjust to judge the position of woman in Islám by our modern standard of what is moral and just. Those who criticise the stipulations in the *Qur'án* concerning women's rights should remind themselves that the equality of women in Germany was realised only recently with the German national constitution of 23 May 1949 and the change of the civil code of laws of 1953. In many parts of the world marriage is still settled in a patriarchal way.[632]

Comparison with Christianity shows that the latter did not fly the flag of the equality of women's rights.[633] It is with the apostle Paul that fear of sex and scorn for women made their appearance in Christianity.[634] Woman, whom Paul calls man's 'vessel',[635] was for him a 'second-class person'[636]—a contrast to Jesus's attitude. Man is the reflection of God and woman only 'the glory of man'.[637] Man was not created for the sake of woman but woman for the sake of man.[638] This is why she must be silent in church and cover her head to show her lowliness.[639] The Father of the Church, Tertullian, tolerated woman only when she was a virgin and described her as 'the open door to the devil'.[640] The same attitude was assumed by the radical enemies of sensuality, the

---

631. ibid., pp. 280–81.   632. See p. 72, note 211.
633. The beginning of the emancipation of women in the nineteenth century was not at all welcome to the churches.
634. I Corinthians 11:3.   635. I Thessalonians 4:4.
636. J. Leitpoldt, *Jesus und die Frauen*, p. 109.
637. I Corinthians 11:7 ff.   638. ibid., 11:9 ff.
639. ibid., 11:13.   640. *Cultu fem.* 1:1.

Fathers of the Church, Hieronymus and Ambrosius. Augustine, who even considered birth to be a dirty process (*'inter faeces et urinam nascimur'*) unreservedly shared this depreciatory view of women. It was through the troubadours and minstrels in the eleventh and twelfth centuries that women were raised to a high rank morally and spiritually. And where does the minstrel's love song come from? It is of Arabic and Islamic origin![641]

Predestination and free will

A concept of Islám widely spread in the West is that by teaching God's omnipotence and man's absolute dependence, Islám leads its followers to the idea of blind fate, of a fatalism which, on the one hand, encourages Muslim warriors to be fearless but, on the other, often causes the 'Muhammadan to persist in an attitude of dull resignation and inactivity . . .'[642] Kellerhals maintains that the devoted Muslim's main virtue, 'Islám' (complete submission to the will of God) and his constant phrase 'inshá'alláh' can only be understood in the following way: 'The sovereign grace of God has been replaced by the despotic and tyrannic whims of an arbitrary power and his royal freedom has been replaced by the enslavement of God by arbitrary chance.'[643] Islám is said to 'bluntly and unreservedly profess that all events are predestined' and to deny 'that man enjoys any free will' or 'has any part in his own actions'.[644] For Kellerhals this alleged solution to the problem of predestination in Islám is a typical example of the way 'the human spirit is lost in hopeless error when it attempts to know and describe God by means of reason which is not disciplined and directed by God's own revelation'.[645]

It is remarkable that this judgment, passed by a clergyman who was acquainting young missionaries with Islám in a seminary of the Basle mission, completely overlooks the fact (which could hardly have been unknown to him) that during the whole history of the Church the problem of man's free will and divine predestination has been violently debated and that there have also been renowned champions in Christianity of this concept of predestination. Paul, the real creator of the Church's doctrine of grace,

---

641. Sigrid Hunke, op. cit., p. 341 ff. Rudolf Erckmann, 'Der Einfluss der arabisch-spanischen Kultur auf die Entwicklung des Minnesangs'.

642. See the Protestant theologian Emmanuel Kellerhals, *Islam, seine Geschichte, seine Lehre, sein Wesen*, p. 200.

643. ibid., p. 199.   644. ibid., p. 198.   645. ibid.

advocated the idea of predestination and later all those who thought as he did rightly quoted him.[646] Augustine took up the idea of predestination, developed and defended it radically. The reformers, too, took over this teaching. According to Calvin, 'man's salvation and damnation' are once and for all established by God's independent decree. Man must resign himself to this 'terrible resolution' which serves the Glory of God. This teaching was accepted by all Calvinist churches at the Synod of Dordrecht (1618–19). Thomas Aquinas, too, championed the doctrine of predestination and thus, in the Catholic Church, Thomists and Molinists fought over the question of the interdependence of grace and freedom without finally coming to agreement. Scholars of Islám who are committed to Church dogma are subjective in their judgments, as is shown by the fact that according to their own position they either show indignation at Muḥammad's alleged teaching or find, on the contrary, the warmest words of praise for it. Thus, Tor Andrae, a dogmatic Calvinist[647] who never misses a chance to criticise Muḥammad and his religion, comments on this teaching of Islamic theology: 'It is a significant proof of the purely religious strength of Mohammed's experience of God that he arrived at this daring conception of the unbounded majesty and omnipotence of God without being influenced as far as I can see, either by Judaism or by Christianity.'[648]

The problem of free will and predestination is the oldest dogmatic controversy in Islám. The starting-point is the teaching of the *Qur'án* about man's complete dependence on the divine will. According to the *Qur'án* God is the Exalted, the Powerful, the Omnipotent. 'All that is in the Heavens and in the Earth praiseth God, and he is the Mighty, the Wise! His is the Kingdom of the Heavens and of the Earth; he maketh alive and killeth; and he hath power over all things! He is the first and the last; the Seen and the Hidden; and he knoweth all things!'[649]

God is supreme, and there are no limits to his absolute will: 'He shall not be asked of his doings.'[650] He sends punishments

646. 'And we know that all things work together for good to them that love God, to them who are the called according to his purpose. For whom he did foreknow, he also did predestinate . . .' (Romans 8:28–9). Compare 9:14–16 and 18.

647. op. cit., p. 90.   648. op. cit., p. 86.   649. *Qur'án* 57:1–3.

650. *Qur'án* 21:23. See also the following quotations: 'But God doth what he will' (2:253); 'God will create what He will; when He decreeth a thing, He only saith "Be", and it is' (3:42); 'God doth his pleasure' (14:32); 'God doth that which He pleaseth' (22:14; 22:19).

when he pleases and when he desires, he is merciful. There is no rule which restrains his will or by which one can determine and evaluate his doings. This sovereign and free will of God is the cause of all that is, and it cannot be altered by man. Early in the history of Islám, Muslim theologians concluded from this omnipotence and man's absolute dependence on it that God's power also extended to the determination of human will-power; man could only want what God had decreed. But if this should be the case, belief or disbelief did not ultimately depend on man's will. Rather it was God who offered or denied man the gift of faith.

But this belief in predestination, in the divine act of grace, is nowhere to be found as an *expressis verbis* teaching in the *Qur'án*. It is a product of theological reflection. The *Qur'án* of course contains numerous verses which could be interpreted in a deterministic sense.[651]

But God is not only almighty; he is just, too. And so, as early as the time of the 'Umayyad Caliphate, there were Muslims who advocated the teaching of man's free will. They were called '*Qadaríyyah*' (from *qadar*, decision) as opposed to the '*Jabríyyah*' who championed determinism (from *jabr*, compulsion). The Qadaríyyah—a thorn in the side of the ruling dynasty of the 'Umayyads[652]—could quote at least as many Qur'ánic verses suggesting that man has free will, for the idea that God is just and

651. 'No soul can believe but by the permission of God: and he shall lay his wrath on those who will not understand' (10:100). 'Verily God misleadeth whom He will and guideth whom He will' (35:9; 74:31). 'Had we pleased we had certainly given to every soul its guidance. But true shall be the word which hath gone forth from me—I will surely fill hell with Djinn and men together' (32:13). 'As to the infidels, alike is it to them whether thou warn them or warn them not—they will not believe: Their hearts and their ears hath God sealed up; and over their eyes is a covering' (2:5-6). 'Truly we have thrown veils over their hearts lest they should understand this Qur'án, and into their ears a heaviness: And if thou bid them to "the guidance" yet will they not even then be guided ever' (18:55-6). 'We had not been guided had not God guided us!' (7:41). 'And thy Lord createth what he will and hath a free choice. But they, the false gods, have no power to choose. Glory be to God! and high let him be exalted above those whom they associate with him!' (28:68). 'And whom God shall please to guide, that man's breast will He open to Islám; but whom He shall please to mislead, strait and narrow will He make his breast, as though he were mounting up into the very Heavens! Thus doth God inflict dire punishment on those who believe not' (6:125).

652. As a proof of the authenticity of their dynasty, they referred to the doctrine of predestination (Goldziher, *Vorlesungen über den Islam*, p. 92).

that each receives the reward his actions deserve is a recurrent reassurance given by Muḥammad.[653]

When the systematic theology of Islám was established at the height of the Mu'tazilite period in the eighth and ninth centuries, and reason ('*aql*) became the source of religious knowledge, the issue was again discussed. As the monotheistic notion of God was purified from all distortions of popular origin, all ideas detrimental to the concept of God's unity and justice were removed. According to the teaching of this school, God is necessarily just. The notion of justice cannot be separated from the concept of God. God is not a despot who populates heaven and hell in an arbitrary and capricious manner. His rule is not an arbitrary one. Man is the master of his actions. The Mu'tazilites—who taught that men are free to follow the teachings revealed for their salvation and are just as free to reject them, whereas God, who is just, must reward the righteous and punish the evil-doers—did not, in the end, meet with the approval of orthodox views which were based on tradition. For through their doctrine God's doings are humanised and ultimately man, who is free, is faced with a God who is not.

These two extreme doctrines are opposed by two intermediary views, one of which is that held by the theologian al-Ash'arí.[654] It is closer to the idea of predestination and has entered scholastic theology[655] without, however, being regarded as the only acceptable view.

653. 'God will not burden any soul beyond its power. It shall enjoy the good which it hath acquired, and shall bear the evil for the acquirement of which it laboured' (2:286). On that day shall every soul find presented to it 'what it hath earned' (3:24). 'But their own works have got the mastery over their hearts' (83:14). Even when 'the sealing up of Hearts' is mentioned, it refers to those who 'follow their own lusts' (47:18). It is not God who hardens their hearts but their own wickedness that they 'become hard like rocks, or harder still' (2:69). God has pointed out the right way to men, but it is up to man whether 'he be thankful or ungrateful' (76:3). 'Say: Every one acteth after his own manner: but your Lord well knoweth who is best guided in his path' (17:86). 'And say: the truth is from your Lord: let him then who will, believe; and let him who will, be an infidel' (18:28). 'This truly is a warning: And whoso willeth, taketh the way to his Lord' (76:29). 'Truly man's guidance is with Us and Ours, the Future and the Past. I warn you therefore of the flaming fire; none shall be cast to it but the most wretched, who hath called the truth a lie and turned his back. But the God-fearing shall escape it, who giveth away his substance that he may become pure' (92:12–18). Therefore God does not become a hindrance to the wicked. He allows him to do evil as he allows the righteous to do good.

654. d. 935 A.D.   655. *Enzyklopädie des Islam*, vol. II, p. 647 ff.

These explanations are given to show that Islamic theology has offered different solutions to this fundamental theological problem —the question of free will and divine predestination—without giving a logically satisfactory answer. The problem cannot be solved by means of logic. However, Goldziher has alluded to an essential fact which is relevant to understanding the problem of free will. A large number of the Qur'ánic verses which are claimed to justify the conclusion that it is God himself who causes man's sinfulness and leads him astray, take on another meaning when the word '*adalla*', which suggests this leading astray is fully understood. *Adalla* does not mean 'to lead one astray' but 'to let him go astray', not to concern oneself with him, not to show him the way out of the difficulty. The verse 'God guides whom he wants and leaves whom he wills to go astray' does not mean that God directly leads the evil-doer to the wrong path but that he punishes him as it were by withdrawing from him the way to grace. Goldziher remarks: 'One can visualise a lonely wanderer in the desert and the Qur'ánic expression about guidance and error has come from such an image. The wanderer errs in unlimited space and seeks the right direction towards his goal. Thus man is wandering throughout life. Whoever has, through his good deeds, deserved God's favour is rewarded with God's guidance. God leaves the evil-doer to go astray and abandons him to his fate, . . . he does not lend him a guiding hand. But this does not mean that he leads him onto the wrong path. This is also why the image of blindness and groping around is so often used to represent sinners[656] . . . The abandonment of men unto themselves, and the withdrawal of loving care, is a predominant concept in the *Qur'án* with regard to people who, through their past behaviour, have made themselves unworthy of divine grace. God forgets sinners, i.e. he does not concern himself with them. By guiding them God rewards the righteous. "God guideth not the ungodly people."[657] He lets them go astray aimlessly. Lack of faith is not the consequence but rather the cause of erring.'[658]

656. 'Now have proofs that may be seen, come to you from your Lord; whoso seeth them, the advantage will be his own: and whoso is blind to them, his own will be the loss' (*Qur'án* 6:104). 'We have sent down the Book to thee for man and for the ends of truth. Whoso shall be guided by it—it will be for his own advantage, and whoso shall err, shall only err to his own loss' (*Qur'án* 39:42).

657. *Qur'án* 9:110.

658. Goldziher, *Vorlesungen über den Islam*, p. 86 ff.; compare also *Qur'án* 61:5: 'And when they went astray, God led their hearts astray; for God guideth not a perverse people'; see also *Qur'án* 4:154; 9:128.

The theologian Ḥasan al-Baṣrí's theory about the sealing up of hearts states: 'God sets a limit to the sins of men; if men reach that limit, their hearts are then sealed up by God who no longer guides them. He abandons them to themselves.'[659]

As we have seen, many different theories were conceived in Islám about the relationship between free will and divine predestination (which 'Abdu'l-Bahá called one of the most essential and abstruse theological problems)[660] without one doctrine, binding on all believers, ever being agreed upon. As the Jesuit Oskar Simmel rightly remarked, there will never be a rationally satisfying solution to the contradictory principles of God's omnipotence and his justice: 'The meaning of the doctrine of grace is not the solving of a metaphysical puzzle, but the fact that a righteous life before God is made possible.'[661]

Regarding this righteous life, it is important that all good and evil deeds have their source in man's free will, that man has the choice between good and evil and is therefore answerable to God for his deeds.[662] Muḥammad never left any doubt as to man's responsibility: each soul receives 'what it deserves'.[663]

As for the alleged fatalism to which Islám is supposed inevitably to lead, the central concept *tawakkul* (to rely on God) exists next to the ideas already partly mentioned of *qaḍa* (divine decree), *qadar* (divine predestination), *jabr* (compulsion, i.e. unalterable destiny). *Tawakkul* and the concept of *islám* (submitting oneself to

---

659. See Goldziher, op. cit., p. 325, note 42.

660. *Some Answered Questions*, LXX. Regarding this concept of predestination, which evolves from the concept of God's omnipotence, 'Abdu'l-Bahá has offered thought which makes the subject easier to understand: the difference between decreed and impending fate. 'Fate is of two kinds: one is decreed, and the other is conditional or impending. The decreed fate is that which cannot change or be altered, and conditional fate is that which may occur. So, for this lamp, the decreed fate is that the oil burns, and will be consumed; therefore its eventual extinction is a decree which it is impossible to alter or to change, because it is a decreed fate. In the same way, in the body of man a power of life has been created, and as soon as it is destroyed and ended, the body will certainly be decomposed, so when the oil in this lamp is burnt and finished, the lamp will undoubtedly become extinguished ... While there is still oil, a violent wind blows on the lamp, which extinguishes it. This is a conditional fate. It is wise to avoid it, to protect oneself from it, to be cautious and circumspect. But the decreed fate, which is like the finishing of the oil in the lamp, cannot be altered, changed, nor delayed ...' (ibid., LXVIII).

661. 'Christliche Religion', *Fischer-Lexikon*, p. 107.

662. Compare 'Abdu'l-Bahá, *Some Answered Questions*, LXX.

663. Compare *Qur'án* 3 : 25.

God), which is closely related to it, are, according to Imám 'Ali, two of the four pillars of faith.[664]

Of course this notion of *tawakkul* is particularly stressed in Islám but it is present in all religions. Trusting in God is one of the attitudes demanded from believers, especially in Judaism and Christianity.[665] The Islamic *insḥá'alláh*, which is criticised so much by Kellerhals and which he quoted to justify his reproach that Islám is fatalistic, is by no means foreign to Christianity. 'God willing' is a condition to which believers of all religions submit their plans, projects and actions. It is hard to understand why this attitude which is common to all religions should become a sign of fatalism when it is Islám that teaches it.

Now there were in early Islám, as in Christianity, ascetic zealots who exaggerated individual teachings and commands of the prophet. It was they who raised the idea of trust in God (*tawakkul*) to the extreme degree of inactive quietism. Goldziher writes about these fanatics: 'They show complete indifference and reject any kind of decision-making in their personal circumstances. They give themselves up entirely to the care of God and to his decree. They seem to be in God's hand as the corpse is in the hands of the corpse-washer, entirely devoid of will and uninterested. In this sense they call themselves *muttawakkilun*, i.e. those who trust in God. A number of their principles have been handed down from which it is evident that they consider it despicable to provide for their own needs. This would be equivalent to violating their trust in God.'[666] The exaggerated trust in God displayed by these sectarians did not correspond to the official Islamic concept of life and this is proved by the polemic literature of the period concerned.[667] It is an excellent example of the way God's religion is always deformed when single teachings or prescriptions given by the prophet are given different values by ignorant zealots, are torn out of their context, brought into a central position and magnified to the extreme. In most religions this is the process by which sects have come into being. Many Europeans look upon the Islamic attitude of *tawakkul*[668] as one of fatalism. This is because they

---

664. Goethe said: 'If Islam means submission to God, then in Islam do we all live and die' (Quoted by P. Eberhardt, *Religionskunde*, p. 91).
665. Compare Psalms 18:31; 118:8; Jeremiah 3:14; II Corinthians 1:9, 3:4.
666. op. cit., p. 151.   667. Compare Goldziher, ibid., p. 152 ff.
668. The greatest theologian of Islám, al-Ghazálí (1058–1111), discussed this concept exhaustively in his work *Minhág al-'Ábidin* (The Path of God's Servants). Franz

have never properly grasped what the real heart of God's religion is: complete submission to his will, that is 'Islám'.

In Islám life on this earth was never a matter of indifference. It always endeavoured to change and shape relations on earth according to God's revealed will. Such an active reorganisation of the social structure would not have been possible by reliance on God alone without committed involvement and activity. The degree to which the religion of Muḥammad was orientated towards this life as well as the next is shown by a *ḥadíth* recognised by Sunnís and Shí'ahs alike and according to which Muḥammad has given his people the following maxim: 'Strive for this life as though thou wouldst live eternally and strive for the next as though thou wouldst die tomorrow.'[669]

Does not this tradition remind one of the Christian *'ora et labora'*? It says even more.

If properly understood, reliance on God in Islám cannot possibly lead to an indifferent passivity and a dull belief in fate. This is shown by another *ḥadíth* which has been carefully preserved: 'A believer asked the Prophet about his camel: "O messenger of God! Should I tie it up and rely on God or leave it free in its movements and trust in God?" The Prophet answered: "Tie it up and rely on God!"'[670] With this advice Muḥammad prevented any kind of fatalism from becoming legitimate.

König in the theological dictionary published by the Catholic publishing trust, Herder (Freiburg, 1956, column 668–9) stresses the fact that it was only after the political decline of Islám that the kind of fatalism described by the Turks as *'qismat'* (fate or 'kismet') appeared. This concept includes the attitude of resignation towards all failures and misfortunes (cf. W. Montgomery Watt, *Free Will and Predestination in Early Islam*, London, 1948).

669. *Majmu'at Warram* (The Compilation of Warram), Najaf, 'Iráq, 1389 A.H. (1969), vol. II, p. 227. The editor Warram was a pious prince who died in 605 A.H. He was a Sunní, but his work is also read by the Shí'ahs as it contains traditions by Muḥammad, the Imáms and other wise and learned men of Islám.

670. I. Jarāhī, *Kashf-ul-Khafā'Wa Muzīl-ul-Ilbās 'Am-ma shtahara min-al-Aḥaditḥi 'Ala Alsinatin-nas*, 2nd edition, Beirut, 1351 A.H. (1931). The title of the work is: 'The Revealer of Things Hidden and the Remover of Confusion about the Traditions which have become known to Men.' The work discusses under consecutive numbers the authenticity of 3281 traditions. The tradition quoted here comes under number 418. The work originates from Anas, one of Muḥammad's servants and companions who died in A.D. 712. It is also recognised by the Shí'ahs, for Tarihi mentions it in his work *Majma'ul-Bahray*, vol. V, Najaf, 'Iráq, without date under the title *Wakala*. This work by Tarihi, who died in 1085 A.H. is a work of reference favoured by the Shí'ahs. Its title means 'The Meeting of Both Seas' (i.e. the *Qur'án* and the traditions).

A few objections against Islám made by Western readers have been presented in the previous sections. On how little knowledge and on how much resentment these widespread and deeply-rooted prejudices rest may now be judged. Nevertheless it is undeniable that progress towards a more understanding evaluation of Islám is visible. As indifference towards religious thinking is increasing, so tolerance towards the non-Christian religions is growing. And the rise of the Arab nations has brought a greater need for strictly objective information in the West about Islám. But only he who has recognised the *Qur'án* to be the Word of God and the Arabian Prophet to be a manifestation of the living God can really give this strictly objective information and a genuine image of Islám.

Conclusion

The religious and historical parallels are obvious: Judaism has
seen in Christianity its rebellious daughter and rejected the Christian claim to truth. Clinging to the literal sense of the Scriptures,
it was not able to believe that the covenant established by Moses
was fulfilled and that the Church was the new Israel.[671] Because it
is God's Law, the Law of Moses[672] is for the Jews unalterable,
complete and utterly perfect; therefore it will be valid for eternity.[673] Moreover, the Messiah they are awaiting and who was
foretold by the prophet will therefore announce no new law or
new teaching but will rather abide by the laws and teaching of
Moses.[674] Because of this doctrine and of a literal interpretation of
the Messianic prophecies, Judaism has rejected the message of
Jesus,[675] as well as the claim of the Church that the fulfilment of
God's promises and prophecies will not take place in the future
but has already come to pass, that the kingdom of God has begun
and can be seen in the Church.[676] Israel still expects the Promised
One.[677]

671. The Jewish answer to the Christians and all those who believe in the com-
pletion of the Torah or in a new revelation, reads: 'But it is said in Deuteronomy
30:12: "The teaching is not in heaven". Therefore do not say that another Moses has
stood up and has brought another Torah from heaven, I testify that nothing from the
Torah has remained in heaven' (*Debarim abba*, VIII; quoted by H. J. Schoeps,
Jüdisch-christliches Religionsgespräch in neunzehn Jahrhunderten, p. 55).

672. See Deuteronomy 4:2, 12:32; Psalms 19:8–10.

673. 'The truth of the covenant of Israel which is rightly called eternal covenant
not "old covenant" is independent of human statements and cannot be lifted or
made redundant by God, for God is not a man that he should lie; neither the son of
man, that he should repent (Numbers 23:19)' (H. J. Schoeps, ibid., p. 153).

674. The difference lies only in the fact that the covenant with God will no longer
be broken in the Messianic age, as it was broken during the flight from Egypt.

675. As well as that of Muḥammad.

676. And also because of the Pauline transformation of the Faith of Jesus into a
faith in Jesus, his crucifix-theology, his theory of the impossibility of fulfilling the

Christianity understands the divine revelation which took place in the history of Israel as an act of revelation which led to the advent of Jesus and found its fulfilment in him, while the prophecies of the Old Testament prophets about the coming of the Messiah and the future of Israel are all interpreted as referring to Jesus and the Church. However, with Christ and the apostles, 'the fulness of the time'[678] was reached; communication and revelation from God himself have 'at the same time met their apex and their end'.[679] This is why the Church expects 'no new revelation addressed to the whole of humanity'.[680] Nevertheless she awaits a future redeeming event: the return of Christ in the last days from which she expects the last accomplishment of God's redeeming works and which will 'make manifest to the whole world God's triumph over sin, death and the devil'.[681] Christianity interprets literally the signs given by Jesus relating to his return and the concepts of 'resurrection' and 'Day of Judgment', and, in rejecting an allegorical interpretation[682] of the Scriptures adopts the same attitude for which it reproaches Judaism. Thus Christian theologians have rejected the post-Biblical religions, Islám and the Bahá'í Faith, and refused to accept them as being the fulfilment of Jesus's prophecies. Christianity, too, expects the fulfilment of its prophecies[683] to take place in the future.

---

law and his teaching that God therefore had to establish another connection with man and out of his infinite love for humanity descended in the flesh, that God was in Christ (II Corinthians 5:19) and he humbled himself, and became obedient unto death (Philippians 2:5 ff.)—all these could not be accepted by the Jews and were bound to appear as a violation of God's absolute transcendence (see also Schoeps, *Jüdisch-christliches Religionsgespräch in neunzehn Jahrhunderten*, pp. 48–58, 149–4).

677. On this question see 'Abdu'l-Bahá: 'The Jews were expecting the appearance of the Messiah, looking forward to it with devotion of heart and soul but because they were submerged in imitations they did not believe in His Holiness Jesus Christ when he appeared. Finally they rose against Him even to the extreme of persecution and shedding His blood. Had they investigated reality they would have accepted their promised Messiah. These blind imitations and hereditary prejudices have invariably become the cause of bitterness and hatred and have filled the world with darkness and violence of war. Therefore we must seek the fundamental truth in order to extricate ourselves from such conditions and then with illumined faces find the pathway to the kingdom of God' (*Bahá'í World Faith*, p. 239).

678. Galatians 4:4.

679. O. Simmel, S. J., 'Christliche Religion', p. 52.

680. ibid.

681. R. Stählin in 'Christliche Religion', p. 194.

682. Rosenkranz (*Die Bahá'í*, p. 59) criticises the Bahá'ís for carrying on 'their allegorical game' with the New Testament.

683. As far as the Christians still take them seriously.

Muḥammad strongly rejected the objection raised by the rabbis about the inalterable quality of the Torah and its eternal validity: '"The hand of God", say the Jews, "is chained up." Their own hands shall be chained up ... Nay! outstretched are both his hands.'[684] 'The Hand of God was over their hands.'[685] However, orthodox Islám, just like the Church, has elevated the teaching of the finality of revelation to the rank of dogma, has rejected the allegorical interpretation of the prophecies and anathematised the claim of the Bahá'ís that these prophecies are fulfilled and that God has once more manifested himself in the twin messengers, the Báb and Bahá'u'lláh.[686] Islám, too, still awaits the fulfilment of her prophecies.

Further parallels: Christianity has led the non-Jewish, Christian world to Sinai and introduced it to Moses and the prophets. Islám has made known to the non-Christian world Jesus,[687] Moses and also the Jewish prophets. The Bahá'í Faith also proclaims to the non-Islamic world the message of him of whom Bahá'u'lláh testifies: 'Followers of the Gospel! If ye cherish the desire to slay Muḥammad, the Apostle of God, seize Me and put an end to My life, for I am He, and My Self is His Self.'[688]

Over the centuries the history of religion has been a sublime testimony to the enlightenment of mankind by the light of divine

---

684. *Qur'án* 5:69.   685. *Qur'án* 48:10.

686. 'Although the commentators of the *Qur'án* have related in divers manners the circumstances attending the revelation of this verse, yet thou shouldst endeavour to apprehend the purpose thereof. He saith: How false is that which the Jews have imagined! How can the hand of him Who is the King in truth, who caused the countenance of Moses to be made manifest, and conferred upon Him the robe of Prophethood—how can the hand of such a One be chained and fettered? How can He be conceived as powerless to raise up yet another Messenger after Moses? Behold the absurdity of their saying; how far it hath strayed from the path of knowledge and understanding! Observe how in this day also, all these people have occupied themselves with such foolish absurdities. For over a thousand years they have been reciting this verse, and unwittingly pronouncing their censure against the Jews, utterly unaware that they themselves, openly and privily, are voicing the sentiments and belief of the Jewish people! Thou art surely aware of their idle contention, that all Revelation is ended, that the portals of Divine mercy are closed, that from the day-springs of eternal holiness no sun shall rise again, that the Ocean of everlasting bounty is forever stilled and that out of the Tabernacle of ancient glory the Messengers of God have ceased to be made manifest ... The utter destitution into which this people have fallen doth surely suffice them, inasmuch as they have been deprived of the recognition of the essential Purpose and the knowledge of the Mystery and Substance of the Cause of God' (*Kitáb-i-Íqán*, pp. 87–8 (Brit.), pp. 136–8 (U.S.)).

687. Of course not as 'Son of God' in the ontological sense, but as a prophet.

688. *Gleanings*, XLVII.

revelation. Innumerable are the examples of active love, of sacrifice, devotion, self-sacrifice and glorification of God; innumerable the signs showing to what heights man can exalt himself when he follows his true destiny, fulfils it and turns to God his Creator. How lofty the brilliance of human cultures which, in their *apogée*, owed their light, their force and their dynamism to nothing else but the Word of God.

But how innumerable, too, are the sufferings inflicted, and the misdeeds which were and still are committed, in the name of religion, through claims to exclusiveness and finality. How much injustice men have had to bear on this planet from followers of other religions or denominations, notwithstanding the teaching common to all religions that all men were created by God.

In an epoch stamped with the stigma of unbelief and nihilism, should it not be the conviction of all religious men that religion should be the cause of love, unity and harmony among men and not the cause of discord, dissension and conflict? In the words of 'Abdu'l-Bahá: 'If religion becomes a cause of dislike, hatred and division, it were better to be without it, and to withdraw from such a religion would be a truly religious act. For it is clear that the purpose of a remedy is to cure; but if the remedy should only aggravate the complaint it had better be left alone.'[689] Would not humanity profit if the precept given by Bahá'u'lláh to his people became the maxim of conduct of the believers of all religions? 'Consort with the followers of all religions in a spirit of friendliness and fellowship.'[690]

---

689. *Paris Talks*, p. 130.

690. *Gleanings*, XLIII. See also *Epistle to the Son of the Wolf*, p. 13: 'That the divers communions of the earth, and the manifold systems of religious belief, should never be allowed to foster the feelings of animosity among men is, in this Day, of the essence of the Faith of God and His Religion . . . Gird up the loins of your endeavour, O people of Bahá, that haply the tumult of religious dissension and strife that agitateth the peoples of the earth may be stilled, that every trace of it may be completely obliterated. For the love of God, and them that serve him, arise to aid this sublime and momentous Revelation. Religious fanaticism and hatred are a world-devouring fire, whose violence none can quench. The Hand of Divine power can, alone, deliver mankind from this desolating affliction.'

Bibliography

'ABDU'L-BAHÁ. Paris Talks. London: Bahá'í Publishing Trust, 11th edn. 1969. (Published in the U.S.A. as *The Wisdom of 'Abdu'l-Bahá*.)
— *The Promulgation of Universal Peace*. 2 vols. Chicago: Bahá'í Publishing Society, 1922. Repr. Wilmette: Bahá'í Publishing Committee, 1943.
— *Some Answered Questions*. Trans. by Laura Clifford Barney. London: Bahá'í Publishing Trust, 1961. Wilmette: Bahá'í Publishing Trust, rev. edn. 1964.
— *The Secret of Divine Civilization*. Wilmette: Bahá'í Publishing Trust, 1957.
ADAM, KARL. *Das Wesen des Katholizismus* (The essence of Catholicism). Düsseldorf, 1927.
ADLER, H. G. *Die Juden in Deutschland* (The Jews in Germany). München, 1960.
AL GHAZĀLĪ. *Der Pfad der Gottesdiener* (The path of God's servants). Trans. from the Arabic by Ernst Bannerth. Salzburg, 1964.
ALTHAUS, PAUL. *Die Ethik Martin Luthers* (The ethic of Martin Luther). Gütersloh, 1965.
AMEER ALI, SYED. *The Spirit of Islam. A History of the Evolution and Ideals of Islam with the Life of the Prophet*. London: Methuen & Co. Ltd., 1965.
ANDRAE, TOR. *Mohammed: The Man and His Faith*. Trans. from the German by Theophil Menzel. London: George Allen & Unwin Ltd., 1936.
ANDRESEN, C. *Logos und Nomos, Die Polemik des Celsus wider das Christentum* (Logos and Nomos, the Polemic of Celsus against Christianity). Berlin, 1955.
ANDRESEN, WILHELM. 'Selbstpreisgabe der Theologie?' (Self-abandonment of theology?), *Deutsches Pfarrerblatt*. Essen: Verband der Evangelischen Pfarrvereine in Deutschland, Jahrgang 62, 1962.
ARNOLD, SIR THOMAS WALKER. *The Caliphate*. Oxford: Oxford University Press, 1924. Re-issued 1965.
Bahá'í Administration. Wilmette: Bahá'í Publishing Trust, 2nd edn. 1960.

Bahá'í News. A monthly magazine. Wilmette: National Spiritual Assembly of the Bahá'ís of the United States.

Bahá'í Procedure. Wilmette: Bahá'í Publishing Trust, 2nd edn. 1942.

Bahá'í World Faith. Selected Writings of Bahá'u'lláh and 'Abdu'l-Bahá. Wilmette: Bahá'í Publishing Trust, 1943.

BAHÁ'U'LLÁH. *Epistle to the Son of the Wolf*. Trans. by Shoghi Effendi. Wilmette: Bahá'í Publishing Trust, rev. edn. 1953.

— *Gleanings from the Writings of Bahá'u'lláh*. Trans. by Shoghi Effendi. Wilmette: Bahá'í Publishing Trust, rev. edn. 1952. London: Bahá'í Publishing Trust, 1949.

— *The Hidden Words*. Trans. by Shoghi Effendi with the assistance of some English friends. London: Bahá'í Publishing Trust, 1949. Wilmette: Bahá'í Publishing Trust, rev. edn. 1954.

— *Hidden Words, Words of Wisdom and Communes*. Chicago: Bahá'í Publishing Society, undated.

— *The Kitáb-i-Íqán. The Book of Certitude*. Trans. by Shoghi Effendi. Wilmette: Bahá'í Publishing Trust, 2nd edn. 1950. London: Bahá'í Publishing Trust, 2nd edn. 1961.

— *Prayers and Meditations by Bahá'u'lláh*. Compiled and trans. by Shoghi Effendi. New York: Bahá'í Publishing Committee, 1938. London: Bahá'í Publishing Trust, 1957.

— *The Proclamation of Bahá'u'lláh*. Haifa: Bahá'í World Centre, 1967.

BALYUZI, H. M. *Muḥammad and the Course of Islám*. Oxford: George Ronald, 1976.

— *Edward Granville Browne and the Bahá'í Faith*. London: George Ronald, 1970.

BARTH, KARL. *Die Kirchliche Dogmatik* (The dogma of the Church). München, vol. I, 1932.

BATES, MINER SEARLE. *Religious Liberty*. New York: Church World Service, 1945.

BAUER, WALTER. *Rechtgläubigkeit und Ketzerei im ältesten Christentum* (Orthodoxy and heresy in earliest Christianity). Tübingen, 2nd edn. 1964.

BAUSANI, Alessandro. 'Babismo' and 'Bahá'ism', *Enziklopedia Cattolica*. Vol. II. Cittá del Vaticano, 1949.

BECKER, CARL HEINRICH. *Islamstudien* (Islamic studies). Leipzig, vol. I, 1924; vol. II, 1932.

BERKENHOFF, HANS A. *Tierstrafe, Tierbannung und rechtsrituelle Tiertötung im Mittelalter* (The punishment and banishment of animals, and legal rites of execution in the Middle Ages). Bühl, 1937.

BRAUN, HERBERT. *Gesammelte Studien zum Neuen Testament und seiner Umwelt* (Collected studies on the New Testament and its background). Tübingen, 1962.

BROWNE, E. G. (ed.) *A Traveller's Narrative* written to illustrate the Episode of the Báb. Vol. II, English Translation and Notes. Cambridge University Press, 1891. Re-issued Philo Press, Amsterdam, 1975.

BROWNE LAURENCE E. *The Eclipse of Christianity in Asia.* Cambridge: Cambridge University Press, 1933.

BULTMANN, RUDOLF. *Glauben und Verstehen* (Belief and Understanding). Band I. Tübingen, 4th edn. 1961.

BURCKHARDT, JACOB. *Weltgeschichtliche Betrachtungen* (Reflections on world history). 1905. Edited by Rudolf Marx. Stuttgart, 1955.

CAETANI, LEONE, Principe di Teano. *Annali dell'Islam* (Annals of Islám). Milan, 1905–20.

— *Das historische Studium des Islams* (The historical study of Islám). Milan, 1911.

Chambers's Encyclopaedia. London: Pergamon Press, new rev. edn. 1966.

CONZELMANN, H. 'Zur Methode der Leben-Jesu-Forschung', (Towards a method of research into the life of Jesus), *Zeitschrift fur Theologie und Kirche.* Edited by Gerhard Ebeling and others. Beiheft I, 1959. Later published by Kaiser Verlag, München, 1967.

DANTE, ALIGHIERI. *The Vision; or Hell, Purgatory, and Paradise.* Trans. by Henry Francis Cary. Oxford: Oxford University Press, 1910.

DERMENGHEM, EMILE. *The Life of Mahomet.* Trans. by A. Yorke. George Routledge & Sons, London, 1930.

DESCHNER, KARL-HEINZ. *Abermals krähte der Hahn* (And again the cock crew). Stuttgart, 1962.

DIEM, HERMANN. 'Dogmatik. Ihr Weg zwischen Historismus und Existentialismus' (Dogma. Its path between history and existentialism), *Theologie als kirchliche Wissenschaft.* München, vol. II, 1955.

DIEZ, ERNST. *Glaube und Welt des Islam* (The belief and world of Islám). Stuttgart, 1941.

DONALDSON, DWIGHT M. *The Shiʿite Religion.* London: Luzac & Co. 1933.

DUPONT-SOMMER, ANDRÉ. *Die essenischen Schriften vom Toten Meer* (The scrolls of the Essenes from the Dead Sea). Tübingen, 1960.

DURANT, WILLIAM JAMES. *The Story of Civilization.* Vol. III, Caesar and Christus. New York: Simon and Schuster, 4th edn. 1944.

EBELING, GERHARD. 'Hermeneutische Theologie?' (Hermaneutic Theology?), *Kirche in der Zeit.* Edited by Günter Heidtmann, Karl Herbert Herborn, Heinrich Reiss. Düsseldorf, Jahrgang 20, 1965.

EBERHARDT, P. *Religionskunde* (The science of religion). Gotha, 1920.

Enzyklopädie des Islam. Edited by M. Houtsma. Leiden, Leipzig, 1927.

ERCKMANN, RUDOLF. 'Der Einfluss der arabisch–spanischen Kultur auf die Entwicklung des Minnesangs' (The influence of Arabic–

Spanish culture on the development of troubadour song). Thesis. Giessen, 1933.

ESSLEMONT, J. E. *Bahá'u'lláh and the New Era*. London: Bahá'í Publishing Trust, rev. edn. 1974.

FRIES, HEINRICH and RUDOLF STÄHLIN. *Gott ist tot?* (Is God dead?). München, 1968.

FÜCK, JOHANN. 'Muhammed—Persönlichkeit und Religionsstiftung' (Muḥammad—personality and religious basics), *Saeculum, Jahrbuch für Universalgeschichte*. Edited by Georg Stadtmüller and others. Freiburg-München, vol. III, Heft I, 1952.

GABRIELI, FRANCESCO. 'Muhammad und der Islam als weltgeschichtliche Erscheinungen' (Muḥammad and Islám as phenomena of world-wide importance), *Historia Mundi, Handbuch der Weltgeschichte*. Bern, Vol. V. 1956.

GEBSER, JEAN. *In der Bewährung* (In the proving). Bern and München: 1962.

GIESE, E. *Die Toleranz im Islam* (Tolerance in Islám). Weimar, vol. VIII, 1915.

GLASENAPP, HELMUTH V. *Die nichtchristlichen Religionen* (The non-Christian religions). Das Fischer-Lexikon. Frankfurt, 1957.

GOGARTEN, FRIEDRICH. *Die Verkündigung Jesu Christi* (The proclamation of Jesus Christ). Heidelberg, 1948.

GOLDZIHER, IGNAZ. *Vorlesungen über den Islam* (Lectures on Islám). Heidelberg, 3rd edn. 1963.

GOPPELT, LEONHARD. *Christentum und Judentum im ersten und zweiten Jahrhundert* (Christianity and Judaism in the first and second centuries). Gütersloh, 1954.

GRASS, HANS. 'Der theologische Pluralismus und die Wahrheitsfrage' (Theological pluralism and the question of truth), *Kirche in der Zeit*. Düsseldorf, Jahrgang 20, 1965.

GRIMM, E. *Die Ethik Jesu* (The ethic of Jesus). Leipzig, 2nd edn. 1917.

GUARDINI, ROMANO. *Das Bild von Jesus dem Christus im Neuen Testament* (The portrait of Jesus the Christ in the New Testament). Würzburg, 1936.

— *Das Ende der Neuzeit*. Basel, 1950. (Published in English as *The end of the Modern World*.)

HARENBERG, WERNER. *Jesus und die Kirchen* (Jesus and the churches). Stuttgart–Berlin, 1966.

HARNACK, CARL GUSTAV ADOLF V. *Entstehung und Entwicklung der Kirchenverfassung und des Kirchenrechts in den zwei ersten Jahrhunderten* (The rise and development of Church constitution and Church law in the first two centuries). Leipzig, 1910.

— *Lehrbuch der Dogmengeschichte*. Freiburg, 1886–9. 5th edition, 1931–2. (Published in English as *History of Dogma*.)

HARTMANN, RICHARD. *Die Religion des Islam* (The religion of Islám). Berlin, 1944.

HARTMANN, WALTER. 'Wer ist der Mensch?' (Who is Man?) *Evangelische Unterweisung*, Dortmund, February 1966.

HAUCK, W. A. *Rudolf Sohm und Leo Tolstoi*. Heidelberg, 1950.

HEER, FRIEDRICH. *Mittelalter* (Middle Ages). Zürich, 1961.

HEILER, FRIEDRICH. *Der Katholizismus, seine Idee und seine Erscheinung* (Catholicism: its ideal and its vision). München, 1923.

HENTIG, HANS V. *Soziologie der zoophilen Neigung* (Sociology of bestial tendencies). Stuttgart, 1962.

HUNKE, SIGRID. *Allahs Sonne über dem Abendland* (Allah's sun over the West). Stuttgart, 1962.

HUTTEN, KURT. *Seher, Grübler, Enthusiästen* (Seers, Meditators, Enthusiasts). Stuttgart, 10th edn. 1966.

JASPERS, KARL. 'Die nicht-christlichen Religionen und das Abendland' (The non-Christian religions and the West), *Die grossen nicht-christlichen Religionen unserer Zeit in Einzeldarstellungen*. Stuttgart, 1954.

JOCKEL, RUDOLF. 'Die Lehren der Bahá'í-Religion' (The teachings of the Bahá'í Faith). Thesis. Tübingen, 1952.

— *Islamische Geisteswelt, von Muhammad bis zur Gegenwart* (The spiritual world of Islám, from Muḥammad to the present day). Darmstadt, 1954.

KAHL, JOACHIM. *Das Elend des Christentums oder Plädoyer fur eine Humanität ohne Gott* (The misery of Christendom, or arguments for a humanity without God). Hamburg, 1968.

KANT, IMMANUEL. 'Kritik der praktischen Vernunft' (Critique of practical reason), 1788. *Kant's Werke*, edited by Th. Knauer Nachfolger. Berlin and Leipzig, undated.

— *Zum ewigen Frieden* (To eternal peace). 1795. Edited by Limes-Verlag. Wiesbaden, 1946.

KAUTSKY, KARL. *Der Ursprung des Christentums* (The origin of Christianity). Stuttgart, 1st edn. 1908.

KELLERHALS, EMMANUEL. *Der Islam, Seine Geschichte, seine Lehre, sein Wesen* (Islám, its history, its teaching, its essence). Basel, 2nd edn. 1956.

KLAUSNER, J. *Jesus von Nazareth, Seine Zeit, sein Leben und seine Lehre* (Jesus of Nazareth, His time, His life and His teaching). Jerusalem, 3rd edn. 1952.

The Koran. Trans. by J. M. Rodwell. London: J. M. Dent & Sons Ltd., 1953.

KÜNNETH, WALTER. *Glauben an Jesus? Die Begegnung der Christologie mit der modernen Existenz* (Belief in Jesus? The encounter of Christology with modern existence). Hamburg, 1962.

LEITPOLDT, J. *Jesus und die Frauen* (Jesus and women). Leipzig, 1921.

LEO, HEINRICH. *Lehrbuch der Geschichte des Mittelalters* (Manual of the history of the Middle Ages). Halle, 1830.

LUTHER, MARTIN. *Von der weltlichen Obrigkeit, wie weit man ihr Gehorsam schuldig sei* (On the authorities of the world, how far one owes them obedience). 1523. Weimar edition, vol. XI.

MAURER, W. *Kirche und Synagoge* (Church and synagogue). Stuttgart, 1953.

MEINERTZ, MAX. *Theologie des Neuen Testaments* (The theology of the New Testament). Bonn, 1950.

MENSCHING, GUSTAV. *Soziologie der Religion* (The sociology of religion). Bonn, 1947.

MEYER, E. *Ursprung und Anfänge des Christentums* (Origin and beginning of Christianity). Stuttgart and Berlin, 1923.

MÜHLSCHLEGEL, PETER. 'Sozialisierte Erlösung' (Socialised Redemption), *Bahá'í-Briefe, Blätter für Weltreligion und Weltbewusstsein*, Heft 36, April 1969.

MUIR, SIR WILLIAM. *The Life of Mahomet*. Smith, Elder & Co., London, 1894.

NESTLE, WILHELM. *Krisis des Christentums* (Crisis of Christianity). Stuttgart, 1947.

NIETZSCHE, FRIEDRICH. *Thus spoke Zarathustra*. Trans. by R. J. Hollindale. London: Penguin Books, 1974.

PARET, RUDI. *Zur Frauenfrage in der arabisch–islamischen Welt* (On the question of women in the Arabic–Islamic world). Stuttgart–Berlin, 1934.

PARRINDER, GEOFFREY. *Comparative Religion*. London: George Allen & Unwin Ltd., 1962.

PERCY, E. *Die Botschaft Jesu* (The message of Jesus). Lund, 1953.

PETRY, GERHARD. 'Das Ende der Theologie?' (The end of theology?), *Kirche in der Zeit*, Jahrgang 18. Düsseldorf, 1963.

PLACK, ARNO. *Die Gesellschaft und das Böse* (Society and evil). München, 7th edn. 1970.

— *Plädoyer für die Abschaffung des Strafrechts* (Arguments for the abolition of criminal law). München, 1974.

PREISKER, HERBERT. 'Christentum und Ehe in den ersten drei Jahrhunderten, Eine Studie zur Kulturgeschichte der alten Welt' (Christianity and marriage in the first three hundred years, a study in the cultural history of the ancient world), *Neue Studien zur Geschichte der Theologie und der Kirche*, Stück 23. Berlin, 1927.

Principles of Bahá'í Administration. London: Bahá'í Publishing Trust, 3rd edn. 1973.

Principles of the Bahá'í Faith. A pamphlet. New York, Bahá'í Publishing Committee, undated.

RABBÁNÍ, RUḤÍYYIH. *Success in Teaching*. Wilmette: Bahá'í Publishing Trust, undated.

RADHAKRISHNAN, SARVAPALLI. *The Recovery of Faith*. London: George Allen & Unwin Ltd., 1956.

RASCHKE, H. *Das Christusmysterium* (The mystery of Christ). Bremen, 1954.

RICCIOTTI, G. *Paulus* (Paul). Rome, 1950.

ROEMER, HERMANN. *Die Babi-Beha'i* (The Bábí-Bahá'ís). Potsdam, 1912.

ROSENKRANZ, GERHARD. *Die Bahá'í. Ein Kapitel Neuzeitlicher Religionsgeschichte* (The Bahá'ís. A chapter in the modern history of religions). Stuttgart, 1947.

RUOFF, FRITZ. *Die Radolfzeller Halsgerichtsordnung von 1506* (The criminal procedure of Radolfzell in 1506). Karlsruhe, 1912.

SABET, HUSCHMAND. *The Heavens are Cleft Asunder*. Oxford: George Ronald, 1975.

SCHAEFER, UDO. 'Die Grundlagen der Verwaltungsordnung der Bahá'í' (The legal basis of the administrative order of the Bahá'ís). Thesis. Heidelberg University Library, 1957.

SCHLATTER, A. 'Die Entwicklung des jüdischen Christentums zum Islam' (The development of Jewish Christianity to Islám), *Evangelisches Missionsmagazin*. Stuttgart, 1918.

SCHNEIDER, CARL. *Das Frühchristentum als antisemitistische Bewegung* (Early Christianity as an anti-semitic movement). Bremen, 1940.

— *Geistesgeschichte des antiken Christentums* (The spiritual history of ancient Christianity). München, 1954.

SCHOEPS, HANS-JOACHIM. *Jüdisch–christliches Religionsgespräch in neunzehn Jahrhunderten* (Judaeo–Christian religious dialogue in the nineteenth century). Frankfurt, 1949.

— *Theologie und Geschichte des Judenchristentums* (Theology and history of Judaic Christianity). Tübingen, 1949.

— *Paulus. Die Theologie des Apostels im Lichte der jüdischen Religionsgeschichte*. Tübingen, 1959. (Published in English as *Paul, The Theology of the Apostle in the light of Jewish Religious History*.)

SCHONFIELD, HUGH J. *Those Incredible Christians*. London: Hutchinson & Co. Ltd., 1968.

SCHOPENHAUER, ARTHUR. *Aphorismen zur Lebensweisheit* (Aphorisms on life). Edited by Rudolf Marx. Stuttgart, 1956.

SCHWEITZER, ALBERT. *The Mysticism of Paul the Apostle*. Trans. from the German by William Montgomery. London: A. & C. Black Ltd., 1931.

SEARS, WILLIAM. *Thief in the Night*. London: George Ronald, rev. edn. 1964.

SEEBURG, REINHOLD. 'Luthers Anschauung vom Geschlechtsleben und der Ehe und ihre geschichtliche Stellung' (Luther's attitude to sex and marriage and their position in history), *Luther Jahrbuch*, No. 7. Berlin, 1925.

SHOGHI EFFENDI. *The Advent of Divine Justice*. Wilmette: Bahá'í Publishing Trust, 1971.

— *God Passes By*. Wilmette: Bahá'í Publishing Trust, 5th repr. 1965.

— *The Promised Day is Come*. Wilmette: Bahá'í Publishing Trust, 1961.

— *The World Order of Bahá'u'lláh*. Wilmette: Bahá'í Publishing Trust, 1965.

SIMMEL, P. OSKAR, SJ, and RUDOLF STÄHLIN. *Christliche Religion* (Christian religion). Das Fischer-Lexikon. Frankfurt, 1957.

SIMON, GOTTFRIED. *Die Welt des Islam und ihre Berührungen mit der Christenheit* (The Islamic world and its contact with Christendom). Gütersloh, 1948.

SOHM, RUDOLF. *Kirchenrecht* (Church law). Leipzig, 1892.

Sonne der Wahrheit. A Bahá'í journal. Stuttgart: National Spiritual Assembly of the Bahá'ís of Germany and Austria, 2nd series, 1947–53.

STÄHLIN, RUDOLF. See FRIES; also SIMMEL.

STAUFFER, ETHELBERT. 'Zum Kalifat des Jacobus' (Towards the Caliphate of Jacob), *Zeitschrift für Religions-und Geistesgeschichte*, Jahrgang IV, Heft 3. Leiden–Heidelberg, 1952.

— *Jerusalem und Rom im Zeitalter Jesu Christi* (Jerusalem and Rome in the age of Jesus Christ). Bern, 1957.

STEINHEIM, SALOMON LUDWIG. *Die Offenbarung nach dem Lehrbegriff der Synagoge* (Revelation according to Synagogue doctrine). Vol. III: Der Kampf der Offenbarung mit dem Heidentum, ihre Synthese und Analyse. Leipzig, 1863.

SUHRAWARDY, SIR ABDULLAH. *The Sayings of Muhammad*. London: John Murray, 1941.

Synopsis and Codification of the Laws and Ordinances of the Kitáb-i-Aqdas. Haifa: Bahá'í World Centre, 1973.

SZCZESNY, GERHARD. *Die Zukunft des Unglaubens* (The future of unbelief). München, 1959.

THIESS, FRANK. *Die griechischen Kaiser. Die Geburt Europas* (The Greek King. The birth of Europe). Hamburg, Wien, 1959.

TILLICH, PAUL. *Religiöse Reden:* 'In der Tiefe ist Wahrheit' (Religious talks: In the depth is truth). Stuttgart, 1957.

TROELTSCH, ERNST. *Die Soziallehren der christlichen Kirchen und Gruppen* (Social teachings of Christian churches and sects). Tübingen, 1923.

TURNELL, MARTIN. (trans.) *Pascal's Pensées*. London: Harvill Press, 1962.

VISSER'T HOOFT, W. A. *No Other Name*. London: SCM Press Ltd., 1963.

WACH, JOACHIM. *The Sociology of Religion*. Chicago: Chicago University Press, 1946.

WATT, W. M. *Free Will and Predestination in Early Islam.* London: Luzac & Co., 1948.

WEINEL, HEINRICH. *Die Stellung des Urchristentums zum Staat* (The attitude of original Christianity towards the state). Tübingen, 1908.

WERNER, MARTIN. *Die Entstehung des christlichen Dogmas problemgeschichtlich dargestellt* (The rise of Christian dogma depicted in historical problems). Stuttgart, 1959.

WINCKLER, HUGO. *Arabisch–semitisch–orientalisch* (Arabic–Semitic–Oriental). 1901.

WINDISCH, H. *Paulus und Christus* (Paul and Christ). Leipzig, 1934.

— *Der Sinn der Bergpredigt* (The Sermon on the Mount). Leipzig, 1937.

WOLLE, W. 'Der Gleichheitsgrundsatz von Mann und Frau' (The base of equality between husband and wife), *Kleine Schriften zum Familienrecht*, vol. 25. Berlin, 1954.

ZAHRNT, HEINZ. *Die Sache mit Gott. Die protestantische Theologie im 20. Jahrhundert* (The Affair with God. Protestant theology in the 20th century). München, 1966.